THE NO-NONSENSE MANAGER'S PLAYBOOK

A GUIDE FOR LEADERS WHO NEED ANSWERS NOW!

BLUE AMERICA EDITION

GARRY W. STANBERRY

BLUE AMERICA EDITION
   Paperback ISBN: 979-8-9921528-3-8
   eISBN: 979-8-9921528-4-5

Published by
Stanberry Books LLC
Oakton, Virginia, USA

Author's website:
garrystanberry.com

To my wife Liz and our son Will

CONTENTS

WHY TWO EDITIONS? ONE RED AND ONE BLUE

Let's be honest. America isn't one nation anymore—it's two. Red America and Blue America don't just disagree; they live in different worlds, guided by different values, principles, and priorities. Nowhere is this divide sharper than on the issue of diversity, equity, and inclusion (DEI). Blue America embraces DEI as a way to create a more just and representative society; Red America often sees it as divisive, discriminatory, and part of the "woke" ideology. So I decided to meet both sides where they are. The Blue America edition includes a section on DEI. The Red America edition does not. Simple as that.

Some will call it opportunism. I call it entrepreneurship—the very heartbeat of America. We've always rewarded those who recognize a market and fill it. That's not division; that's innovation. And if the Founding Fathers were alive today, I suspect they'd raise a glass to anyone bold enough to turn political polarization into profit.

HOW TO READ THIS BOOK—AND WHY

There's no need to read this book from cover to cover.

- **It is a handbook for ready reference.**

- **Here's what sets this *management* book apart:**
  - Unlike most management books that gives you general advice, this book provides concrete guidance on what to do and *how to do it*. For example, while others say to address problem employees promptly, few explain how. Worldwide, the majority of managers don't speak to problem employees because they don't know what to say.[1] In this book, you'll find eight scripts for the eight most common reasons you need to talk to problem employees, including poor performance, inappropriate language, and bad attitudes.
  - The book covers 34 essential management topics—dealing with problem employees is just one. Truly effective managers need practical know-how in all of them.
  - You'll find more than 160 illustrative stories that make every topic memorable and reinforce the lessons.
  - The book draws on dozens of recent research studies and global surveys, reflecting a dramatic increase in new insights over the past few years.

- **Here's why this book's format is very different:**
  - Unlike traditional books that follow the Chicago Manual of Style, this book uses a much easier-to-follow format, explained below. Two independent reviewers even named my radically different approach the "Stanberry Style."
  - It's the first management book written in the outline format. This allows the reader to find the material they are looking for quicker, and me to be understood with far fewer words.
  - Designed for millennial and Gen Z managers, it embraces microlearning: concise, actionable information you can apply right away.
  - Each section stands alone, so you can get the information you need without reading the entire book.
  - Complex topics are broken down into step-by-step tables, each paired with practical examples for easy understanding.
  - Symbols (like %$&@#) are used instead of words, as the human brain processes symbols more quickly.
  - If your employees have different political views than you, or if you don't know whether they do, simply cut off the top right-hand corner of your book cover. Then your employees won't know your political affiliation.

Becoming an Effective Manager

The No-Nonsense Manager's Playbook is a comprehensive manager's guide that shows you how to deal effectively with your employees, bosses, peers, customers, and unions; how to hire, develop, and retain the best employees; work cooperatively with unions at a time when unions are on the rise; the importance of empowerment in the decision-making process; new research on the effectiveness of electronic brainstorming meetings; all you need to know to be successful at coaching and mentoring; the misunderstood importance of recognition and appreciation; methods to improve the level of employee engagement and why it is critical for productivity and retention; why women are better managers than men; how to improve your bottom line by embracing diversity; how to be the best manager possible using the latest research; and much more. My book will help managers navigate using battle-tested, proven management methods.

The No-Nonsense Manager's Playbook discusses how to respond to recent changes to the working world that are here to stay: significant increases in artificial intelligence, telework, robotics, telemedicine, e-commerce, cloud computing, big data analytics, encryption, text mining, voice and speech recognition, image processing, and video conferencing. It also covers substantial improvements to work-life balance for many workers, radical changes in office floor plan configurations, trends in supply chain management, and much more.

A 2024 Society for Human Resource Management (SHRM) study found that 64% of U.S. workers rated their managers as highly effective.[2] An earlier SHRM study found that 84% of workers blame badly trained managers for generating needless stress and work.[3]

Sadly, almost all of us have worked with managers who were ineffective or worse. *The No-Nonsense Manager's Playbook* tackles the poor performance of these managers and discusses how to turn this around using the latest research. Jennifer, a hypothetical person, is a model employee selected to manage. While excited about the promotion, she also worries whether she has the skills to succeed. Whether you are an engineer, a tech worker, an educator, or a worker in many other fields, your chances of becoming a manager increase with each promotion. You may get no additional training, but suddenly, you are in charge of people and outcomes. You are not alone. What managers need to know to be successful is in this book. It is an easy-to-understand how-to guide that you will quickly find essential.

The No-Nonsense Manager's Playbook is the first book to offer research-based guidance on dealing effectively with employees, bosses, peers, customers, and unions in a single volume. This research is often behind paywalls and so voluminous as to be impossible to read while still having time to do your job. So, I did all the work for you using the latest research. The book is a quick reference guide with examples of real-world challenges managers face and how they have successfully dealt with them.

Examples of the types of information in *The No-Nonsense Manager's Playbook* are:

- Do you know how to attract, develop, and retain the best employees? You will learn how in Chapter 2: Hire, Develop, and Retain a Great Team. Hint: The answer is not money.

- Do you know the fundamentals of coaching and mentoring and their importance to millennials and Gen Zers? Section 2.2, Coaching and Mentoring, has everything you need to know.

- The COVID-19 pandemic set new expectations for telework. In Section 3.7, Flexible Work Arrangements, you will learn the best approach to deciding who should telework and when.

- Do you know what you should accomplish in your first few weeks at a new job? Studies show you need a strong start in your new management job for long-term success. Section 3.1, Your First Weeks at a New Job, will help you achieve this with a complete list of tasks and the order to do them.

- Do you know what it takes to create the best organization at little to no cost? Chapter 10, How to Build the Best Organization Possible, lists initiatives to improve recruiting and retention that cost little or nothing.

The No-Nonsense Manager's Playbook starts with the understanding that readers have limited knowledge of business terms. The book carefully defines dozens of terms in the fewest words possible.

I spent seven years researching and writing this book, with months at the world's largest and most comprehensive library, the Library of Congress. I could access dozens of management subscription services from around the world, books, scholarly papers, research studies, surveys, videos, magazines, and newspapers. All industrialized countries conduct management research, and the Library of Congress is one of the few places in the world where most of the vast research materials can be found in one place. Most of the material is not on-line, you must be in the Science and Business Reading Room, 5th floor, John Adams Building, the Library of Congress, Washington, D.C., to do management research. In addition to research, I draw directly from my experience of successfully managing hundreds of employees over more than four decades.

This book offers guidance for how to:

- Provide employees with competitive pay and benefits (Chapter 1)

- Hire, develop, and retain great employees (Chapter 2)

- Be an effective manager at work (Chapter 3)

- Use all these managers' tools (Chapter 4)

- Partner with your peers (Chapter 5)

- Partner with your bosses (Chapter 6)

- Partner with your unions (Chapter 7)

- Excite your customers (Chapter 8)

- Be the best manager possible (Chapter 9)

- Create the best organization possible (Chapter 10)

All generations place a high value on work-life balance. A 2013 Stanford University study shows that increases in output are small as hours rise beyond 50 hours a week. There are no productivity increases in working more than 55 hours per week.[4] I recommend limiting work to no more than 50 hours per week because those are the hours in which you are fully productive. Of course, the 50-hour-per-week maximum includes managers. My goal is to help you become effective managers by giving you practical advice on getting all your work done in less than 50 hours per week. Managers deserve a life outside of work, too.

For over a generation, people have been told to find their passion, leading them to their profession. You may have heard or read a version of the sentiment, "If you find something you love to do, you'll never work a day in your life." Unfortunately, that's not how the human brain works. Very recent research has established that your passion is not in your DNA. What you become passionate about requires your investment and growth over time.[5] Effective managers are made, not born. *The No-Nonsense Manager's Playbook* will help you become an effective manager.

You may find that making your staff successful is rewarding. If you do, you will not get many pats on the back. Lao Tzu, a Chinese philosopher and the founder of Taoism, said in 600 BCE, "A leader is best when people barely know he exists, when his work is done, his aim fulfilled, they will say: We did it ourselves."[6] Nothing has changed in the ensuing 2,600 years.

I have had a nearly lifelong interest in writing a how-to management book. It began when I completed a business management undergraduate degree at Southern Methodist University in 1971. On the last day of class, a popular professor asked his graduating seniors if anyone had any final questions before he sent us out into the business world. A red-haired man who rarely spoke slowly raised his hand. This student asked if the professor had any advice on how to deal with employees. He explained that since many of us would soon be managers, we should know how to deal effectively with our employees. The man asked if that discussion was saved for the last day. The professor smiled and said we would not be discussing that topic. Without further questions, the professor congratulated us and wished us all bright futures. This book is a response to the red-haired man's very insightful question. I have been working on this book officially since 2014 and unofficially since 1971.

One of the most thought-provoking quotes I have ever heard is from Madame Ellen Johnson Sirleaf, the former president of Liberia, who said, "If your dreams do not scare you, they are not big enough." One of my big dreams is to help all managers worldwide be highly effective while achieving a work-life balance. Why can't you be an effective manager, work at or under 50 hours a week, enjoy your work, and have time for your pursuits of happiness? This book tells you how.

ACKNOWLEDGMENTS

Ms. Mary Parker Follett (1868–1933) was the first to investigate how to create effective management and advocate for constructive human relations in the workplace. Noted management theorist Warren Bennis said Ms. Follett's enormous contribution to management practice is the basis for almost all management writing today.[7]

My thanks to the staff at the Library of Congress for their help navigating their countless books, subscription services, research studies, scholarly papers, surveys, videos, magazines, and newspapers. Thanks also to the many authors whose work I have cited here. I chose their works because they are the most original, logical, and relevant—my sincere thanks to each of these talented writers.

Sir Isaac Newton said it best:

"If I have seen further, it is by standing on the shoulders of giants."[8]

If there are any errors in this book, they are mine alone.

CHAPTER 1

Introduction

To be an effective manager, you must do everything possible to help your employees succeed. You can learn how to become an effective manager.[9] This book tells you how.

1.1 DEFINITIONS

Out of necessity, I wrote many of the definitions in this book. While researching this book, I learned that almost all management terms have multiple definitions. Some are confusing, others are contradictory, and many are just too wordy. My definitions use the fewest and smallest words possible. I have never liked lengthy definitions using big words. Who are they trying to impress?

I provide a brief history of the terms *management* and *leadership* below to give you an idea of how unnecessarily complicated and confusing definitions can become. I also provide you with clear definitions of these two terms, explaining the difference and in what context these terms are customarily used.

> **Classic definition of management:** "The art of getting things done through the efforts of other people."[10] —Mary Parker Follett (1868–1933), a pioneer in organizational theory and behavior

According to Henri Fayol (1841–1925), who developed a general theory of business administration, management consists of five functions: planning, organizing, commanding, coordinating, and controlling.[11]

Definition of planning: A dynamic process of developing strategic goals and actionable and measurable objectives that show how the organization plans to differentiate itself within its marketplace and create sustainable value, and how it plans to bridge the gap between its strategy and implementing it day-to-day. For more information, please see Section 3.11, Strategic Planning.[12]

Definition of organizing: Recruiting, developing, retaining, training, and organizing workers. For more information, please see Section 2.1, Hire and Retain Great Employees, and Section 2.3, Training.

Definition of commanding: Managing, motivating, creating expectations and priorities, and establishing goals and objectives for each direct report that align with the organization's goals and objectives. This book will teach you how to manage people effectively. Please see Section 3.8, Motivation, Recognition, and Appreciation, and Section 2.4, Performance Development.

Definition of coordinating: Ensuring that all activities are coordinated to achieve the strategy, goals, and objectives. Please see Section 3.11, Strategic Planning, for more information.

Definition of controlling: Monitoring progress toward achieving goals and objectives while systematically looking for ways to improve processes, performance, and outcomes. For more information, please see Section 2.2, Coaching and Mentoring, Section 2.4, Performance Development, Section 3.4, Decision-Making, and Section 3.11, Strategic Planning.

Definitions of Management Versus Leadership

Definition of management (abridged): Overseeing the work of one or more people to ensure that a task or tasks are done correctly and on time. Effective managers empower, encourage, and motivate their employees so they want to do the work.

- Please note that the word management is often used in contexts other than managing people. For example, you can manage a program without managing people. In this book, the word management will primarily be used to refer to managing people.

> **Definition of management (unabridged):** Overseeing the work of one or more people to ensure that a task or tasks are done correctly and on time. Managers should monitor employees progress in completing the task(s). Managers use their judgment in giving autonomy to their employee(s) to complete tasks based on the employee(s) position, experience, judgment, and technical, professional, and people skills. Once the manager delegates responsibility for the task(s), the manager and employee(s) share ownership. A manager never loses responsibility for the successful completion of tasks. Effective managers empower, encourage, and motivate their employees so they want to do the work.

- Management principles apply equally to all industries, non-profits, government bodies, and military services.[13]

> **Definition of leadership:** In 1991, a leadership studies professor at an American university read all the available literature on leadership published between 1900 and 1991. The results: He found over 200 different definitions of leadership. The only common denominator was that leadership was "good management."[14] In 2012, Dr. Barbara Kellerman, founding director of the Harvard Kennedy School Center for Public Leadership, said there are about 1500 definitions of leadership and 40 leadership theories.[15] Peter Drucker, one of the foremost management writers of the 20th century, writes that management and leadership are "precisely" the same.

- Some people, however, associate charisma with leadership. Drucker dispels the notion that leaders always have charisma or possess similar personality traits. He cites examples of highly effective leaders who were not charismatic. These include Dwight Eisenhower and Harry Truman. Drucker also points out that leaders do not have leadership qualities or personalities. He says that Winston Churchill, Douglas MacArthur, and Franklin Roosevelt were highly effective leaders but shared few, if any, personality traits.[16] For those still thinking there is a difference between leadership and management, please identify one skill, characteristic, talent, or outcome that one has and the other does not. I rest my case.

- *The Essential Drucker: The Best of Sixty Years of Peter Drucker's Essential Writing on Management* remains a top-selling management book after more than 20 years.

○ In 2012, Dr. Kellerman wrote that our understanding of how to develop effective leaders or slow or stop the bad ones had not changed much in the past millennia.[17] I offer this book as a resource to develop effective leaders. Regarding slowing or stopping bad leaders, we can choose from the traditional options of the boot, the ballot, or the bullet.

  - Dr. Kellerman's book *Bad Leadership: What It Is, How It Happens, Why It Matters* explains how bad leadership arises when unethical or incompetent leaders are tolerated, resulting in widespread harm and how followers comply or fail to resist harmful behavior.

○ There is often a difference in the context in which the words *leadership/leader/lead* and *management/manager/manage* are used. For example, *presidents lead nations, and generals lead armies.* You are far less likely to see the words *presidents manage countries, and generals manage armies,* but they do. For example, the American president manages three million federal government employees in the Executive Branch. Generals also manage armies. By way of illustration, throughout most of recorded history, more soldiers have been killed or incapacitated by disease or non-battle injuries than in combat. In the United States, this began to change during World War II with the introduction of improved casualty care. Better health management of injured soldiers ensures that more soldiers can be returned to combat sooner.

○ All managers delegate work and ensure it gets done. Effective managers also *empower, encourage,* and *motivate* their employees so they want to do the work. These three verbs are more often associated with leaders than managers, but they apply equally to both.

○ In this book, I will use the words *management/manager/ manage* or *boss.*

> **Definition of effective management:** To be an effective manager, you must do everything possible to help your employees succeed. This book tells you how.

1.2 WHAT EMPLOYEES WANT

What employees want changes over time. A 2022 Gallup survey of over 13,000 U.S. employees shows that 64% of respondents feel it is very important to have a large increase in income or benefits, and 61% want better work-life balance and personal well-being. Interestingly, in Gallup's earlier 2015 survey, the respondents' desire for more income or benefits was in fourth place. Since then, the low unemployment rate and competition for talent have increased employee expectations.[18] People accept jobs from organizations that offer good pay and benefits. Good employees remain only if their immediate boss is effective.[19]

Let me dispel the notion that employees leave for more money. A study by the Saratoga Institute shows that 89% of managers are convinced that their employees leave for more money, but only 12% of them actually leave for more money.[20] A staggering 57% of employees leave because of their immediate boss.[21]

Generational differences exist in terms of what each wants in the workplace. However, there are far more similarities in workplace interests than differences among the generations. Let us look at both.

- A meta-analysis of 20 studies assessing workplace generational differences found no significant ones. Any differences between generations are likely due to their life stage rather than their generation.[22] Every new generation of young people is significantly more narcissistic than older generations. These selfish young people mature as they age.[23] Effective managers help orient and motivate new employees through coaching and mentoring. Please see Section 2.2, Coaching and Mentoring, for more information.

What employees in every generation want, in addition to those things mentioned the 2022 Gallup survey results above:

- Good benefits and perks.

> **Definition of benefits and perks:** Employee benefits are nonwage compensation, such as paid health insurance, paid time off (PTO), retirement benefits, dental and vision insurance, and disability insurance. Employees will pay for these benefits if organizations do not. Perks include telework, wellness programs, financial wellness programs, employee discounts, etc. These typical perks are often low or no cost but, in some cases, like telework, are very important to employees.[24]

- The "big three" traditional benefits, health insurance, PTO, and retirement benefits, are universally recognized as essential by all generations. These benefits play a crucial role in employee satisfaction and retention.
  - Health insurance.
    - The U.S. Census Bureau reports that 86% of private-sector workers were offered employer-sponsored health insurance.[25]
    - The Patient Protection and Affordable Care Act (PPACA) requires organizations with 50 or more employees to provide health insurance to their employees and their dependents or incur penalties. The PPACA established the Small Business Health Options Program for organizations with fewer than 50 employees who choose to offer health coverage.[26] Please consult a tax attorney for further details on this law.
    - An increasing percentage of organizations offer health care coverage for same-sex spouses. Of the organizations that offer spouse health benefits, the percentage that offer same-sex health care increased dramatically from 43% in 2016 to 74% in 2020.[27]
    - The PPACA does not require that employers provide dental coverage. The U.S. Bureau of Labor Statistics estimates that 44% of American civilian workers have access to a dental insurance plan. Not all employees who are offered a dental plan elect to enroll. Of those eligible, 81% take part in a dental insurance program. As a result,

only 36% of American workers participate in a dental insurance plan.[28]

- Paid time off (PTO)

> **Definition of paid time off (PTO):** A benefit in which employees take time off for anything while still getting paid.

- ☐ PTO is used for personal appointments, sick time, and vacations. Organizations sometimes offer PTO rather than specific personal, sick, or vacation days.[29]

- ☐ According to the Center for Economic and Policy Research, 91% of full-time U.S. employees are offered vacation/PTO, but 54% do not take all their vacation/PTO because they fear that they will be replaced if they do. Most Americans have no job security except those in unions or have written contracts.[30] Effective managers ensure that each employee takes all their vacation days every year. No exceptions. If employees take their vacation/PTO, they will be less stressed and will do more and better-quality work. This book contains guidance on how managers can reduce errors when their staff members are on well-deserved time off. Encouraging your employees to take all of their time off each year improves recruitment and retention and costs nothing. Please see Section 4.6, Policies, Procedures, and Checklists for more information.

ILLUSTRATIVE STORY

One CEO motivates his staff to take vacation days. This CEO sets an example by taking three weeks of vacation each year and posting his vacation photos on social media.[31]

- A 2019 Harvard analysis of a Glassdoor survey found that noncash benefits, such as the freedom to take vacation days, improved job satisfaction more than bigger paychecks.[33] Employees of all ages who see their immediate boss as a partner are much happier with their lives. Life satisfaction is worth more than doubling their income for middle-aged workers.[34] For more information, please see Chapter 6: Partner with Your Bosses (Okay, You're the Junior Partner).

- Retirement benefits.
  - 69% of private-sector organizations offer employer-provided retirement plans, while only 52% participate.[35]
  - In addition to the "big three" benefits above, employees in every generation want work-life balance.

> **Definition of work-life balance:** Employees spend an adequate amount of time at work, but not more than 50 hours per week to remain fully productive, while having enough time for their pursuits of happiness, such as spending time with family and friends, worship, volunteering, and reading this book.[36]

- A 2022 Pew Research Center poll found that among employed adults who seldom or never worked from home before the COVID-19 pandemic and currently work from home at least some of the time, 64% say it is now easier to balance work and personal life.[37] Effective managers discuss with their employees how much telework they can take and still develop social cohesion, allowing the sparks of creativity to generate new ideas. New ideas most often come from face-to-face collaboration.[38] For more information, please see Section 3.7, Flexible Work Arrangements (also Workplace Flexibilities).

- What baby boomers, born 1946–64, want in addition to the "big three" benefits and what's included in the Gallup poll results at the beginning of this section:
  - Legal advice for wills; estate planning; planning for eldercare; health care coverage until employees are eligible for Medicare (age 65 unless they have a disability); work-life balance; and phased retirement, gradually reducing hours and responsibilities.[39]

- What Generation X, born 1965–80, wants in addition to the "big three" benefits and what's included in the Gallup poll results at the beginning of this section:
  - Opportunities for growth and advancement, help with student loans, financial wellness education, wellness programs, and work-life balance.[40]

- What millennials, or Generation Y, born 1981–1996, want in addition to the "big three" benefits and what's included in the Gallup poll results at the beginning of this section:
  - Flexible work arrangements, student debt help, professional development, financial wellness education, wellness programs, and work-life balance.[41]
  - According to PricewaterhouseCoopers, 71% of millennials want to work outside their native countries, but the specific countries survey respondents are willing to work in vary greatly.
    - 58% of respondents said "yes" to working in the United States.
    - 48% of respondents said "yes" to working in the United Kingdom.

- 39% of respondents said "yes" to working in Australia.

- 11% of respondents said "yes" to working in India.

- 2% of respondents said "yes" to working in mainland China.[42]

- What Generation Zers, born 1996–2012, want in addition to the "big three" benefits and what's included in the Gallup poll results at the beginning of this section:

  - Wellness benefits, career growth, financial wellness education, diversity, inclusion and equity, and work-life balance.[43]

  - In 30 years, Gen Zers will want the same perks that baby boomers want now.

  - In 2024, there were more Gen Zers in the U.S. workforce than baby boomers.[44]

  - The Bureau of Labor Statistics calculates that Gen Zers will make up approximately 30% of the U.S. workforce by 2030.[45]

  - Over half of Gen Zers plan to work for their present employer for under three years.[46] One of the reasons that Generation Z workers want to leave in less than three years is that most bosses are ineffective or worse. They will stay, however, if you create an environment with effective managers (see Chapter 9, How to be the Best Manager Possible) and a good organization (see Chapter 10, How to Build the Best Organization Possible).

  - Rest assured that you will soon see articles on how demanding Gen Zers are. This happens with each generation as they enter the workforce. In time, they will amaze us with their hard work, creativity, and grasp of technology.

Final thought:

- "If the whole world depends on today's youth, I can't see the world lasting another 100 years."[47] —Socrates, Greek philosopher (470–399 BCE)

1.3 U.S. DEMOGRAPHIC TRENDS

- Demographic trends that are changing the U.S. workforce.

  - In 2022, almost 46.2 million immigrants lived in the United States, the largest number since census recordkeeping began in 1790. Immigrants' share of the U.S. population has significantly increased from a record low of 4.7% in 1970. In 2022, immigrants comprised 13.9% of the total U.S. population, just under the record high of 14.8% in 1890.[48]

  - The population of people identifying as "two or more races" is expected to be the fastest-growing ethnic or racial group in the United States over the next 20 years. Asian Americans are the second fastest-growing group, followed by Hispanic Americans.[49]

  - In 2019, 41.2% of mothers were their families' primary or sole breadwinners, making at least half of their total household income.[50]

  - Beginning with the baby boomers, each succeeding U.S. generation has been increasingly diverse. Baby boomers, born 1946 to 1964, were composed of 19% racial and ethnic minorities as of 1969. Gen Zers, born 1996 to 2012, were composed of 48% racial and ethnic minorities as of 2019.[51]

  - The United States will have no ethnic or racial majority by 2043. While the non-Hispanic white population will continue as the largest distinct group, no group will be the majority.[52]

  - The United States will experience significant demographic changes over the next two decades. By 2030, all baby boomers will be over age 65, and one in five Americans will be of retirement age.[53] Due to the aging population, immigration will represent 75% of the overall increase in the U.S. population by 2033. The remaining 25% will be the net amount of natural increase (the excess of births over deaths). By 2043 and beyond, all population growth will come from immigration.[54]

A final thought on U.S. demographic trends:

- America is the world's leading migrant destination.[55]

CHAPTER 2

Hire, Develop, and Retain a Great Team

The most challenging management decisions are those that deal with people. Promoting, hiring, firing, etc., are the most difficult to remedy.[56] This chapter's step-by-step guidance will help you skillfully navigate hiring, developing, and retaining great employees.

2.1 HIRE AND RETAIN GREAT EMPLOYEES

In 2023, Development Dimensions International surveyed 529 CEOs of organizations with an average of 16,000 employees in ten industries worldwide. The survey shows that the CEOs' top concerns are hiring, retaining, and developing top talent and keeping their workforce engaged.[57] These should be your top priorities, too.

As Jesse Schell, CEO of Schell Games, says, "The main way to reduce stress in the workplace is by picking the right people."[58] This quote is a perfect summary of this chapter.

Before beginning the hiring process, it is crucial to consult a labor attorney for your questions about unions or an employment attorney for all other employment questions. I treat each step as though I expect a lawsuit, and you should, too. **It can be costly and embarrassing to be told by your attorney that you should have spoken to them before a mistake was made.** When in doubt, please seek legal advice as early as possible. I have never had an attorney say, "Hey, Garry, you're asking for advice too soon."

Steps in the Hiring Process

Please do every step in the hiring process below in the order listed. You cannot afford to cut corners with hiring. At the same time, you must move quickly before other organizations hire the best people. A 2021 Society of Human Resource Management survey found that 96% of job candidates accept their first job offer.[59] To help speed up your hiring process, there are several dozen companies that offer software that manages the recruiting and hiring process. Application tracking systems (ATSs) have been around since the late 1990s and are used by 99% of Fortune 500 companies, 66% of large companies, and 35% of small companies.[60] These ATSs do many of the following tasks:

- Write job descriptions

- Cast a wide net to find strong candidates

- Select the best candidates using assessment tools and simulation exercises

- Create interview questions

- Schedule video or in-person interviews

- Conduct background and reference checks

- Conduct initial interviews

- Notify applicants where their application is in the hiring process

- Send offer letters

- Create onboarding checklists

- Allow new employees to complete all onboarding documents online before their first day of work

- Enable new employees to review and sign an acknowledgment of the employee handbook along with frequently asked questions and answers

Many companies offer ATS software. These companies continue to merge, and others go out of business. You should choose ATS software from companies that offer superior services and will likely be around for the long term. Several companies will help you make smart software choices. These include Gartner, G2.com, Forrester, TrustRadius, International Data Corporation, Spiceworks, IT Central Station, Frost & Sullivan, Nielsen Holdings, eMarketer, GetApp, and others.[61] An assessment of these companies can be found at bstrategyhub.com/gartner-competitors-alternatives. I have no financial interest in any of these companies. My interest is in ensuring that you purchase the best software for your needs from a company that will be around long term. I do not recommend that you decide just by listening to several of these companies give sales pitches. They will not tell you if they are barely hanging on and may be out of business soon. Some will also tout capabilities that are merely in development and are not immediately available. Buyer beware.

As a manager, you are always looking for talent, whether they are a good fit for your team or another in your organization.

- A significant 82% of job applicants expect employers to regularly update them on where their applications are in the hiring process.[62] Some ATSs will notify applicants where their applications are in the hiring process.

1. Do you need to fill the job vacancy?

- Most organizations are dynamic and continually changing. Just because someone leaves the organization does not necessarily mean you need to replace them.
  - A job analysis by your human resources (HR) staff can help you decide whether you need to fill the vacancy.

> **Definition of job analysis:** identifying the job duties and responsibilities; requirements for skills, work experience, qualifications, education; and work conditions of a specific job. This information is used to create a job description that ensures that a person with the right skills, knowledge, and abilities is hired.[63]

- ○ Can you distribute their duties to others? A job analysis by your HR staff can help you decide.

> ***ILLUSTRATIVE STORY***
>
> *At one organization, a senior manager and a manager reporting to her were hired at about the same time. They both soon recognized that the lower-level manager had too many employees. Those employees were eager for more work as they were underemployed and bored. Two employees agreed to transfer to new roles outside their offices because the new jobs suited their skills well. Over the next few months, departing employees were not replaced, and their workload was distributed to others. During this time, the number of employees dropped from 25 to 18, and morale improved. Their performance went from "satisfactory" to "outstanding." Too many employees can be as bad as too few.*

- Effective managers find the correct number of employees with the right skills, which helps improve recruiting and retention. HR will help you do this.

- How is it possible that organizations can have too many employees? Some managers are empire-builders who hire too many staff members to satisfy their egos.

- Has your organization taken on new work that it has not done in the past? Ask HR to do a workload analysis.

> **Definition of a workload analysis:** A workload analysis will determine the number of necessary employees, and the skills, knowledge, and abilities needed to perform the existing or projected workload.[64]

2. Is the job description current? If not, update it as accurately as possible. Why be so precise? People will apply based on the job duties that you advertise. If those duties are inaccurate, you will miss out on the most qualified people. If you hire a new employee based on an outdated job description, they will be unhappy that the job does not resemble the advertisement and will likely quit.

- An effective job description states what the person doing the job is expected to accomplish and can help sell the job. It should consist of the following elements:

  - A descriptive job title: business development manager, project manager, graphic designer, safety engineer, budget analyst, software engineer, etc. Avoid using unusual words.

  - A brief summary of what your organization does and what makes yours unique

  - A description of the employee's duties and responsibilities, with the most important listed first and the least important last. Include the expected percentage of time spent on each significant duty. Include relevant keywords so your job can be found easily.

  - The job location

  - Your telework policy

  - Any travel requirements, including locations and frequency

  - What is the boss's title?

  - A salary range

  - List of benefits and perks

  - The number of staff: How many people will the person who will fill this vacant position manage, if any?

  - Physical requirements, which may include lifting, sensory requirements, and potential exposure to extreme conditions such as cold, heat, noise, confined spaces, and high places. The Americans with Disabilities Act requires these disclosures.[65]

  - Required work experience

  - Required skills (job proficiency from experience or training), knowledge (specific information needed for the job), and abilities (capability to apply skills and knowledge to get the job done)[66]

  - Equipment used on the job, such as specific software, tools, or machinery

- ○ Qualifications such as specific college degrees, certifications, licensing, and special training

- ○ The application submission deadline. Please see the details below.

- ○ A direct link to the online application

- According to a study conducted by Google, 53% of mobile users quit if a website takes more than three seconds to load.[67] You must meet or exceed this demanding standard to hire the best millennials and Gen Zers. Effective HR managers test their websites regularly to find out how long they take to load.

3. Advertise the job using the revised duties.

- Most new hires come from referrals. The number of new hires your employees refer says a lot about how pleased they are working for your organization. Reward employees if you hire someone they refer.[68]

  ILLUSTRATIVE STORY
  Over the years, my best new employees have been referred by other employees. Employees are conscientious when referring people for jobs in their organization as they know their reputations are on the line. Of course, you should also do background and reference checks on referrals and always hire the most qualified candidates.

- Be sure to advertise *all* jobs internally. Each job you advertise internally signals your employees that you are interested in internal hiring and promotions. Just program your ATS to also post all jobs internally.

- You may want to advertise certain jobs internally only if you have a sufficient number of qualified people on staff. Your staff will notice and appreciate it.

- Some union agreements require that certain jobs be advertised internally first. Please consult a labor attorney with questions.

4. Advertise the job and include an application submission deadline.

- The length of time that you should advertise a job varies. It can be as brief as two weeks if you have highly qualified candidates in-house. Most jobs are advertised for 30 days. It may take several months to fill senior positions, like CEOs and university presidents. These last two jobs may involve hiring executive search firms.[69]

- Some organizations have no application submission deadlines for specific jobs. This would be the case for jobs with continuous openings, such as fast-food workers with high turnover.

- Accept applications until the job is filled.

5. Screen applications based on the job description.

- The job description is your job selection criteria. Use the same job selection criteria when screening each résumé. When reviewing résumés, look for job experience, educational requirements, etc., that match your job description.

- The Equal Employment Opportunity Commission (EEOC) estimated that 83% of all employers, including 99% of Fortune 500 companies, filter job applications using AI.[70] For those organizations that still have people screen résumés, using more than one screener helps ensure that good candidates are not overlooked.

- A comprehensive study published in *Development and Learning in Organizations* linked higher college grade point averages (GPAs) with successful job performance and more helpful behavior.[71] That is why asking job candidates for their GPAs is a good interview question, providing you recognize the qualitative differences in colleges.

- Has the applicant changed jobs often? The Bureau of Labor Statistics calculates that 4.1 years is the median number of years that hourly wage and salary workers have been at their current organizations. This number varies by age, industry, and occupation. Workers from age 25 to 34 have a median tenure of

2.8 years. Workers from age 55 to 64 have a median tenure of 9.8 years.[72] If the applicant has had several jobs within a one-to-two-year span, please ask them for an explanation. They may have been laid off or quit because of an ineffective manager. There are also a small number of people who are perpetual job hoppers.

- A StandOut CV survey found that over half of the job applicants surveyed admitted to lying on their résumés.[73] While most organizations now use AI to screen applications, background and reference checks are essential to help catch lies in résumés.

- 51% of hiring managers do not consider candidates with dishonest résumés; 40% said it would depend on what the lie was about.[74]

  - There are many ways in which applicants create lies on their résumés. Some of the more common ones include inflating responsibilities and job titles, claiming a college degree they do not have or never completed, and falsifying technical abilities. Why would a person be hired even though they lied on their résumé and were caught? Some organizations are desperate to fill specific vacancies, such as information technology (IT) technicians, and may overlook lies. In these cases, organizations should contact as many references, former bosses, and fellow employees as possible. Managers should also be extra observant during their probationary period.

6. Use predictive hiring analytics.

- Predictive analytics are used in many disciplines. Predictive hiring analytics identifies the best candidates, improve the hiring process by speeding it up, and improves retention by analyzing data from current employees, including performance data, engagement data, and retention data.[75]

  - They identify the best candidates. These systems offer self-assessments, personality tests, and simulation exercises that allow organizations to test candidates in role-play exercises to see how they do in real-world scenarios. These scenarios gauge a candidate's ability to think strategically, create effective solutions, etc. While hiring analytics has improved the hiring process, you still need to conduct the interviews and do background and reference checks.[76]

○ Your hiring speed is crucial. If you consider someone a great candidate, other hiring managers will, too. The organization with the most efficient hiring process gets the best candidates.

○ Retention is important. A 2018 BambooHR study shows that 31% of new hires quit within six months.[77] This is completely avoidable. Detailed information on how to retain employees is found later in this chapter.

- All applicants selected during the application screening, Step 5 above, should be asked to complete the online self-assessments and personality tests and participate in any simulation exercises. The results of these tests will help determine which applicants to interview.

- This step should be done at the same time as Step 7.

7. Create interview questions.

- ChatGPT can create interview questions based on the job description and the industry. Some ATSs generate interview questions also.

- Interview questions should encourage interviewees to describe their specific work experience to demonstrate their skills and abilities and how they will meet your needs.[78] Below are frequently asked interview questions. The usefulness of each is noted. Some answers will not necessarily give you much helpful information on the candidate's skills and abilities.

○ "Please tell us about yourself." Good question. Many interviewees expect this question first. It often helps them get started on a positive note.

○ "Please tell us why your skill set will help us." Good question. This gets to the heart of the interview. Does this person have the skills you need?

- ○ "What is your greatest strength and weakness?" This question is ineffective. Candidates can google this question and find answers. If people can find the right answers to a question online, it is not a useful question.

- ○ "Why do you think you are a good fit for this job?" Good question. The candidate can explain how their skills and abilities will help your organization. It will also tell you how much research the candidate did on your organization.

- ○ "Where would you like to be in your career five years from now?" This is an ineffective question. More than a few will respond that in five years, they see themselves in your job. You will learn nothing about their skills and abilities from this question.

- ○ "Please tell us about a professional mistake you made, what you learned from that mistake, and how you have applied that lesson in your work."[79] Good question. Everyone makes mistakes. The best candidates explain how they recovered.

- ○ "What is your ideal company?" Ineffective question. Many will respond, "Yours!" You will learn nothing about their skills and abilities from this question.

- Now, it is the interviewee's turn to ask any questions. "Do you have anything you would like to ask us?" Good question. This is always my last interview question. The best response I ever received to this question was, "Yes, when do I start?" I burst out laughing. Yes, we did hire her because she was easily the most qualified. She turned out to be an outstanding employee.

- Avoid questions about anything not related to the job. These include but are not limited to age, marital status, children, spouse, sexual orientation, race, color, ethnicity, national origin, native language, religious beliefs, disability status, medical history, arrest record, garnishments, or political affiliations.[80] **A complete list of subjects to avoid during interviews will change over time. Please consult an employment attorney with questions.**

- Before we get to the interview questions below, you first need to know the definitions of *goals*, *objectives*, and *milestones*.

> **Definition of a goal:** An outcome that an individual or organization plans to accomplish in a set amount of time *without* specifying how this outcome will be achieved.
>
> **Definition of an objective:** A series of *measurable* steps to achieve a goal. Section 2.2, Coaching and Mentoring, outlines the steps to creating objectives using the SMART objectives model.

  - The words *goal* and *objective* are frequently used interchangeably. You can usually tell which one is meant by the context. In case you hear someone use goal or objective incorrectly, please smile and nod your head.

> **Definition of a milestone:** a predetermined point toward achieving an objective. Measurements calculate progress toward achieving objectives and milestones.

- Even better interview questions are below. These questions are grouped according to the experiences you want to learn more about. Some of these questions apply to hiring managers, but most apply to hiring at all levels.
  - Establishing relationships[81]
    - Describe a working relationship you fostered to achieve a mutual objective.
    - Describe a time when office politics came into play and how you handled it.
    - Tell us about a time you worked with someone with an unpleasant personality. How did you handle it? What was the outcome?
    - Tell us about a time when you had difficulty establishing a relationship with an important person. How did you handle it? What was the outcome?

- Dealing with change[82]
  - Have you ever disagreed with your boss on a change? What did you do? What was the outcome?
  - Tell us your process for achieving objectives.
  - Give an example of how you have handled an unexpected challenge.
  - How do you approach a new task?
- Effective judgment and decision-making[83]
  - Were you ever asked to make a difficult decision? What was the outcome? What were the steps you took?
  - Tell us about a time when you did not have all the information you needed to make a decision. What was missing? What was the outcome?
  - Explain your experience with technology and how you use it to achieve objectives.
  - Have you ever faced an unexpected change at work? What was the outcome? What steps did you take?
- Achieving outcomes[84]
  - Tell us about a time you achieved results that pleased your boss.
  - How do you measure customer service?
  - Tell us about a time you juggled competing priorities.
  - Tell us about a project team you led. How did it turn out? What did you learn?
- Effectively managing people[85]
  - Tell us about a time you motivated a group to achieve a shared goal or objective.
  - Tell us about a time you successfully resolved a disagreement between employees.
  - Have you ever given feedback to a difficult person? Please describe what happened.

- Tell us about a time when your office shared a goal or objective with another office. How did you divide the tasks? How did you track progress?
  - Another good question is: "Please tell us how you prepared for this interview?"[86] This will tell you how much the applicant wants this job.

- An illegal interview question in 21 states is: "What is your current salary?" As of February 2022, 21 states prohibited employers from asking questions about salary history. Some additional states are considering outlawing it because some people of color and women are paid less for the same work. Using salary histories to determine new hires' pay continues this trend. Omitting questions about salary history helps to address this inequity.[87] I have omitted a list of the states that still allow salary questions, as there are no circumstances where this is okay. Women and people of color know that if a salary history question is asked, you may decide to hire them. However, they may not want to work for you. Remember that interviewees are assessing you as you are assessing them.

8. Conduct the interviews

- A Resume Builder survey of nearly 1,000 employers in 2024 found that 68% plan to use AI in the hiring process by 2025. Of these, 83% of these companies planned to use AI to review résumés, 42% planned to use AI to scan social media, and 28% planned to use AI for onboarding.[88] While AI interviews can speed up the hiring process, organizations must ensure that their AI is bias-free. AI that is programmed with biased data could result in unfair hiring practices.[89] AI may make some selections, but please remember to do background and reference checks in all cases.

- Face-to-face (F2F) interviews are better than videoconferencing (VC). According to a survey published in *Management Decision* in 2013, applicants in VC interviews received lower scores than those in F2F interviews and were less likely to be hired. The applicants in VC interviews thought the interviews were less job-related and had less favorable views of the interviewers than those in F2F interviews.[90] Applicants prefer F2F interviews. Since applicants are assessing you as you are considering them, you are wise to use the F2F interviews whenever possible.

- Interview panelists should always be friendly because the interviewees are considering you and your organization as you are considering them. Also, friendliness can help reduce interviewee nervousness. I always give each interviewee a bottle of water as the interview starts. Some interviewees get a case of dry mouth when they get nervous.

- Describe the job accurately and honestly to the applicant. If you leave out something important, such as frequent travel, the candidate you select may later feel that they were deliberately misled and quit soon after taking the job.

- During the interview:

  ○ Please allow the interviewee to do almost all of the talking.

  ○ Ask each interviewee the same questions. While you should stick to the script, an interviewee's answer may prompt you to ask another question for clarification. That is okay as long as the question is for clarification. You can ask additional questions during the interview to clarify items on their résumé as well. In these cases, you can ask questions like the following: "I see on your résumé that you have only been at your present job for five months. Why are you looking to leave so soon?" Another example is: "I see you have a college degree. What was your GPA?"

  ○ Be aware that implicit bias may affect your selection. This bias stems from our preference for people who are like us. We begin to treat people unlike ourselves differently within a fraction of a second of seeing them. To fight this tendency, select interview panel members with dissimilar backgrounds (discussed later in this chapter), recruit where minorities are more likely to be found (many ATSs can do this), ensure your job descriptions are bias-free, assess each résumé and interviewee using the job description as a baseline, and ensure that you hire the most qualified person.[91]

- Offer reasonable accommodations, such as a sign language interpreter for a deaf candidate. Employers cannot refuse to hire people who need accommodations because they have a disability or because the person requires a reasonable accommodation to do the job.[92] The majority of people with disabilities do not need any accommodations. The average cost of an accommodation is only $500, and organizations may be eligible for tax incentives to cover these costs.[93]

- Some candidates deliberately do not always make eye contact.

  - In some cultures, interviewees avoid eye contact as a sign of respect and courtesy.[94]

  - Remember that between one-third to one-half of Americans are introverts.[95] Some introverts may look away to avoid distractions while they think about their answers.

    ILLUSTRATIVE STORY

    At one organization, a senior manager, Danielle, served on an interview panel with her director of information technology (IT). Following an interview with Anthony, the IT director criticized him for his lack of eye contact and slow response to questions. It was clear to Danielle that Anthony was an introvert. As an analyst, his lack of eye contact and delayed responses were unimportant because he would work primarily alone. His employment record as an analyst was very impressive. He was hired and did outstanding work.

- How many times should applicants be interviewed? LinkedIn recommends two to three interviews for most jobs, to allow sufficient time to assess the candidates. Conducting too many interviews can cause good candidates to decline further interviews.[96] Google researched its interview practices and reduced its number of interviews from twelve to four or fewer for non-technical jobs and five for technical jobs. Should senior or longtime employees have more say in who is hired? The answer from Google's team is no. Tina Malm, Google's people analytics manager, said that regardless of the seniority or longevity of the interviewers, every interviewer's score had the same weight. Google has not found that senior or long-time employees are better at picking the best employees.[97]

ILLUSTRATIVE STORY

In the latter part of my career, I was often the most senior person on the interview panel. As the most senior panelist, I instructed the other panelists on the ground rules before our first interviews. I would tell them that I would call on the most junior person on the panel first when we began our discussion immediately following the last interview. I would ask them for their assessment of each candidate and their first and second choice for the job. Then I would go to the next most junior person, and so on. I spoke last. I asked the panelists to give their assessments in this order so that the more senior people did not influence those who were more junior. I asked the panelists for their top two choices because their first choice may have declined the job, or we may have found something unacceptable during the background and reference checks. Of course, the interview panel members sometimes agreed that none of the job candidates was good enough to be the primary or backup choice.

- For jobs in the low-skill service sector, hiring tests help identify the best applicants better than interviews.[98] Hiring tests also take less time than interviews.

9. Perform background checks, reference checks, and social media checks.

Definition of a background investigation or check: A background check determines whether a job applicant is unqualified due to criminal history, bad credit history, falsified academic history, falsified work history, or inappropriate information on social media.[99] Some ATSs do background checks, which can help speed up your hiring process.

- Too many applicants embellish their records, expecting that they will not get caught, and too often, they do not. An increasing percentage of people get their jobs by falsely presenting their backgrounds and job skills.

- o Pre-employment screenings can include civil litigation history, criminal conviction history, credit history, driving record, drug testing, education verification, employment verification, military discharge records confirmation (DD Form 214, Certificate of Release or Discharge from Active Duty), palmistry (reading lines on the palm), sex offender registries, Social Security number confirmation, tarot card readings, terrorist watchlist checks, workplace violence checks, and checking zodiac signs. No list of pre-employment screening questions can be all-inclusive, and this list will change over time. Please consult an employment attorney with questions. Most states recognize an employer's legal responsibility to check the references and backgrounds of applicants seeking positions that include high levels of public contact. Organizations that do not do these screenings can be found liable for the harm or injury that may result from their negligent hiring and retention practices.[100] Hiring employees with background problems will also hurt morale and affect retention. Please see Section 2.7, Problem Employees, for more information.

- o Some organizations give math, literacy, or other job-related skills tests. The EEOC and the U.S. Departments of Labor and Justice have created guidelines for such tests. All literacy tests for applicants must be job-related and adequately evaluate the applicant's ability to perform the job.[101]

Definition of a reference check: Asking former bosses, coworkers, direct reports, and educators to verify the job applicant's previous career and educational information and to gain insight into their character, conduct, work knowledge, skills, abilities, and level of engagement. These checks must be done before making a job offer. Some ATSs do reference checks, which can help speed up your hiring process.

- o You must call all references to find any problems. Hire respectful people by eliminating all potentially difficult people as soon as possible during the hiring process. Help create an organization where you would want your children to work. I have worked with the occasional difficult employee, and many of you have also. Often, the great mystery is how these people got hired in the first place. It was likely that people in the hiring process were in a hurry and left out steps like the background and reference checks. You will spend a lot more time if you hire the wrong person than if you follow these steps closely the first time.

- ○ Applicants carefully choose references who provide only positive comments. Former bosses or coworkers are far more likely to accurately describe the applicant's strengths and weaknesses than references. However, they may be reluctant to criticize former employees because they believe such criticisms could lead to lawsuits. **Many states have laws that protect employers who give factual accounts of an employee's performance to a potential new employer. Please consult an employment attorney with any questions.**[102]

- ○ Frequently asked questions of references include:

  - What were the applicant's beginning and ending dates of employment with your organization? What positions did they hold?[103]

  - How long have you known the applicant? What was your work relationship?[104]

  - Tell me about the quantity and quality of the applicant's work, and please give examples.[105]

  - Why did this applicant leave your organization?[106]

  - Let me briefly describe the job that the applicant applied for with our organization. Do you think the applicant has the skill sets to be successful in this job?[107]

  - Would you rehire the applicant? If not, why?[108]

  - How do you score their courteousness and tact on a 1–10 scale, 1 (poor) and 10 (best)?[109]

- An essential question for a reference is: "Does the job applicant freely do their best at work?" Employers should actively recruit employees who are already showing high engagement.[110] Please see Section 3,6, Employee Engagement, for more information.

  ○ Be aware that former bosses may sometimes discuss their former employees carefully.

    - Listen for subtle cues from former employers. Remember that they never get in trouble for praising applicants.

    - Do they quickly and enthusiastically endorse the applicant?

    - Do they carefully select their words and speak slowly?

    - Do they limit their responses to only acknowledging the employment start and end dates? This may be the organization's policy. If you are not sure, ask.

    - You can always ask the job applicant's references for the contact information of others who know the applicant well. You may get more frank information from them. I ask: "I am tasked to get one additional reference. Would you please give me the contact information of someone who knows the applicant well? Thank you."

ILLUSTRATIVE STORY

At one organization, an IT manager, Robert, selected the most qualified candidate to fill a job vacancy. The interview went so well that Robert decided not to waste time calling the interviewee's references. The new employee became extremely difficult to work with after the probationary period ended. When Robert's boss asked him if he had checked the employee's references, he sheepishly said no. The organization's employment attorney instructed Robert on how to counsel the difficult employee. He was unable to persuade the difficult employee to improve his negative attitude. The employee was ultimately dismissed. This dismissal took a large amount of staff time to complete successfully. The lesson of this example is that you must call all references in every case and ask the questions listed above or similar questions.

- Be careful when using social media to screen applicants.

  ○ Social media, i.e., blogs, bulletin boards, chat rooms, personal websites, etc., are online sites that allow people and organizations to share information, videos, and other content. Some examples are Facebook, Instagram, LinkedIn, WhatsApp, Snapchat, and YouTube.

  ○ Organizations often use social media to recruit and investigate current employees. Hiring managers use social media sites, such as LinkedIn, to look for suitable candidates. However, social media checks risk introducing biases to the applicant screening process. Interview panel members are frequently influenced by factors such as age (Lahey, 2008) (Weiss & Maurer, 2004), facial attractiveness (Tews, Stafford, & Zhu, 2009), gender (Riach & Rich, 2002) (Swim & Hunter, 1995), obesity (Roehling, 1999) (Swami, Chan, Wong, Furnham, & Tove'e, 2008), race (Cesare, 1996) (Pager, 2003), and sexual orientation (Drydakis, 2009) (Weichselbaumer, 2003). These factors allow hiring managers to consider information from social media sites that constitute legal, professional, and ethical violations.[111]

  ○ Still, social media sites offer valuable information, such as relevant volunteer experience, hobbies, and language skills, that employers can legally consider. Employers also review social media to corroborate the information on an application or résumé. Social media profiles also likely contain legally protected information such as age, disability, gender, or race, which cannot be legally considered when hiring. Employers should be aware that a lawsuit may result if they collect and assess legally protected information about a job applicant from a social media site, and this information is alleged to be the basis for not selecting the candidate. For example, what if the applicant is a practicing adherent of a non-traditional religion and reveals these or other nontraditional spiritual beliefs on their social media profile, and evidence shows that an organization screener reviewed their social media profile and decided not to hire them? It will be difficult to convince a jury that access to this legally protected information did not influence their hiring decision.[112]

- A photo alone can reveal protected traits such as age, disability, gender, or race that cannot legally be considered when hiring.

- Here are some good practices when using social media to screen applicants:

  - Review social media sites after conducting interviews to minimize bias.

  - If you find anything questionable on social media, print a copy, date it, and include a memo describing why it is questionable because this online page may be removed later.

  - Use your HR staff or an outside organization to screen social media to ensure that your hiring panel members do not see any information online that they cannot legally consider.[113]

  - I strongly recommend that you follow the recommendations above to avoid introducing biases to the screening and selection processes. These biases may cause a less qualified applicant to be hired or lead to lawsuits or both.

10. Select the most qualified candidate.

- Always hire the most qualified applicant.

  - American women's performance as managers and workers is impressive.

    - Are American women or men better managers? Answer: women. A Gallup survey published in the *Gallup Business Journal* in 2014 showed that 35% of male managers were engaged at work compared to 41% of female managers. In all working-age generations, female managers were more engaged than male managers. Remarkably, female managers with children living in their households were also more engaged than their male counterparts. Higher engagement means higher levels of workplace performance.[114]

- Are American workers more productive if they work for men or women? Answer: women. The same Gallup survey showed that 35% of female workers and 29% of male workers who worked for female bosses were engaged, while only 31% of female workers and 25% of male workers were engaged when they worked for male bosses. Engaged workers are more productive.[115]

- Are women or men workers more engaged in the United States and Canada? Answer: women. A 2024 Gallup survey conducted in the United States and Canada showed that 35% of women were engaged at work compared to 31% of men. By comparison, the engagement rate worldwide for both genders is just 23%.[116] Please see Section 3.6, Employee Engagement, for more information.

- Does having at least one woman on the board of large-cap companies yield lower leverage, higher valuations, and higher return on equity than those that do not? Answer: Yes, according to a Credit Suisse Research Institute global analysis of 2,400 large-cap companies. Those with at least one woman on the board outperformed large-cap companies with no women on the board by 26%.[117]

- Are men or women managers fairer in deciding how much to compensate employees? Answer: women. A 2012 Karlsruhe Institute of Technology study showed women award 13% more pay to their employees than male managers when circumstances allow.[118] Since the 1600s, women have sometimes been referred to as the fairer sex. It took 400 years for studies to show that women are indeed fairer.

- Despite the benefits of hiring women as managers, women hold 47.4% of U.S. jobs overall but only 42.1% of U.S. management jobs.[119]

- Once these survey results become widely known, the percentage of women managers, including women of color, will soar.

- Since surveys show that women are more engaged as managers and are fairer in determining compensation, and because introverts are critical thinkers, better strategists, and better at solving your most challenging problems,[120] the percentage of introverted women, including introverted women of color, in management will soar.

- Women are not more effective in the workplace because they are smarter than men; men must deal with the effects of testosterone, which affects their behavior.[121]

  ○ What happens when you do not hire the most qualified applicant?

  ILLUSTRATIVE STORY

  The interview panel did not select the most qualified applicant at one organization. The interview panel consisted of two finance managers and an HR manager. Weeks after selecting an inexperienced junior finance manager, the senior HR manager confided to a peer that the two other interview panel members had outvoted her. This panel passed up two highly qualified candidates and hired someone far less qualified. The organization suffered from the new, decision-delaying finance manager. This manager was performing just well enough to avoid getting fired. Why did this panel hire a less qualified candidate? This is likely because the selected applicant matched the gender, age, and ethnicity of two interview panel members, while the two more qualified applicants did not.

- Most new employees are placed in a "probationary period" status, generally 90 days, but this period can be six months or longer. This allows the managers to decide whether the new employee is a good fit. If they are not considered a good fit, they will be dismissed. Other employees may be placed in a probationary period if they are demoted, promoted, reemployed, or laterally transferred. Probationary periods are not required by federal law.[122]

> **ILLUSTRATIVE STORY**
>
> *In one organization, new employees were told that they would only be given a six-month contract. They were promised that if additional funds were found, their contract could be extended. This approach is a thinly veiled probationary period. If the employee did not work out, they were told that there was no money available to extend their contract. This example comes from an economic time in which jobs were scarcer, and employers could be very selective. Of course, at present, this practice would not work because there are often more job openings than qualified candidates. When the labor market again has more candidates than jobs, you can expect to see the six-month contract option return.*

- One major study shows that 52% of recent college graduates are working in jobs that do not use their degrees. This underemployment has long-term earnings implications.[123] That means that the majority of hiring panels select candidates who will be working in areas unrelated to their college degrees. During the interview, you are encouraged to ask these applicants why they are interested in a job outside the area of their college education or current employment.

- What to expect when hiring internal and external candidates. External hires are those hired from outside the organization. New external hires are paid approximately 18% to 20% more than internal hires because they often have more education and work experience. However, external hires get much lower job performance evaluations for the first two years than internal hires. External hires need about two years to become familiar and knowledgeable in their new jobs and build relationships. External hires are more likely to be fired or leave voluntarily during the first two years. The new external hire's boss is responsible for helping them get oriented and up to speed in their new jobs. Once external hires have been on the job for over two years, they overtake internal hires to get the most promotions.[124] As a manager, if you hire an external candidate, you must spend more time coaching them to ensure their success. Also, please show them this paragraph and tell them to hang in there. The extra coaching will help keep them from leaving voluntarily. Please see Section 2.2, Coaching and Mentoring, for more information.

- What do you do if your top choice declines your job offer? Try to prepare for that possibility in advance. Following the last job interview, when the interview panel selects the most qualified candidate, discuss your second choice. The interview panel should decide whether the second choice is acceptable if the most suitable candidate declines the job offer.

- A 2022–2023 Gartner study showed that half of all new hires surveyed accepted a job, changed their mind, and began working for another company.[125] This is certainly compatible with a 2021 Society of Human Resource Management survey that found that 96% of job candidates accept their first job offer.[126] The art and science of retaining great employees is discussed later in this chapter.

- Occasionally, you will have two outstanding applicants. Of course, you must hire the most qualified person. Then consider your second strong applicant for vacant or soon-to-be vacant jobs for which they would be a good fit.

  ILLUSTRATIVE STORY
  Occasionally, fellow interview panel members suggest ill-advised solutions should the top two candidates' backgrounds and skills be almost identical. These suggestions may include hiring a less experienced candidate because they will be cheaper, hiring a person because of their relation to a current employee, etc. After sitting on many interview panels, I can assure you that there are never two candidates that are exactly alike. Always hire the most qualified person based on your selection criteria. As Mark Twain said, "Do the right thing. It will gratify some people, and astonish the rest."[127]

- Warren Buffett's advice on hiring is to look for people with integrity, intelligence, and energy.[128]

11. Notify the selectee. The HR staff is generally responsible for notifying the selectee by phone and presenting a job offer letter. The HR staff also ensures that the job selectee accepts the job and salary in writing. Senior HR staff members are generally responsible for negotiating if the selectee asks for more money or benefits. These senior HR staff members often have a limitation on how much additional salary or benefits they can approve.

- Some job selectees are slow to respond to job offers. In these cases, selectees are likely waiting for other job offers since many applicants apply for multiple jobs. Employers usually give job selectees a week to decide, but depending on the job, this time varies from a few days to a few weeks. An HR employee should follow up with selectees within a few days if they have not received the signed job acceptance letter.[129] Another option is to ask the selectee's teammates to contact him or her to ask if they have any questions about the job or organization.

- I have rewritten several job offer letter templates. The information in these letters will change over time, but often, no one bothers to review this information to see if it is still current. Do not expect the HR clerks who fill in the blanks on these letters to notice they are outdated. Effective managers ensure that all letters like this are attached to policies to be reviewed regularly but not less than yearly. For more information, please see Section 4.6, Policies, Procedures, and Checklists.

12. Notify the non-selectees. Once the most qualified selectee has accepted the job and salary in writing, email all non-selected people, thank them for applying and let them know that someone else was selected. Please ensure that an employment attorney reviews your email template to non-selectees. If you treat non-selectees courteously, they may apply for other positions in your organization and recommend other qualified applicants. If any organization fails to send you a courtesy notice that someone else was hired, will you ever consider applying to that organization again?

13. Onboard your new employees.

- Before their first day:

  - Schedule a Zoom call with the new employee as soon as possible so their boss and coworkers can welcome them aboard. The boss and coworkers should introduce themselves and say something about their lives outside the office, i.e., hobbies, interests, hometown, etc. The boss should go last. Building relationships early is important. It helps create a bond that will pay great dividends. A 2019 meta-analysis of 32 studies published in *BMJ Open* shows that teamwork positively influences productivity.[130] In this first meeting, the boss should also briefly summarize recent group achievements quickly for the new employee. Do not single out individual employees, however great their achievements. Following these introductions, the sponsor (defined in the next section) should tell the new employees what to expect in their first few weeks. This discussion should be one-on-one. No need to tie up others' time.

  - Arrange for all the coworkers to meet with the new employee for lunch as soon as possible after being hired but before their first day. The primary purpose of the lunch will be socializing and allowing the new employee to get to know their new coworkers. The boss should not attend this informal lunch, or it will feel like a business meeting. There will be a second meeting of this group on the new employees' first day to discuss projects and where the new employee fits into the group.

  - Send new employees a New Employee Onboarding Checklist. These checklists ensure that no onboarding steps are overlooked. The U.S. Department of the Interior has a good onboarding checklist at: https://www.doi.gov/sites/doi.gov/files/uploads/OCIO-Employee-Checklist.pdf.[131]

  - Ask your new employees to complete all their onboarding forms online before their first day using e-signature software. This should be part of your ATS if you're using one.

- On their first day:

  - You only have one chance to make a good first impression (a cliché, but true). Your employees' first day must be carefully orchestrated to ensure that they have a very positive experience. A Gallup survey showed that only 12% of responders said their onboarding experience was great,[132] while 80% of new hires with unsatisfactory onboarding experience plan to quit.[133] By following the steps in this chapter, new employees will be impressed. Also, employees will be far less likely to leave. Detailed information on how to retain employees is found later in this chapter.

    ILLUSTRATIVE STORY

    I was hired by an internationally known and respected organization and arrived at HR on time for my onboarding. Each of us new employees filled in a few forms to begin our pay and life insurance. The HR technician then gave each of us a six-inch-high stack of HR booklets and left the room. We all remained because we thought she would return and answer our questions. Eventually, one of the new employees tracked her down and asked if she was planning to return to answer questions. She looked surprised and said no.

  - Delight your new employees on their first day:

    - In the morning, new employees should attend the HR onboarding meeting, where they will receive a warm welcome from the most senior staff member available, begin their pay, get answers to employee handbook questions, and more.

    - Their boss should give each new employee a building tour and take them to lunch. Please schedule at least 90 minutes to two hours for this.

    - On the afternoon of their first day, new employees should meet again with their coworkers. Allow coworkers to discuss ongoing projects in a friendly, relaxed manner. They should also discuss how the new employee is connected to these projects. The new employees' coworkers will run the meeting. The boss is invited to this meeting but only as an observer.

- Assign each new employee a sponsor, often a coworker, to get them settled, schedule the new employee for all necessary meetings and training, answer questions, get their company-owned equipment, including computers, phones, etc., introduce them to others they will work with, prevent any lulls, and escort them for the first few days until they finish their onboarding checklist.

- An astonishing 89% of new hires want to meet their bosses on their first day at work, and 83% want to meet their work colleagues.[134] Based on the schedule I'm offering here, your new employee will meet their coworkers before their first day and meet their boss for lunch on their first day. HR directors are great folks who will gladly add time for these meetings above to the first day's onboarding schedule. Just show them the statistics in this paragraph.

- As soon as you can schedule:
  - Employees should begin any job-specific training as soon as possible. The most qualified person should teach the training, and this is often the new employee's boss or a coworker.

  - Managers should set goals, objectives, and milestones with new direct hires as soon as possible—this certainly includes your remote workers. These goals, objectives, and milestones must be mutually agreed upon, and of course, they can be adjusted over time. A surprising 60% of companies fail to develop new employees' goals, objectives, and milestones, leaving these new employees anxious and questioning whether they are progressing.[135] For more information, please see Section 2.2, Coaching and Mentoring, and Section 2.4, Performance Development.

  - Each new employee's immediate boss should meet with them briefly at the end of each day for the first two weeks.[136] After that, employees should meet with their boss (coach) at least weekly. Managers should ask each new employee to suggest ways to improve the organization at any time. No idea is too small for you to consider.

> **ILLUSTRATIVE STORY**
>
> *My father, Raymond Stanberry, was the general manager of a large industrial bakery. He encouraged each new employee to suggest ideas to improve the bakery operation. My dad knew from experience that new employees are the ones who produce great ideas. They bring their experiences from other organizations and view your processes with fresh perspectives. Encourage your new employees to suggest ideas for improvements. They will amaze you.*

- "Great minds discuss ideas, mediocre minds discuss events, small minds discuss personalities."[137]—Eleanor Roosevelt, an American political crusader, activist, and diplomat

- How long does onboarding last? As long as it takes for the new employee to be fully productive. Onboarding takes eight months on average to be fully productive, 27% of organizations say it takes at least a year, and 25% say it takes three months or less.[138] Managers continue to help new direct hires understand their roles during their weekly coaching meetings. Please see Section 2.2, Coaching and Mentoring, for more information on coaching.

14. Remember these other considerations in the hiring process.

- Your hiring speed is crucial. Remember that applicants have likely applied for multiple jobs. If you consider someone a great candidate, other hiring managers will, too.

  - The organization with the most efficient hiring process gets the best candidates.

  - A Glassdoor study in 25 countries shows that hiring takes an average of 23.7 days. The hiring time varies by job title; for example, systems engineers take longer than receptionists. If you have not selected a candidate by the average time it takes by job title, your top pick may be hired elsewhere. Here are some examples of the average number of days it takes to hire people for various job titles in the United States: business systems analyst (45 days), software development engineer (41 days), finance manager (40 days), HR manager (32 days), receptionist (13 days), barista (10 days), machine operator (9 days) and waiter (8 days).[139]

- The ATS is an important tool to speed up the hiring process. Select interview panel members with dissimilar backgrounds.

- Dissimilar interview panel members help reduce unconscious bias and show interviewees you are serious about inclusion, diversity, equity, and accessibility.[140] When multiple interviewers conduct interviews, their collective eyes and ears catch more information about each interviewee. It also reduces unconscious bias and provides witnesses who can respond to claims of discriminatory or inappropriate questions. Courts praise diverse interview panels as fair and effective.[141]

- Consider the list below when creating interview panels. I am not suggesting that you must have representatives of each category on each panel. That would involve too many staff members and may overwhelm some interviewees. Three interviewers in an interview panel is a healthy balance between having enough to create a dissimilar group and not too many that it will overwhelm interviewees.[142] Of course, each interviewer can represent more than one category below:

  - Gender diversity.

  - Ethnic diversity.

  - Racial diversity.

  - The immediate boss of the person who will fill the vacancy.

  - A technical expert who understands the job firsthand, as the other panel members may not. In small organizations, consider asking an external technical expert to sit on your interview panel. This person does not have a vote but should be asked how they rate each candidate's technical skills and why.

- A person outside your office who will work closely with the new employee. This person would be invested in helping the selectee become successful.

- Voting members of the interview panel should primarily be from positions equal to or higher than the vacant position.

> ***ILLUSTRATIVE STORY***
>
> *At one organization, a senior official suggested changing the organization's hiring policy to require interview panel members with dissimilar backgrounds following the criteria outlined in the section above. The policy committee, which included the organization's senior staff, approved this recommendation but changed one word. An experienced employment attorney recommended that the interview panels "should," rather than "must," have dissimilar backgrounds. The attorney explained that if they use the word "must" without including representatives of each category in every interview panel, they will have difficulty defending their selections in court because they failed to follow their own policy.*

- American labor turnover

  - In 2021 and 2022, tens of millions of Americans voluntarily quit their jobs.[143] Some refer to this record-setting turnover as the Great Resignation. A Pew Research Center survey found that inadequate pay, no opportunities to advance, and not feeling respected at work were the primary reasons Americans quit their jobs in 2021.[144] Effective managers can address these issues. The Great Resignation is now over. U.S. workers are now staying put because of high inflation, mass layoffs, and slowing wage growth.[145] Advice on how to Retain Great Employees is provided later in this chapter.

  - Employee turnover is costly.

    - According to a 2019 Gallup survey, American businesses lose a trillion dollars to voluntary turnover each year. This is mostly avoidable. The replacement cost for departing staff ranges from half the employee's annual salary to two times their annual salary. Effective managers will reduce this cost by improving employee retention.[146]

- Employee turnover costs include:
  - Recruiting and hiring a replacement.
  - Lost productivity and possibly lost business.
  - Training, orienting, and developing the new hire.
  - Loss of organizational knowledge.
  - Other employee replacement costs include safety issues (e.g., for manufacturing), errors due to lower staffing, and morale damage.[147]

Retain Great Employees

- Be the best manager possible. Do everything possible to make your employees successful. As an effective manager, you must hire, develop, and retain great employees; give them flexibility in their work hours and place of work; ensure they have adequate resources; hire a dissimilar group so they challenge each other to do their best; empower them; give them motivation, mentoring, and training; grow employees through future-focused coaching that include the creation and tracking of mutually agreed-upon performance expectations that includes goals and objectives that align with the organization's goals and objectives; establish accountability for results; treat them as partners; share responsibilities with them; always show respect; give them choices to learn and grow; and use every tool in this book. When appropriate, give them recognition and appreciation, i.e., thank you. Then please stay out of their way. Always remember that if anything goes badly, managers take all the blame. If anything goes well, employees get all the credit. There is more on this subject in Chapter 9, How to Be the Best Manager Possible.

- Hire the right people who already show engagement at work. Please see Section 3.6, Employee Engagement, for more information.

- Employees of all ages who see their immediate boss as a partner are much happier with their lives. Life satisfaction for these employees is worth more than doubling their income for middle-aged workers.[148] Effective managers know that working closely with their direct reports costs nothing but improves their morale, performance, recruiting, and retention. Please see Chapter 6: Partner with Your Bosses (Okay, You're the Junior Partner) for more information.

- The Society for Human Resource Management site surveys show that most responders say that *respect* was an important contributor to their job satisfaction.[149] Effective managers will ensure that everyone is treated respectfully.

- Give your employees fair pay and benefits. Larger salaries are not the answer to retention, but effective management is. More on this is in Section 1.2, What Employees Want.

- Ensure your staff is not approaching burnout. A surprising number of managers and their high-potential employees are approaching or suffering from burnout. According to a report, *Development Dimensions International: Global Leadership Forecast 2023*, a shocking 72% of managers surveyed are exhausted at the end of each day, which is a strong sign of burnout. This is an increase from 60% in 2020.[150] How do you deal with this? First, show empathy. Second, work with them through coaching to help them through tough patches and encourage them to look for more work to delegate. Third, are they working more than 50 hours per week? A 2013 Stanford University study shows that increases in output are relatively small as hours rise beyond 50 hours per week. There are no productivity increases from working more than 55 hours per week.[151] Fourth, Gallup reports that workers receiving gratifying recognition are 90% less likely to feel burnout. Effective managers use their weekly coaching meetings to recognize the accomplishments of their direct reports.[152] Finally, do they need more staff? When in doubt, conduct a workload analysis.

- Use every tool in this book to retain great employees.

Laying Off Employees

- Managers sometimes wait too long to tell people they are being laid off. Others fail to express sympathy. Finally, some managers neglect to tell departing employees about severance and other benefits.[153] A checklist of subjects to cover during layoff notifications will ensure that these meetings go smoothly. As with all procedures and checklists, this checklist should be affiliated with an HR policy and reviewed regularly but not less than annually. Please see Section 4.6, Policies, Procedures, and Checklists, for more information.

- Steps in the layoff process:
  - The CEO addresses the entire staff to explain what happened that required a layoff.
  - Managers are responsible for notifying their employees of layoffs. They must be completely truthful. Here is a sample script:
    - "We are very upset to lose such outstanding employees. It is our failure and not yours. Thank you for your important contributions to our organization. We genuinely appreciate all you did for us. Our HR staff will work with each of you individually to discuss timing, severance packages, and healthcare benefits. They will also work with you to revise your résumé and help you find new jobs. Again, we are very disappointed to have to let you go and will do everything we can to get you resettled in a new job." Of course, if your organization can rehire some of these employees later, their respectful treatment during layoffs will help them decide whether they want to return.[154]

> ***ILLUSTRATIVE STORY***
>
> *At one organization, the HR staff told an employee that she was being laid off per company policy to lay off the newest employees first. In spite of the explanation, she was still upset. Her boss, Rachel, took her to lunch to talk. Rachel explained that there was nothing wrong with the quality of her work and that she was an outstanding employee whom Rachel did not want to lose. She offered to provide an excellent reference and rehire her when possible. Rachel stayed in contact with the employee until she had a new job and said she would contact her if a job became available and that would be a good fit. Would you agree to work for this manager again if they treated you this well during a layoff?*

○ A January 2023 survey of 300 HR officers shows that 98% of their companies use algorithms to decide whom to cut.[155]

> **Definition of an algorithm:** A process in which precise instructions are programmed into a computer to calculate the optimal solution.

Dismissing (firing) an employee: Please see Section 2.7, Problem Employees.

When Employees Retire or Quit

- For all employees who retire or leave, HR must provide a checklist to ensure that all administrative "offboarding" matters are completed before their last day. This checklist is written and updated by HR, given to departing employees, collected before they leave, and reviewed to ensure that every checklist item is done. The offboarding checklist should include such items as calculating final pay; when the money should be in their bank account; turning in company-owned property to include badges, deactivating computers and other electronic equipment; reminding them that they signed an agreement that they would not share your company's proprietary information; conducting exit interviews; and ensuring the departing employee has completed the Job-Related Information for Your Successor Form provided in the Appendix, etc. This offboarding checklist is, like the onboarding checklist, attached to an HR policy, reviewed regularly, and updated as needed.

- It is customary to have a goodbye event for departing employees. This is an excellent opportunity to highlight their accomplishments, thank them for their work, and give them your best wishes for continuing success.

A final thought on managing good employees:

- "The best executive is one who has sense enough to pick good people to do what they are tasked to do, and self-restraint enough to keep from meddling with them while they do it."[156] —Theodore Roosevelt, 20th President of the United States

2.2 COACHING AND MENTORING

> **Definition of coaching:** A process where coachees (aka direct reports) develop their own solutions to job-related issues through their coach's (boss's) skillful listening and insightful questions. Creating their own path forward makes the coachee more committed to their own success.[157]

"You cannot teach a man anything. You can only help him discover it himself."[158]

—Galileo Galilei (1564–1642), astronomer and polymath

- Coaching is a powerful tool that encourages beneficial personal development for the long term and consistently improves outcomes. This is an important no-cost management tool that enhances productivity, recruiting, and retention.[159]

- Micromanaging is the opposite of coaching. It's a management style in which managers closely control every aspect of their employees' work, including their decision-making. These managers have difficulty delegating responsibility, and employees are not empowered to be creative and innovative. Employees want a sense of control and autonomy.

- Remember that managers need coaching, too.

- Only the coach and coachee participate in coaching meetings.

- The coach is almost always the coachee's (direct report's) boss.

- Direct reports' coaching responsibilities:

  - Provide their immediate boss with weekly updates on performance measurements for both recurring work and nonrecurring work (definitions below), decision requests, and any sensitive information on employees.

    - Performance measurements. Your most important performance measurements are those that align with your organization's strategic plan. See Section 3.2, Now That

You're Settled In, for more information on performance measurements and Section 3.11, Strategic Planning.

- Recurring and nonrecurring work

> **Definition of recurring work:** Recurring work is routine work that does not usually require any direct involvement by the manager if the performance measures meet the pre-established thresholds.

  - For example, tracking the number of call center phone calls is recurring work. Of course, if a percentage of these calls is not resolved within pre-established time thresholds, this must be reported to the manager as soon as possible but not later than the next coaching meeting.

  - Updates on recurring work in which the performance measures meet the pre-established thresholds are provided to your boss "for your information only."

> **Definition of nonrecurring work:** Nonrecurring work requires the manager's involvement, though this may be as little as receiving an update at a weekly coaching meeting. An example of nonrecurring work is tracking the construction of additional office space to accommodate an increasing number of staff. The direct report should provide the status of the project, i.e., whether it is ahead or behind schedule, is the expenditure rate higher than projected, etc.

- Decision requests. Direct reports should ask their bosses for decisions on matters that cannot be resolved at their level. Here is an example of a decision requested of you, the manager. In this example, the HR director asks for additional office space. Requests for your decisions should include a summary of alternatives, the pros and cons of each, and a well-thought-out recommendation. Below is an example of a complete but abbreviated decision request.

  - Decision request: The HR director requests additional office space.

- Summary of request: The HR director asks for 550 square feet of additional office space to ensure the privacy of conversations, which often involve sensitive personal information.

- Option 1: Rent additional office space to give each staff member a private office.

  - Pros: This will achieve the objective of ensuring privacy.

  - Cons: It will cost $250,000 to construct and lease "swing space" to house employees during construction.

  - Cons: This will take six months to plan and construct and will cost $25,000 to lease the additional space each year.

  - Cons: This will be very disruptive during the construction phase.

- Option 2: Use white noise (a whooshing sound that most think is air handling) to help mask nearby conversations and ringing phones.

  - Pros: This has a high probability of achieving the objective of ensuring privacy.

  - Pros: This will incur a one-time cost of a few hundred dollars, including installation.

  - Pros: This will cause minimal disruption in installing the white noise machine and speakers. If you want no disruptions, install the noise machine during the weekend.

  - Cons: While installing a white noise machine is highly likely to work successfully, there is no guarantee until it is installed and tested.

- Option 3: Allow HR staff to telework, reducing demand for office space. You will need to work with your staff to determine how many days each can telework. Use AI to help you determine who should be at the office on the same days.

- Pros: No cost.
- Pros: Improves morale and work-life balance.
- Cons: If the amount of office space is reduced due to telework, employees will not have the same desk each time they work in the office.

□ Option 4: Do nothing or delay the decision until later. These are good options on occasion.

□ Recommend Options 2 and 3: white noise and telework. Instruct the HR staff to let you know if the white noise is effective. Remember that there is a volume control on the white noise machine. If the device does not appear to be working, please see if it is on full volume. In this example, the device worked well after the volume was turned up. Most white noise speakers are installed in open areas, not offices. In this case, two more white noise speakers were installed in individual offices at their request. Their air-handling ductwork allowed conversations to be heard between these two offices. Telework is always an option whether you need more space or not.

- Sensitive information on employees. Though most briefing subjects will be electronic, sensitive subjects, such as staff disciplinary matters, should be briefed from memory or notes and not sent electronically unless told otherwise. Occasionally, emails containing sensitive subjects are inadvertently forwarded to unintended recipients. Also, please remember that both emails and notes can be used as evidence in court.

○ Other coaching meeting considerations:

- Decision requests should be made face-to-face, if possible. For these meetings, encourage your direct reports to bring people on their teams who are most familiar with the decision subject. It is a good experience for them, and you get to know them better. This allows you to recognize and thank your direct reports for their accomplishments and efforts. Of course, before the meeting, you should contact your direct reports about their direct reports' accomplishments. Imagine the morale lift for these employees, from wondering whether you know who they are to receiving recognition and appreciation for their accomplishments and efforts. For more information, please see Chapter 9, How to Be the Best Manager Possible.

- Brief your bosses on specific subjects that are "out of cycle" if something occurs that they need to know about sooner. Problems do not get better with time.

○ Limit weekly coaching meetings to 30 minutes. Of course, in some situations, coaching meetings can be scheduled for more time. Be careful if you schedule more than 30 minutes for each coaching meeting. Since managers in the United States manage an average of ten direct reports, scheduling 60 minutes for each will require 10 hours of your 50-hour week and 15 hours per week if you schedule 90 minutes for each coaching meeting. A 30-minute weekly coaching meetings encourage both parties not to waste time.

○ Direct reports ask their coach for additional coaching meetings beyond the weekly scheduled meeting as needed.

- Coach's coaching responsibilities:

○ A 2024 Gallup report stated that 80% of employees who received worthwhile feedback in the past seven days were very engaged. This high level of engagement applied to all workers regardless of the number of days they teleworked. The Gallup report stated that these meaningful conversations that provide direct reports with worthwhile feedback should last between 15 and 30 minutes weekly. The 30-minute weekly coaching meetings allow coaches to get updates on all performance measurements and for coaches to provide coachees with worthwhile feedback.[160] After recognizing their accomplishments (recognition), please remember to say thank you (appreciation). A 2022 Quantum Workplace survey showed that employees want one-on-one meetings weekly with their bosses, too. The 30-minute weekly coaching meetings satisfy this need perfectly. These meetings will increase engagement and make your job easier.[161]

- Let direct reports make their own decisions as often as possible. Ask insightful questions to guide them toward their own solutions. Direct reports do not want to hear how you fixed a similar problem.

- Coaches and coachees use the GROW and SMART models described below. The GROW model helps to improve goal-setting, decision-making, problem-solving and personal development.[162] The SMART model ensures that objectives are (S) specific, (M) measurable, (A) achievable, (R) relevant, and (T) time-limited.[163]

- Your coaching meetings should be on the same day of the week. Same place. Same time. Minimum chance of being interrupted.

- Schedule additional meetings as needed.

- Coaches should spend the great majority of their time listening.

- Never interrupt your direct reports.

- When to coach direct reports: At least weekly, also at milestone completion, at the end of a project or task completion, when external changes affect the task completion timeline, and when performance changes, whether for better or worse.

- Below is an example of a coaching meeting discussion.

Direct report: My staff and I are working on an impossible deadline. Our software engineers tell us that completing the project within the time allocated is not possible.

Coach: Can you get a deadline extension?

Direct report: We asked for an extension but were told our customer needs the new software by our agreed-upon deadline.

Coach: Will more resources help?

Direct report: It is not a resource problem. The critical path cannot be compressed any further. The critical path is the longest order of sequential tasks, from beginning to end, that shows the minimum time to complete the project. The completion date will be delayed if there is a single delay along this path. Our software engineers have reviewed it and agree that we cannot meet the deadline.

Coach: What limitations does their existing software have? What are we being paid to fix or revise?

Direct report: The revised software will add new functions to the existing software for our customer. Some of the functions are more important than others. I just realized we could first focus on writing code for our customers' essential functions. That may meet their immediate needs, giving us additional time to complete their less important tasks.

Coach: Great idea! What is your next step?

Direct report: I will work with our contracting office and our customer to see if we can build their critical new functions first to meet their immediate needs.

Coach: That is perfect! How can I help you?

Direct report: Nothing, for now, thanks. I will arrange a meeting with our contracting staff and our customer.

Coach: Great thinking! Thanks for all you do!

- The GROW coaching (and mentoring) model:[164] Both coaches and coachees should use a coaching model such as the GROW model to improve goal setting, decision-making, problem-solving and personal development. GROW stands for (G) Goal, (R) Reality (current), (O) Options or Obstacles, and (W) Will or Way Forward. Let us look at each of these four steps:
  - Goal questions:
    - Describe the outcome once this objective is achieved.

- Does your goal have must-have and nice-to-have objectives? If so, what are they, and what criteria did you use to determine that some are must-haves and others are nice-to-haves?
- Who did you partner with to create this goal? Your employees? Customers?
- Does your goal require the involvement of other offices? If so, who are they, and what is their involvement?

○ Current Reality questions:
  - Why are you doing this? What is broken?
  - What do you need to change?
  - What is currently happening (who, what, when, where, and how)?
  - What is your next step, and why?

○ Options (Obstacles) questions:
  - What options are you considering for achieving the goal or objective?
  - What obstacles do you see, and how do you plan to resolve each?
  - Have all team members and customers had a chance to review and comment on the options?
  - Describe the pros and cons of each option. (An interesting fact: Ben Franklin created the pros and cons list. He described it to Joseph Priestly, the discoverer of oxygen, in a 1772 letter.)[165]
  - How will these options impact others outside of our organization?

○ Will or Way Forward questions:
  - Which option did you choose, and why did you choose it?
  - Who helped you choose this option?
  - Can you realistically achieve your goal in the time allotted? If not, what will it take to meet the timeline?
  - Do you need additional staff or funds?

- ○ Sir John Whitmore developed the GROW model and described it in his book *Coaching for Performance Fifth Edition: The Principles and Practice of Coaching and Leadership.*[166]

SMART Objectives model:[167] Both coaches and coachees should use a coaching model such as the SMART model to create objectives that are (S) specific, (M) measurable, (A) achievable, (R) relevant, and (T) time-limited.

SMART Objectives Model with an Example

SMART	STEPS[168]	SMART Objectives[169]	Example
S	Specific	Specify the outcome you want to achieve.	Improve online customer satisfaction ratings.
M	Measurable	Identify measurements that will allow you to calculate progress toward achieving your objective.	Improve average review ratings from 4.5 to 4.7 on a rating scale of 0 (poor service) to 5 (outstanding service).
A	Achievable	Is the objective achievable? Do you have the right skill sets and resources?	The objective is achievable, but additional resources are needed. We must select and deploy advanced website engagement tools.
R	Relevant or Realistic	Is this objective aligned with your strategic plan? Is this objective realistic and achievable?	This software tool will help us achieve our objective, and it is aligned with our strategic plan. Yes, this objective is realistic and achievable. Studies show that advanced website engagement tools will help us achieve our review ratings goal.
T	Time-Limited	Does the deadline reasonably allow you to achieve your objective?	Yes, the deadline is reasonable. Studies show that our allotted time is sufficient to deploy this tool and improve our review ratings to the level we set as an objective.

- More SMART questions
  - ○ "Specific" questions:
    - ■ Who was involved in creating this outcome? Did your staff and stakeholders have an opportunity to comment on this outcome?

- What do we want to accomplish? What are the benefits?
- Will this give us the outcome we want?

  - "Measurable" questions:
    - What measurements will tell us we are on track to achieve our objective?
    - How difficult will it be to capture these measurements?
    - Is there research to show the likelihood of our success in the time allotted?
    - How will we know when our objective is complete?

  - "Achievable" questions:
    - Can we achieve this objective in the time we are given?
    - Do we have the financing necessary?
    - Do we have people with the suitable skills to accomplish this objective?
    - Do we need to partner with another office? If so, who are they, and what is their role?

  - "Relevant or Realistic" questions:
    - Do we have the resources to complete this objective?
    - Is this objective even achievable?
    - Why is it important?
    - Is this the right time to tackle this objective?

  - "Time-Limited" questions:
    - What is our deadline? Who decided on this date?
    - Can we realistically complete this objective in the time given to us?
    - Will this date affect any other projects? If yes, who should we notify?

- George T. Doran introduced the SMART model in his 1981 article, "There is a S.M.A.R.T. Way to Write Management's Goals and Objectives" published in *Management Review*.[170]

> **Definition of a stretch goal:** A deliberately challenging goal or objective. Setting a stretch goal means attempting to do more than you think you can.

- Stretch goals give you an entirely different approach to achieving your goal. You will learn to do more with less and find shortcuts that you would not have otherwise. A stretch goal should be the direct report's decision. Thank them for even trying. If they fail, ask them what they learned, but never criticize.

Mentoring

> **Definition of mentoring:** A long-term partnership in which mentors support the personal and professional growth and development of mentees (aka proteges or direct reports) in areas such as career development, job skills development, employee engagement, management skills development, networking, etc.[171]

- Only the mentor and mentee participate in mentoring meetings.

- Mentees may have more than one mentor at the same time. For example, the boss can serve as a mentor to their direct reports for such areas as employee engagement, management development, communications skills development, work-life balance, etc. If your direct report is in the accounting field and you are not, you should help your direct report find someone in the accounting field who can serve as their mentor in such areas as career development, job skills development, networking, etc.

- The use of mentors continues to grow in corporate America. A remarkable 84% of Fortune 500 companies have mentorship programs.[172] Mentoring is a low-cost management tool that improves recruitment, retention, and outcomes.

- A 2018 PricewaterhouseCoopers survey reveals that women worldwide do not believe their boss's advice on pay, promotions, or what would help or hurt their careers.[173] A 2023 LeanIn.Org and McKinsey & Company study showed that women remain underrepresented in corporate America. In 2022, women filled 47% of entry-level positions. They comprise 40% of managers, 36% of senior managers/directors, 33% of vice presidents, 28% of senior vice presidents, and 28% of positions in the C-Suites.[174] Although women are underrepresented in corporate America, their performance is impressive. A Gallup survey shows that 35% of male managers are engaged at work compared to 41% of female managers. In all working-age generations, female managers are more engaged than male managers. Remarkably, female managers with children living in their households are also more engaged than their male counterparts. Higher engagement means higher levels of workplace performance.[175]

- Mentees' responsibilities:
  - Initiate requests for mentors' guidance (some mentees and mentors are matched by their organization or a professional association).

  - Come prepared to meetings with specific questions on career development, developing better communication and management skills, networking, improving work/life balance, etc. Mentees should think through their questions and then prepare potential solutions for their questions and the pros and cons of each.

- Mentors' responsibilities:
  - Schedule your meetings on dates and times you are least likely to be interrupted.

  - Mentors should spend the great majority of their time listening. Never interrupt your mentees, please.

  - If you do not have the background to answer all of your mentee's questions, please refer them to someone who can answer the ones you cannot.

  - Remember that mentors need mentoring, too.

- Some mentors prefer to ask questions to help mentees develop their own options. Here are a few examples of a mentor's questions:

  - Do you know what your strengths are? Have you taken Gallup's CliftonStrengths Assessment online? For more information, please see Section 3.6, Employee Engagement.

  - What is the highest-level job you would like to attain and when?

  - What job do you want next, and what training and experience will you need to be competitive to be selected?

  - What job activities do you enjoy the most and least?

  - What could you do to help achieve your career goal? Join a committee or project?

  - Would it be helpful to shadow someone in a job you aspire to?

  - Is there a professional association you could join?

  - What are your career goals for the next three years? How can I help you get started?

- When to mentor employees: Your first meeting should be scheduled for 90 minutes to 2 hours and preferably face-to-face, allowing the mentor to learn the mentee's background and career goals. All other meetings should be one hour monthly.

A final thought on coaching and mentoring:

- Coaching and mentoring are must-use management tools for the 21st century and beyond. They are very effective and low-cost, and millennials and Gen Zers expect to receive both.

2.3 **TRAINING**

Managers only have motivation and training to improve employee output. You are failing to use a vital tool if you are not training your employees.[176] Training is also an important recruitment and retention tool.

> **Definition of training:** Teaching an employee knowledge and skills to improve their ability to do a specific job.[177]
>
> **Definition of upskilling:** Teaching an employee new knowledge and skills to improve their ability in their current job.
>
> **Definition of reskilling:** Teaching an employee new knowledge and skills to improve their ability to do a different job.

- Types of training:
  - On-the-job training (OJT)
    - Specific job training for employees new to the job. This is usually provided by a manager or coworker familiar with the job and is often conducted one-on-one.
    - Training for employees who provide backup when the primary person is unavailable.
    - Written policies, procedures, and checklists can be very helpful for training new employees. It allows them to get "up to speed" quicker and be more accurate sooner. For more information, please see Section 4.6, Policies, Procedures, and Checklists.
  - Other job-related training examples:
    - Reskilling
    - Upskilling
    - Managers' training
    - Safety training

- Professional credentials training (required of physicians, nurses, etc.)

- Quality training

- Ethics training

- Strategic plan training so everyone knows how their work unit's goals, objectives, and milestones support the organization's strategic goals, objectives, and milestones

- Training employees to do the work of others creates depth in your organization

○ Training outside your employees' current job area. Most millennials and Gen Zers accept the first job offer, and many feel they did not get their ideal job. In fact, in one major study, 52% of recent college graduates are working in jobs that do not use their degrees. This underemployment has long-term earnings implications.[178] Often, these employees are looking to leave. Once people are on the wrong career track, moving to their chosen career track can be challenging. Training in their chosen field will help them move to a preferred career track. Offering them training outside their career area can incentivize them to perform well and consider other jobs in the organization that may be a better fit.

ILLUSTRATIVE STORY

Andrew, a millennial with a college degree, was an administrative assistant for nearly eight years. He felt stuck in that field and asked his boss, Elizabeth, for advice. Elizabeth said colleges give you a broad education but no practical job skills. She suggested that Andrew gain valuable job skills in his preferred career field. Elizabeth recommended that Andrew follow his interests and complete a ten-week training course in budget and finance. Within a year, Andrew completed all the classes. He also worked in the evenings to keep up with his office work. The same week Andrew completed his final course, he was hired by the organization's finance office, receiving a promotion and pay increase.

There were over 300 applicants for this job. Andrew dazzled the interviewers with the detailed information he learned in his training courses. Within a year, he earned another promotion. Like Andrew, many millennials accept a job that is not in their field of choice. The longer they spend in an undesired career field, the harder it is to leave for a more desired one. Acquiring the right job skills is an excellent way to transition to a different career field. Andrew said that without Elizabeth's training recommendation, he would likely be working elsewhere as he was already applying for jobs outside the organization.

Now, he is much happier and fully productive in the same organization. Which training courses would you recommend to employees? Encourage your employees to contact senior people in their chosen career fields for advice. If you know someone in their preferred career area, contact them and ask if they could spare time to chat with an eager employee seeking career advice. When I have done so, no one has ever turned me down. These "information interviews" are opportunities to ask what credentials and courses are the most recognized in their field and get other information to help them transition. Encourage these interviewees to prepare questions and deliver a hand-written thank-you letter as soon after the meeting as possible.

- Why training is essential:
  - Training is the only way to keep workers' job knowledge and skills current in an age of rapid technological changes.
  - Demand for training will increase. A 2023 World Economic Forum survey shows that by 2027, 60% of employees will require training, but only half will have access to training opportunities. The top priority for skills training is analytical thinking, followed by creative thinking.[179]
  - On-the-job training ensures new employees can perform their jobs better, be productive earlier, and make fewer or no mistakes.
  - Job training ensures employees know what is expected of them.

- ○ Job training maintains professional credentials (e.g., medical professionals).

- ○ A 2021 Gallup and Amazon poll found that 71% of U.S. workers who participated in job upskilling said it increased their job satisfaction, 65% said upskilling raised their standard of living, and 69% said upskilling improved their quality of life.[180]

- Training considerations

  - ○ Millennials and Gen Zers prefer microlearning, which involves the presentation of concise information that is quickly understood and ready to apply immediately. This book is written in the microlearning format.

  - ○ Onboarding and training should be as visual as possible. Gen Zers are visual learners who grew up watching YouTube.[181]

  - ○ Training can be prepared and presented by the company, provided commercially, or a combination of these. For larger companies, bringing the trainer on-site may be more cost-effective. The training costs per person are usually less, and your employees will have no travel expenses. Here is an illustrative story to bring this subject to life.

    ILLUSTRATIVE STORY
    One large organization brought a trainer onsite, lowering costs. They also had a higher attendance rate because the training was now more convenient for the employees.

  - ○ It is crucial to ensure that your instructors have current and firsthand experience in the subjects they teach. This not only enhances the credibility of the training but also ensures that the content remains relevant and up to date, making the training more trustworthy and valuable for your employees.

- When to discuss training options and what to cover

  - ○ With a new direct report:
    - ■ During onboarding

- Any training required by the position, such as on-the-job training
  - The training funds reserved for this employee for the current fiscal year
- With all direct reports:
  - Whenever the employee asks
  - At least twice yearly to discuss the employee's training requests, any required training, your training recommendations, and the amount of training funds set aside for the employee

ILLUSTRATIVE STORY

The best trainers have experience in the subjects they teach. At one organization, a senior manager, Jessica, taught a course on management. This was the top-scoring course in the organization's prestigious management training program. A training staff member who wanted to begin teaching the class asked for her slides. Jessica kindly replied that her training course was proprietary and that she would not allow anyone else to teach it. She also knew that an instructor who had never managed would not be an ideal candidate to teach a management course.

ILLUSTRATIVE STORY

One large organization had a very high rate of staff turnover. A mid-level manager was aware that training was a strong retention tool. She recommended that the senior management team expand the training budget to help reduce turnover. One of the senior managers replied, "I do not want to waste money on training because the employees will leave anyway." This does make you question how people like this become senior managers.

> ***ILLUSTRATIVE STORY***
>
> *In a forward-thinking organization, each employee is allocated $5,000 annually for training. The funds cover training fees, travel, hotel, and food expenses. With most training opportunities available locally, employees are encouraged to train in their area, allowing them to take more courses. Many employees even opt for online courses to maximize their learning. This commitment to employee development is a testament to the organization's stated value of continuous learning.*

A final thought on training:

- Bill Gates says that training is a fundamental form of knowledge sharing that all organizations need to help stay competitive.[182] It also helps recruitment and retention.

2.4 PERFORMANCE DEVELOPMENT

Gallup's research underscores the need to replace traditional performance management with performance development, a future-focused management tool that fosters employee growth through coaching. Performance development includes the creation and tracking of mutually agreed-upon performance expectations to include goals and objectives that align with the organization's goals and objectives. Finally, it establishes employee accountability for results and gives them autonomy.[183] To be an effective manager, it is crucial to do everything possible to help your employees succeed. A significant part of this support is provided in your coaching meetings.

> **Definition of traditional performance management:** A process of creating employee goals and objectives, measuring employees' progress in completing them, and providing formal, written performance appraisals at the end of the reporting period, often annually, that reflect the degree to which each objective was accomplished. Traditional performance management, including giving report cards, demoralizes employees.

- The outcome of traditional performance management is disastrous; it destroys teamwork and encourages rivalry. Performance ratings create anxiety and leave people upset.[184] Despite the overwhelming evidence that performance appraisals are counterproductive, one study shows that a surprising 63% of companies still use them.[185] A 2020 Gallup poll showed that 86% of employees felt their annual performance appraisals were inaccurate. Even worse, a 2018 Adobe Inc. study found that 22% of responders said they were so upset during their annual performance appraisal discussion that they burst into tears.[186] Effective managers should use performance development exclusively. Show your boss this chapter to convince them to move immediately from traditional performance management to performance development.

ILLUSTRATIVE STORY

In one organization, a highly regarded employee won a prestigious, national-level award. Brenda was so well-liked that she was given a long, heartfelt standing ovation when she received the award. If you asked Brenda about the award, she would say, "I was just doing my job," and she meant it. A few months after she received the award, Brenda's boss retired, and Richard became her new boss. Richard soon met with Brenda to discuss what it would take for Brenda to get the top performance evaluation. In this organization, 65% of employees receive the top rating. (I do not recommend performance ratings because they make employees compete for the top ratings. This is traditional performance management, and it kills cooperation.) Richard laid out a set of performance standards that would be impossible to achieve. Brenda quickly realized that these unachievable performance standards would earn her a rating that would place her in the bottom 35% of employees. When Brenda tried explaining this, Richard smiled, said everyone needs stretch goals, and dismissed her concerns. Brenda discussed this situation with her family and decided to retire early. She also did not want to get another job and start over at her age. Richard was asked to leave the organization within six months of Brenda's retirement. Why didn't Brenda go over Richard's head to complain? It was a personal decision not to tie up her senior boss's time with her problem. The organization unnecessarily lost a valuable employee when she was most productive. If there had been no traditional performance management program, Brenda would have happily kept doing her outstanding job for several more years.

ILLUSTRATIVE STORY

In 1977, the U.S. Air Force introduced an officer performance management system that required senior officers to decide which of their officers were rated in the top 22% (an overall rating of 1), those in the top 23% to 50% (an overall rating of 2), and all others were in the bottom half (an overall rating of 3). The way senior officers handled this new system was to give an overall 1 rating to officers being considered for promotion that year. As a result, for example, if you were a junior captain and not eligible for promotion for several years, you could expect to get an overall 3, no matter how hard you worked. This reduced cooperation and destroyed morale. Many highly effective officers chose to leave the Air Force because of this ill-advised officer performance management system. Within 18 months, a new, fairer performance program was introduced.

> **Definition of performance development:** Management actions that grow employees through future-focused coaching. It includes the creation and tracking of mutually agreed upon performance expectations to include goals and objectives that align with the organization's goals and objectives, establishes employee accountability for results, and gives them autonomy.[187] Performance development improves recruitment, retention, productivity, and engagement.

- Benefits of performance development:
  - There is no scorecard or rating as with traditional performance management appraisals.
  - Employees understand what is expected of them, which improves engagement and retention. For more information, please see Section 3.6, Employee Engagement.
  - It ensures that employees' goals and objectives align with the organization's goals and objectives.
  - Most discussions are future-focused, allowing managers to coach employees to create and track goals and objectives that align with the organization's goals and objectives. Please see Section 3.11, Strategic Planning, for more information.

- It establishes employee accountability for results. Please remember that the manager and the direct report always share responsibility for task completion. Please see Section 3.5, Delegation and Empowerment, for more information.

- It gives employees autonomy so they can achieve the mutually agreed upon goals and objectives their way. People want maximum control over their lives and work. Effective managers give that to them.

- It enables managers to coach employees, which is what effective managers, millennials, and Gen Zers want. Employees get feedback on achieving their objectives at their weekly coaching meetings. A 2024 Gallup report states that 80% of employees who received worthwhile feedback in the past seven days are very engaged. This high level of engagement applies to all workers regardless of the number of days they telework. These conversations should last between 15 and 30 minutes weekly, which makes them ideal for your coaching meetings.[188] Please see Section 2.2, Coaching and Mentoring, for more information.

- Performance development improves recruitment, retention, productivity, and engagement.

- Performance development should provide a summary of employee accomplishments. Traditional performance management usually consists of two parts:

  - The performance appraisal, which reviews the reporting period just ending to determine how well employees achieved objectives against preset standards (not useful), and

  - A summary of accomplishments (still useful). Employees should receive a summary of their accomplishments every six months, and a copy placed in their HR records. Why every six months? Because millennials and Gen Zers want frequent feedback, and a written summary of accomplishments every six months helps achieve this.

Managers should ask each employee for a list of their accomplishments so that nothing is overlooked when preparing the written narrative. Managers cannot remember or document everything their employees have accomplished, and leaving out important information will disappoint them. Why is keeping a summary of accomplishments a good idea? These summaries:

- Are positive feedback to the employee;

- Are a permanent record of each employee's accomplishments and any individual or group awards received;

- Are useful when showing future hiring managers what an employee has accomplished; and

- Help determine whether internal employees are qualified for other positions or promotions. A summary of accomplishments should contain no negative information. No semiannual summary of accomplishments should be completed on problem employees. If you have a problem employee, please follow the guidance in Section 2.7, Problem Employees

○ Some of you may be concerned that if you cannot give a problem employee a low rating on their performance evaluation (traditional performance management), you cannot change their behavior or fire them. Section 2.7, Problem Employees, contains guidance on how to fire employees.

■ There are tools that can help you change the behavior of or fire problem employees whether or not your organization has transitioned from performance management to performance development. Some of these include the following:

  - For problem employees who have the potential to improve, consider a performance improvement plan (PIP). This is discussed in Section 2.7, Problem Employees.

  - Guidance on how to counsel problem employees is found in Section 2.7, Problem Employees. Problem employee behavior includes frequent late arrivals or early departures that are not part of an accommodation; excessive or unexcused absenteeism; inappropriate language (abusive, disrespectful, harassing, etc.); poor job performance in one area, with otherwise satisfactory work; poor performance because he or she cannot grasp the job, but is trying and has a good attitude; poor performance, but has the potential to improve and has a good attitude; frequent complaining or gossip that affects morale; and bad attitude toward the organization or coworkers.[189]

- Dismissing (firing) an employee is your last option after you have exhausted all other options.

- There are circumstances in which employees' behavior is so egregious that they can be dismissed without counseling. Here is a partial list: theft, violence, substance abuse, insubordination, misconduct including fraud, criminal behavior, bullying, etc.[190] In all cases, before firing any employee, check with an employment attorney to ensure you have sufficient justification and documentation for dismissal.

2.5 INCLUSION, DIVERSITY, EQUITY, AND ACCESSIBILITY

Workforces worldwide are becoming increasingly inclusive, diverse, equitable, and accessible. How well you embrace inclusion, diversity, equity, and accessibility will also directly affect your employee hiring, retention, productivity, and your bottom line. Do prospective employees see others like themselves in your organization?

The following four definitions are from an Executive Order dated on June 25, 2021, entitled Executive Order on Diversity, Equity, Inclusion, and Accessibility in the Federal Workforce. While this executive order was written for the federal workforce, the definitions are universal.

Definition of inclusion: " . . . the recognition, appreciation, and use of the talents and skills of employees of all backgrounds."[191]

Definition of diversity: " . . . the practice of including the many communities, identities, races, ethnicities, backgrounds, abilities, cultures, and beliefs of the American people, including underserved communities."[192]

Definition of equity: " . . . the consistent and systematic fair, just, and impartial treatment of all individuals, including individuals who belong to underserved communities that have been denied such treatment."[193]

Definition of accessibility: " . . . the design, construction, development, and maintenance of facilities, information and communication technology, programs, and services so that all people, including people with disabilities, can fully and independently use them. Accessibility includes the provision of accommodations and modifications to ensure equal access to employment and participation in activities for people with disabilities, the reduction or elimination of physical and attitudinal barriers to equitable opportunities, a commitment to ensuring that people with disabilities can independently access every outward-facing and internal activity or electronic space, and the pursuit of best practices such as universal design."[194]

Definition of a best practice: A process that has proven to produce the best results and is acceptable for widespread use.[195] Before implementing a best practice, discuss it with your employees, customers, and even your peers. Your employees will be implementing it, and your customers will live with the outcome. Your peers have backgrounds that can contribute to the best outcome. Please see Section 4.7, Continuous Process Improvement, for more information.

- Inclusion
  - Inclusion happens when everyone feels respected and welcome. Effective managers know that inclusion requires constant work.[196]
  - In a 2023 Pew Research Center survey, 56% of U.S. workers responded that increasing attention to inclusion, diversity, and equity was good.[197] Many organizations believe that they encourage an inclusive and diverse culture, but only 40% of their employees believe their manager promotes an inclusive workplace.[198] Effective managers, you know what to do here.

- Diversity
  - Diversity happens when you hire, develop, and retain a diverse team. Effective managers know that this requires constant work.
  - A group of people with diverse backgrounds is more creative, better at decision-making and problem-solving, more innovative, and likely to improve financial performance.[199]
  - A McKinsey & Company report shows that companies in the top quartile for ethnic diversity have a 39% increased probability of outperforming those in the bottom quartile. Also, companies in the top quartile for gender diversity, with greater than 30% women on their executive teams, are more likely to outperform companies that have fewer than 30% women.[200]
  - A diverse workforce keeps organizations in touch with an increasingly diverse customer base. Thus, organizations are wise to reflect the people they serve.
  - When possible, create diverse teams to work together on projects.
  - Ensure that your interview panels are diverse. Please see Section 2.1, Hire and Retain Great Employees, for more information.
  - Generations define diversity differently. Baby boomers and Generation Xers often see diversity as different genders, races, religions, ethnicities, and sexual orientations. Millennials

take these types of diversity for granted. In addition, they also value cognitive diversity, or diversity of ideas, thoughts, and philosophies.[201]

- Equity
  - Equity happens when each employee feels treated fairly and justly and given equal opportunity at success regardless of their gender, race, religion, ethnicity, and sexual orientation. Effective managers know that equity requires constant work.
  - With equality of reasonable accommodations, everyone is offered equal accommodations. With equity, accommodations are based on individual needs.[202]

- Accessibility
  - Accessibility happens when all restrictions, physical and attitudinal, are removed, and people with disabilities are able to contribute equally with all others.[203] Effective managers know it requires constant work.
  - 25% of today's 20-year-olds will become persons with disabilities before age 67.[204]
  - National employment studies, including a 30-year analysis by DuPont de Nemours, reveal that people with disabilities have less absenteeism, perform equal to or higher than others, and have better retention.[205]

> **Definition of accommodation-sensitive individuals:** Individuals who are completely dependent on work accommodations.[206] The majority of people with disabilities do not need any accommodations. For those who do need accommodations, the average cost is only $500, and organizations may be eligible for tax incentives to cover these costs.[207]

  - The Employer Assistance and Resource Network on Disability has a page on its website called "Resources for Finding Candidates with Disabilities." This is a complete one-stop resource to locate highly qualified people with disabilities in your area with the precise skills your organization needs.[208]

- Encourage your staff to ask for workplace accommodations as needed and provide them willingly when asked. Accommodations can include building ramps, modifying a restroom, modifying a workspace, providing a sign language interpreter, adjusting work schedules to accommodate medical appointments for those with chronic medical conditions, etc.

ILLUSTRATIVE STORY

In 1941, Konrad Zuse developed the first fully programmable digital computer, the Z-3, in Germany. Mr. Arnold Fast was hired to program the Z-3 and became the world's first programmer. Mr. Fast was blind.[209]

ILLUSTRATIVE STORY

Ludwig van Beethoven became deaf at age 29. He went on to compose his Ninth Symphony and other world-famous compositions.

ILLUSTRATIVE STORY

Stephen Hawking, an English theoretical physicist and cosmologist, was diagnosed with amyotrophic lateral sclerosis, or Lou Gehrig's disease, a neurodegenerative disease, at age 21. He went on to propose a theory of cosmology, collaborated on gravitational singularity theorems and predicted that black holes emit radiation.[210]

ILLUSTRATIVE STORY

At age 18, Frida Kahlo was severely injured in a bus accident that left her with lifelong pain. She became one of Mexico's greatest painters.

- Incorporate inclusion, diversity, equity, and accessibility roles into your organization.
  - Your senior executives should:
    - Appoint a chief inclusion, diversity, equity, and accessibility officer (chief IDEA officer). The chief IDEA officer should report to your chief executive officer, chief operating officer,

or another senior official.[211] Not creating or filling these positions will signal to your staff that you do not consider your IDEA program important. In smaller organizations, the chief IDEA officer's responsibilities may be fulfilled by a senior official along with their other duties. I include responsibility for *accessibility* in this position, so there is a high-level official responsible for ensuring that all physical and attitudinal barriers are removed and people with disabilities are able to contribute equally with all others. This can only be done effectively at the highest level of the organization.

- Include IDEA goals and objectives in your strategic plan. The IDEA objectives must be measurable. Senior executives should be updated at least quarterly to review progress toward achieving them.[212]

- Direct pulse surveys on how you are achieving your IDEA goals and objectives.

> **Definition of pulse surveys:** Shorter and more frequent surveys that are designed to take a much more frequent "pulse" of the organization.

  - Results are combined and analyzed over time. Assess the results, compare them to previous survey results as well as other national and international survey results, and act to continually improve IDEA in your organization. Instruct your staff to research IDEA programs from other organizations to find best practices that benefit your programs.

- Encourage employees to create employee resource groups (ERGs) and participate in their meetings and activities.

> **Definition of employee resource groups (ERGs):** Sometimes called affinity groups, ERGs are groups based on common interests, shared characteristics, or life experiences.

- ☐ ERGs allow people with similar backgrounds to connect, such as the Women's ERG, Interfaith ERG, African American ERG, Asian American ERG, Hispanic American ERG, Military Veterans ERG, People with Disabilities ERG, Needlepoint ERG, etc. ERGs can provide mentoring, networking, and socializing, help foster inclusion for your organization, give underrepresented groups a voice, build social networks, and provide community volunteers.[213] Another advantage of ERGs is that they allow employees to make friends at work. An O. C. Tanner Company global study concludes that having a good friend at work improves an employee's work performance, job satisfaction, productivity, and loyalty, provides a sense of belonging, and these employees are more satisfied with their lives overall.[214] Senior managers should give ERGs assignments such as helping attract a diverse workforce and improving retention and workplace culture. ERGs can also arrange organizational events around themes such as Veterans Day, organizational social events, etc. ERGs can also sponsor recognition month events for Asian Americans, Hispanic Americans, African Americans, etc., to include outside speakers. To improve diversity recruiting, ERG members can attend minority hiring events along with HR staff. Minority applicants attending a hiring fair are likelier to speak with recruiters who look like them. Make it clear to your ERGs that you expect them to be a real influence on the business and that they will get the support of senior management. ERGs cost nothing and improve retention.

ILLUSTRATIVE STORY

At one organization, staff members were encouraged to create ERGs. Groups such as the Military Veterans ERG quickly formed. This ERG included over 130 military veterans eager to help the homeless veterans in their area. At the same time, the People with Disabilities ERG started but had few members because almost no employees identified as persons with disabilities. The few that joined initially had family members with disabilities. After the senior management expressed interest in hiring people with disabilities, one division hired Nicholas, a highly qualified person. He was the first person with a disability employed by this organization that anyone could remember. Nicholas did a superb job helping hundreds of customers around the world. He is deaf and deals with all his customers via email. This success led to the organization hiring more people with disabilities. When I checked back a few years later, both ERGs were going strong. Both also had members who were neither veterans nor people with disabilities. People join ERGs for a variety of reasons, but all are welcome.

ILLUSTRATIVE STORY

In the 1990s, Mary Barra, CEO of General Motors, created the precursor to GM WOMEN, which stands for "Women Offering Mentoring, Expertise, and Networking." GM WOMEN offers guest speakers and career planning sessions. Ms. Barra is a remarkable CEO who returned GM to profitability after the government bailout in 2008.[215]

- Ensure diverse representation exists throughout all senior levels, boards, committees, and organization units.

- Participate in the organization's IDEA initiatives.

- Support and attend events celebrating other cultures.

- Create a strong succession plan.

> **Definition of a succession plan:** A formal written long-range plan that identifies and prepares high achievers in your organization to advance to top management jobs.

- ☐ Ensure that succession planning includes women, African Americans, Asian Americans, Hispanic Americans, and other underrepresented employees such as those with disabilities.
- Your chief IDEA officer should:
  - Partner with senior executives to improve business performance by ensuring that all organizational entities have inclusion, diversity, equity, and accessibility. Be involved in every aspect of the organization, including strategic planning, staff diversity, recruiting, retention, etc.[216]
  - Encourage the creation of ERGs and attend their meetings and events.
  - Brief the board of directors at least quarterly on progress with achieving IDEA goals and objectives.
  - Ensure that the diversity strategy, which is centered on attracting and retaining a diverse workforce, is linked to the organization's strategy.
  - Ask employees for suggestions for improving your IDEA programs.
  - Provide IDEA training.
  - Support and attend events celebrating cultures.
- Your HR staff should:
  - Advertise all jobs to a diverse group of potential employees.

ILLUSTRATIVE STORY

At one organization, the chief recruiter attended recruiting events with limited minority participation. These were the same events his predecessor had taken part in for years. A senior manager, realizing the recruiter's limited recruiting range, compiled a list of recruiting events attended primarily by African Americans, Hispanic Americans, Asian Americans, etc. There were many of these events available in their large metropolitan area. When the recruiters took part in these events, they invited senior African American, Hispanic American and Asian American staff members to go with them. People are more likely to approach a recruiting booth if it has people who look like themselves.

- Ensure that all job openings have diverse applicants.
- Include questions about IDEA in employee surveys.
- Ensure that all interview panels are diverse.
- Encourage the creation of ERGs and attend their meetings and events.
- Participate in the organization's IDEA initiatives.
  - Your managers should:
    - Actively support all IDEA initiatives.
    - Ensure that an adequate number of diverse candidates are considered for all job vacancies.
    - Ensure that interview panels are diverse.
    - Encourage the creation of ERGs and attend their meetings and events.
    - Participate in the organization's IDEA initiatives.
  - All employees should:
    - Actively support all IDEA initiatives.
    - Participate in one or more ERGs and create new ones.
    - Provide feedback to improve IDEA initiatives.
    - Ask work colleagues about their cultures, races, religions, and backgrounds.

- Discrimination is costly to businesses. According to a Citigroup study, discrimination cost the U.S. economy $16 trillion over the past 20 years.[217]

- Much work is still needed. A 2021 Gallup study showed that 75% of Black and 42% of white survey participants reported workplace discrimination the previous year. The same survey shows that women suffer a higher job-related burnout rate than men. There was a three-percentage-point difference between women and men in 2019 that increased to an eight-point difference in 2021.[218]

Final thoughts:

- **A final thought on inclusion and diversity:** Recent research by Korn Ferry, a global organizational consulting firm, underscores the power of inclusion and diversity: inclusive and diverse workgroups make better decisions an impressive 87% of the time.[219]

- **A final thought on diversity:** The idea that diversity is an essential source of progress is not new. "It is hardly possible to overrate the value . . . of placing human beings in contact with persons dissimilar with themselves, and with modes of thought and action unlike those with which they are familiar . . . Such communication has always been . . . one of the primary sources of progress."[220] —John Stuart Mill (1806–73), the most influential English language philosopher of the nineteenth century

- **A final thought on equity:** As Melinda French Gates says, equity is ensuring that whatever your circumstances, you have an opportunity to live a productive and healthy life.[221]

- **A final thought on accessibility:** Some progress has been made in eliminating physical barriers to accessibility. Now, we need to eliminate the attitudinal barriers.

2.6 INTROVERTS AND EXTROVERTS

Organizations need *introverts* and *extroverts*. Effective managers ensure that the work environment allows both to reach their full potential.

> **Definition of introversion:** A personality type characterized by a preference for quiet and being alone. Introverts are reserved and more deliberate.
>
> **Definition of extroversion:** A personality type characterized by outgoingness and talkativeness. Extroverts draw energy from social interactions.

- Think of introversion and extroversion as a continuum. Many people show characteristics of both at different times. A third middle personality category is called ambivert, with characteristics of both introverts and extroverts.[222]

- Is there a physiological difference between introverts and extroverts? Yes. Introverts have a thicker prefrontal cortex, which is associated with decision-making and deep thought. Extroverts have thinner prefrontal cortexes, which are associated with processing information faster and more impulsively. For example, extroverts have a larger dopamine reward network, which makes them more motivated and excited when planning a social event. Introverts are less excited and can even feel a sense of dread when planning a similar event. Introverts have more acetylcholine receptors, which makes them feel good when calm and quiet. This allows them to reflect and focus.[223]

- Is there a difference between introversion and shyness? Yes. Introversion is a healthy ability to be more comfortable with one's thoughts and feelings than with anything external. Shyness is a tendency to feel tense and a desire to withdraw in social situations. Shyness is generally considered a learned behavior.[224] Introversion and shyness can overlap, such as when a person is introverted and is also uncomfortable with public speaking.[225]

- Western cultures favor extroverts. Introverts, therefore, feel pressure to be more outgoing, which can cause lower self-esteem and anxiety.[226]

  ILLUSTRATIVE STORY

  At a small organization, Ryan was the ninth employee hired. His boss began teasing him about being so quiet. At one point, Ryan's boss smiled and said, "We just want you to come out of your shell and be more social." Ryan was an outstanding employee and an introvert. As an introvert, he was uncomfortable being told to be more social. He soon found a new job.

- Strengths of introverts and extroverts include:
  - Introverts are critical thinkers, better strategists, and can solve your most challenging problems.[227]
  - Extroverts excel at multitasking and dealing with information overload.[228]
  - Introverts prefer writing to speaking and are good listeners.[229]
  - Extroverts are more inclined to be successful and happier and are more often selected as managers.[230]
  - Introverts earn more graduate degrees and have more Phi Beta Kappa keys.[231]
  - Extroverts and introverts are equally intelligent.[232]
- Managing introverts
  - Let introverts know what is expected of them as soon as possible. For example, send out meeting agendas in advance so introverts can prepare and think through their responses. This will allow them to make better contributions.[233]
  - Create workplace options where introverts can work without noise and interruptions. Offices can be made available when owners are away so introverts can do their best work without distractions from today's open office plans.[234] Please see Section 4.5, Physical Work Environment, for more information.

- ○ Give projects that one person can accomplish to introverts. When possible, assign introverts to smaller teams.[235]

- ○ Introverts prefer written communication. They can prepare their responses carefully without interruption.[236]

- ○ Try not to put introverts on the spot in meetings. If you do so, you may not get their best answer.[237]

  ILLUSTRATIVE STORY
  At one organization, the senior management decided to create open floor plans. Like countless business offices worldwide, walls came down so everyone could communicate more efficiently and enjoy natural light. The organization also saved money on leases because they did not need as much office space. One senior manager walked around the building and asked people about the new open floor plans. Many introverts responded that the constant noise and disruption affected their ability to get work done as effectively as before.

- Managing extroverts

  - ○ Extroverts are self-starters who draw energy from groups. Some tend to dominate conversations. Effective managers gently work with these extroverts to encourage them to make their points in fewer words and listen more carefully.

  - ○ Allow extroverts extra time to socialize. Please encourage them to take breaks together.

- What if you are an introverted manager?

  - ○ Introverted managers can often produce better results. They ask others for their thoughts, which allows the best ideas to surface.[238]

  - ○ Schedule yourself solitary breaks. Close the door to eat lunch or walk around the block to recharge. Do not feel guilty for doing this. Once recharged, you can be more available to your employees and others. Introverted managers who take solitary breaks are good role models for their introverted employees.[239]

○ Introverts tend to dislike small talk. As an introvert, I ask people about themselves or their latest projects; I only need to listen and smile. I also learn a lot.[240]

> **ILLUSTRATIVE STORY**
>
> *I am an introverted manager and am unable to be spontaneous. I always prepare my remarks in advance for things like a recognition event. Rather than attempt jokes, I always use relevant quotes. Because my preparation is so thorough, my comments about people are always filled with their accomplishments. One of my secrets is to ask honorees what they want me to include in my comments about them. I certainly do not want to leave out anything important. If it is important to the honoree, it is important to me. After the recognition event, I always ask the honorees if they would like the copy of the remarks I referred to during the ceremony. They always smile and say yes.*

- Bias against introverts is a prevalent issue in our workplaces, schools, and places of worship, all of which are typically designed for extroverts. This bias leads to a significant loss of talent and drive, resulting in unnecessary stress and unhappiness. No organization can afford to restrict human talent, our most crucial resource, and remain competitive.[241]

- Are introverts or extroverts better managers? It depends on the type of employees they manage. Introverts are better at managing proactive employees who take the initiative to generate ideas, create new work processes, state opinions, etc. Introverted managers are more likely to listen to suggestions and support their proactive employees. Extroverted managers are more effective with passive employees. Extraverted managers like to create structure and direction and take charge. Extraverted managers can feel threatened by proactive employees. They also can be less receptive to new ideas, discouraging employees from offering suggestions.[242]

  ○ Half of American workers are doing the minimum work required (quiet quitters), and 16% are actively disengaged (loud quitters) and are undermining managers and goals. These two groups together make up 66% of American workers and are best managed by extroverts.[243] Introverts are better at managing employees that are thriving at work (very or fully engaged) because they listen and support their proactive employees." "State of the Global Workplace 2024 Report: The Voice of the World's Employees," *Gallup Workplace*, p. 3, https://www.gallup.com/workplace/349484/state-of-the-global-workplace.aspx?thank-you-report-form=1.

- A survey published in *Industrial Psychiatry* showed that only 2% of introverts become top executives.[244] A ten-year study published in the Harvard Business Review shows that introverts are *moderately more likely* to exceed the expectations of their investors and corporate boards.[245] This is a massive disconnect between the effectiveness of introverted CEOs and the tiny percentage selected as CEOs. Corporate boards know that their selection of CEOs is their most important responsibility and can spell success or failure for their organizations. Once this survey and study become widely known, the percentage of introverts as corporate CEOs will soar. In Section 2.2, Coaching and Mentoring, you learned that women managers are more engaged than men.[246] As a result, I will revise my prediction above to read: Once this survey and study become widely known, the percentage of introverted women as CEOs will soar.

Final thoughts on introverts and extroverts:

- Every organization needs *introverts* and *extroverts*. When hiring, consider this: Do you want an extrovert in strategic planning or an introvert in public relations?

- Ask a shy introvert to prepare a presentation and an extrovert to deliver it. In this example, both are using their strengths, making it a win-win situation.

2.7 PROBLEM EMPLOYEES

Effective managers do not condone employees' problem behavior and must quickly take appropriate action. One survey found that employees rated only 31% of managers as likely to confront a poor performance.[247] That means that 69% of managers do not address poor performance and should not be managers.

> **Definition of a difficult or problem employee:** An employee whose inappropriate behavior causes difficulty for their manager, coworkers, or customers.[248]

Difficult or problem employee behavior includes frequent late arrivals or early departures that are not part of an accommodation; excessive or unexcused absenteeism; inappropriate language (abusive, disrespectful, harassing, etc.); poor job performance in one area, with otherwise satisfactory work; poor performance because he or she cannot grasp the job, but is trying and has a good attitude; poor performance, with the potential to improve and a good attitude; frequent complaining or gossip that affects morale; and bad attitude toward the organization or coworkers.[249]

- Steps for dealing with problem employees:
  - The objective when dealing with problem employees is to try to correct the problem.
  - Managers must speak with poor performers as soon as possible. Failing to address inadequate performance or inappropriate behavior drives away high performers and makes staff members question whether their boss is effective.

> **Definition of progressive discipline:** Progressive discipline addresses the problem of employee behavior in increasingly severe steps that are designed to correct a problem.

- These steps can include verbal warnings, written warnings, demotion, suspension, and termination.[250] These steps can vary by organization and can be spelled out in the labor-management agreement. **Please consult a labor**

attorney with questions on labor-management agreements and an employment attorney for all other questions dealing with counseling, disciplining, and dismissing employees.

○ Firing an employee should be your last option when all other options have failed. For more details, please see "Dismissing (firing) an employee" later in this chapter.

○ In all circumstances, please keep a positive attitude toward all problem employees.[251]

○ Has the employee's work performance dropped? They may be facing a crisis, e.g., a death in the family, health issues, divorce, etc., which is affecting their job performance. Meet privately with the employee and tell them their work quality is declining and you are concerned. You should not ask if they are having personal problems. If they are, they will likely tell you. Listen carefully. If the problem is unrelated to work, avoid getting involved. Refer these employees to the Employee Assistance Program (EAP). If the problem persists after the short-term counseling, the EAPs will refer employees for additional counseling or treatment, such as that offered by their health insurance plan.[252] Most organizations have EAPs, even if they are not well-publicized. If there is no EAP, refer the employee to HR for an outside referral.

> **Definition of an Employee Assistance Program (EAP):** An organization-funded program that offers confidential assessments and short-term counseling for stress, substance and alcohol abuse, grief, etc.

○ Problem behavior usually develops over time rather than occurring as a single incident.[253]

○ Three components often define a problem employee:
  - The problem is persistent.
  - There is a negative effect on job performance.
  - There is a pattern.[254]

- Problems occur in all of our lives, such as having a one-time late report due to a sick child, being late to work because of a car problem, etc. You will know when problems become a pattern and when there is a negative effect on the employee's work.

- Determine if the job-related problem is minor or major.

  - For minor job-related problems:

    - Coach the employee for a minor problem, e.g., misunderstanding tasks.

    - Consider whether training can improve employee performance.

    - If the problem persists or worsens, you will be grateful that you documented the problem from the beginning.

  - For major job-related problems:

    - Examples include frequent late arrivals or early departures that are not part of an accommodation; excessive or unexcused absenteeism; inappropriate language (abusive, disrespectful, harassing, etc.); poor job performance in one area, with otherwise satisfactory work; poor performance because he or she cannot grasp the job, but is trying and has a good attitude; poor performance with the potential to improve and a good attitude; frequent complaining or gossip that affects morale; and bad attitude toward the organization or coworkers.[255]

    - Document every problem and conversation you have with the individual.

    - If other staff members observe the problem behavior, ask them for written statements. If they do not want to give you statements, write one yourself based on discussions with them. Some witnesses may complain verbally but fear retribution from the difficult employee for providing a statement. Do not penalize employees for not providing a witness statement.

ILLUSTRATIVE STORY

I have had many instances of employees reporting others' problem behavior. I always thank the witnesses for coming forward and ask each for a written summary. Most, but not all, will comply. That is the employee's decision, and I never criticize them for not providing a statement. In all cases, I write summaries of my conversations with the witnesses as soon after our conversations as possible. If I had waited to receive a witness statement only to find out they had decided not to submit one, my memory of the details would not have been as complete. Also, in my experience, the employment attorneys would rather have my written summary of the conversations with witnesses than no written statements.

○ A performance improvement plan is another manager's tool to help employees improve their work performance.

> **Definition of a performance improvement plan (PIP):** A PIP is a formal, written and signed agreement between a manager and their problem employee that identifies precisely why the employee's productivity is unacceptable and what acceptable performance looks like so there is no misunderstanding.[256] The objective is to improve their work performance. The PIP also contains manager/employee agreed-upon, measurable objectives to improve performance within a prescribed timeline that generally ranges from 30 to 90 days. The PIP timeline can extend beyond 90 days if you feel it will reasonably take longer than 90 days to successfully achieve all the PIP objectives.

■ You can use the SMART objectives model in Section 2.2, Coaching and Mentoring, to help in preparing PIP objectives. The PIP includes all potential outcomes of completing or failing to complete the performance objectives. This can include completing all PIP requirements successfully and continuing the job, transferring the employee to a job that may be a better fit, demoting the employee to a similar but less demanding job, or dismissal.[257] **If you are**

considering dismissing an employee, consult with an employment attorney to ensure that you have sufficient justification and documentation to support the dismissal. An employment attorney must also review draft PIPs. The employee should sign and date one copy of the PIP, which acknowledges receipt and understanding of the PIP. Ensure that the employee understands they are responsible for their improvement and have your support. Follow up at regular intervals and document every conversation. You should always invite a witness to all PIP meetings. Please ask them to prepare a memo describing your meeting.

- If you anticipate that an employee may try to blame others for their poor performance, practice your conversation with a peer. For more information, please see Chapter 5, Partner with Your Peers

ILLUSTRATIVE STORY

In one organization, an employee frequently gossiped about fellow employees, saying things that were not confirmed as true. Her boss, Patricia, quickly counseled this employee, telling her not to make further inappropriate remarks. Months later, the employee once again said something inappropriate about a fellow employee. During the counseling session, Patricia told the employee that if there were any more inappropriate remarks, the employee would be fired. Less than two weeks later, the employee repeated the offense. Patricia had carefully documented both earlier discussions. She went to the employment attorney to ensure that she had sufficient justification and documentation to dismiss the employee. The employee was dismissed.

○ Transfer the employee to another position that better suits their skills, knowledge, and abilities. **Please consult with an employment attorney if you are considering transferring an employee to another job. If a union represents the employee, please notify the union through your ELR staff, and notify your labor attorney.**

> **ILLUSTRATIVE STORY**
>
> *I have worked with several HR officers throughout my career. The more experience these HR officers have, the more likely they are to consider moving an employee who is trying hard but unable to accomplish work in their current job. As a manager, you may not always have the luxury of working with an experienced HR officer. You may need to take the initiative to suggest a job move in cases like these.*

- Do not ever discuss any employment issues with your staff. If someone has been fired, tell your staff, "Joe no longer works here." Never explain why.

Scripts for the Eight Reasons You Talk With Problem Employees

- Before each counseling meeting with a problem employee, you must discuss your draft counseling remarks with an employment attorney. In addition, please provide the attorney copies of all previous counseling documents, performance improvement plans, witness statements, physician assessments, police reports, and any other documents that deal with the employee's behavior and performance throughout their time with the organization.

- I handle each discussion with a problem employee as though I expect a lawsuit to result. This is one of the most challenging management tasks. That is why I strongly urge you to consult a labor attorney with questions on labor-management agreements and an employment attorney for all other questions dealing with counseling, disciplining, and dismissing employees to ensure that everything goes smoothly. The cost of an attorney's advice is always far less than the cost of an error that results in the loss of a lawsuit.

- You should always have a witness at every problem employee meeting. A witness can confirm what was said. Otherwise, it is your word against the employees if they file a lawsuit. Ask your witness to take notes so they can write a statement on the discussion and outcome of the meeting. If you have more than one discussion with a problem employee, invite a different witness to each meeting to prepare a summary. This will mitigate the risk of the employee claiming that you personally dislike them and only inviting an ally to attend the discussions to write negative summaries. Also, having a witness in the meeting(s) will protect you if the employee says they were verbally abused or physically assaulted or denies the meeting occurred.

ILLUSTRATIVE STORY

I have dealt with employees diagnosed with various disruptive mental health disorders. I only learned about their disorders when the employees were disciplined or dismissed. Their attorneys then present evidence of their client's mental disorders to attempt to reduce or eliminate the disciplinary action or dismissal. You are likely not qualified to diagnose mental health disorders, but you know when an employee exhibits disruptive and abnormal behavior.

ILLUSTRATIVE STORY

An experienced employment attorney once advised me that failing to have a witness when counseling problem employees is a rookie mistake.

- When counseling problem employees, you should start the conversation with positive comments such as these (choose one):
  - "We all need helpful feedback from time to time. I want our talk to be positive and productive."
  - "We all need helpful feedback from time to time. I want to give you helpful feedback, but I am concerned that you may take it wrong."[258]
  - "We all need helpful feedback from time to time. This conversation will be difficult for both of us, but we need to talk."[259]
  - Never say: "We need to talk because several people have complained." This dodges your responsibility and will only embarrass the employee.[260]

- Please begin and end all counseling meetings on a positive note. Each of the eight scenarios below has sample beginning and ending remarks.

1. Frequent late arrivals or early departures that are not part of an accommodation.

- Opening line options (Please start the meeting on a positive note.): "We all need helpful feedback from time to time. I want our talk to be positive and productive." Or: "This conversation will be difficult for both of us, but we need to talk."[261]

- Overall performance line (if appropriate): "You are a solid (or outstanding) performer, and this behavior is out of character for you."

- Define the problem: "This is the second time you have been late to work in the past two weeks. Coming in late is not acceptable. You need to be here when the store opens. This is the second time we have talked about this. We agreed that you would not be late again when we last talked. I want to find out why you cannot meet our agreed-upon goal."

- Discuss the problem and agree on a solution: Listen carefully to the employee and then agree upon a solution, timelines, and milestones. Explain the consequences if the solution is not achieved on time. "Frequent late arrivals or early departures are spelled out in the employee handbook, which cites dismissal for this infraction. The handbook was discussed with you during your first week here. I have already discussed this issue with our employment attorney."

- Summarize the major points: You or your employee should briefly summarize the major points to avoid misunderstandings later. "So that there is no misunderstanding, please summarize the problem, our solution, and timelines/milestones for me." Whether you or the employee summarize the meeting is your decision. If your employee has a positive attitude, you may wish to do the summary yourself. If not, you can instruct the employee to summarize it. The employee may stumble through it, and you may need to assist.

- Closing lines (Please end the meeting on a positive note.): "You are a valuable employee. Your work ethic, teamwork, and sales are satisfactory (or excellent). Or: "We need you to show up on time." Finally, "Do you have any questions?"

- Document the meeting: Ask your witness to write a summary memo immediately after the meeting ends. If there are additional counseling meetings, please have a different witness attend each.

2. Excessive or unexcused absenteeism.

- Opening line options (Please begin the meeting on a positive note.): "We all need helpful feedback from time to time. I want our talk to be positive and productive." Or: "This conversation will be difficult for both of us, but we need to talk.[262]

- Overall performance line (if appropriate): "You are a solid (or outstanding) performer, and this behavior is out of character for you."

- Define the problem: "You have had two unexcused days off in the past two weeks. I want to find out why you were absent without giving sufficient notice. When you do not show up without notifying us, we must interrupt one of your coworkers on their day off and ask them to come to work without notice."

- Discuss the problem and agree on a solution: Allow the employee time to respond and listen carefully. Agree upon a solution, timelines, and milestones. You can say, "Unexcused and excessive absenteeism is spelled out in the employee handbook, which cites dismissal for this infraction. The handbook was discussed with you during your first week here. I have already discussed this issue with our employment attorney."

- Summarize the major points: You or your employee should briefly summarize the major points to avoid misunderstandings later. "So that there is no misunderstanding, please summarize the problem, our solution, and timelines/milestones for me." Whether you or the employee summarize the meeting is your decision. If your employee has a positive attitude, you may wish to do the summary yourself. If not, you can instruct the employee to summarize it. The employee may stumble through it, and you may need to assist.

- Closing line options (Please end the meeting on a positive note.): "You are a valuable employee. Your work ethic, teamwork, and sales are satisfactory (or excellent). Or: We need to know when you cannot work as far in advance as possible." Finally, "Do you have any questions?"

- Document the meeting: Ask your witness to write a summary memo immediately after the meeting ends. If there are additional counseling meetings, please have a different witness attend each.

3. Inappropriate language (abusive, disrespectful, harassing, etc.)

- Opening lines options (Please begin the meeting on a positive note.): "We all need helpful feedback from time to time. I want our talk to be positive and productive." Or: "This conversation will be difficult for both of us, but we need to talk."[263]

- Overall performance line (if appropriate): "You are a solid (or outstanding) performer, and this inappropriate behavior is out of character for you."

- Define the problem: "You have used some offensive language recently. It must stop. This is spelled out in our employee handbook, on which you were briefed your first week here." Next, describe the specific remarks, dates, times, and locations when the employee made the remarks so there is no misunderstanding.

- Discuss the problem and agree on a solution: Allow the employee time to respond and listen carefully. Agree upon a solution. Since you have sufficient documented evidence, say: "The employee handbook explains the consequences of inappropriate language, which includes dismissal. I have already discussed this matter with our employment attorney. If you make any further inappropriate remarks, you will be dismissed."

- Summarize the major points: You or your employee should briefly summarize the major points to avoid misunderstandings later. "So that there is no misunderstanding, please summarize the problem and our solution." Whether you or the employee summarize the meeting is your decision. If your employee has a positive attitude, you may wish to do the summary yourself. If not, you can instruct the employee to summarize it. The employee may stumble through it, and you may need to assist.

- Closing line options (Please end the meeting on a positive note.): "I know you can continue to be an asset to our organization. We would not be having this conversation if I did not, and you would already be gone." Or: "Correcting mistakes and showing improvement is a sign of good character." Finally, "Do you have any questions?"

- Document the meeting: Ask your witness to write a summary memo immediately after the meeting ends. If there are additional counseling meetings, please have a different witness attend each.

4. Poor performance in one area, with otherwise satisfactory work.

- Opening line (Please begin the meeting on a positive note.): "We all need helpful feedback from time to time."

- Overall performance line (if appropriate): "You are a solid (or outstanding) performer, but you are having difficulty performing satisfactorily in one area."

- Define the problem: "This is the second time your reports have been over two days late. As you know, your reports contribute to organization-wide reports that go to our senior managers. We cannot be late with this report, but your tardiness almost caused us to be late again. I would like to know what is causing you to be late."

- Discuss the problem and agree on a solution: Allow the employee time to respond and listen carefully. Agree upon a solution, milestones, and timeline. This may include a performance improvement plan.

- Summarize the major points: You or your employee should briefly summarize the major points to avoid misunderstandings later. "So that there is no misunderstanding, please summarize the problem and our solution." Whether you or the employee summarize the meeting is your decision. If your employee has a positive attitude, you may wish to do the summary yourself. If not, you can instruct the employee to summarize it. The employee may stumble through it, and you may need to assist.

- Closing lines (Please end the meeting on a positive note.): "You are a valuable employee. Your work is excellent (or good) overall; it is just sometimes unacceptably late. Based on our discussion, I hope your reports will be on time from this point forward." Finally, "Do you have any questions?"

- Document the meeting: Ask your witness to write a summary memo immediately after the meeting ends. If there are additional counseling meetings, please have a different witness attend each.

5. Poor performance because they cannot grasp the job despite trying and having a good attitude. Please see if you can find another job that is a better fit. This employee should not have been hired, and you should find out why. Most likely, it was a failure to do background and reference checks.

- Opening line (Please begin the meeting on a positive note.): "We all need helpful feedback from time to time. I want our talk to be positive and productive."

- Overall performance line (if appropriate): The overall performance is in the following line.

- Define the problem: "You have struggled with your work even though we have tried additional training."

- Discuss the problem and agree on a possible solution: "I know you are trying. However, your work remains unsatisfactory overall. If you are interested, I will try to find another job in our organization that may be a better fit for you. I make no promises that I will be able to do so. Unfortunately, I will have to let you go if I cannot find another job for you." Remember that to dismiss employees, you need a legal justification and sufficient documented evidence. Please consult with an employment attorney for additional information.

- Summarize the major points: "I will summarize what we discussed. We have agreed that I will try to find another job in our organization that may be a better fit for you. I may not be able to do so. You understand that if I am unable to find another job for you, I will unfortunately have to let you go."

- Closing lines (Please end the meeting on a positive note.): "I can see that you are trying, which is very important. I need to check with the HR staff to look at current and projected job vacancies. I will get back to you as soon as I can. I cannot promise we can find another job that would better fit you, but we will do our best." Finally, "Do you have any questions?"

- Document the meeting: Ask your witness to write a summary memo immediately after the meeting ends. If there are additional counseling meetings, please have a different witness attend each.

6. Poor job performance but has the potential to improve and has a good attitude. This can result from an inability to learn new skill requirements or personal issues that affect their work, like substance abuse, divorce, financial problems, etc. If the employee has good potential and a good attitude, put them on a PIP. If the problem is personal, avoid getting involved. Refer these employees to the Employee Assistance Program (EAP). Most organizations have EAPs, even if they are not well-publicized. If there is no EAP, refer the employee to an HR staff member for an outside referral.

There are two kinds of people who are not doing satisfactory work: those who would if they could but can't, and those who could but won't. Attitude is everything.

- Opening line (Please begin the meeting on a positive note.): "We all need helpful feedback from time to time. I want our talk to be positive and productive."

- Overall performance line: Since the employee has performed their job poorly, it is inappropriate to make a positive comment about their performance. In this example, you state that their work is not satisfactory in the next sentence.

- Define the problem: "As we have discussed, your work is currently not satisfactory. You are having difficulty learning new job skills which is a requirement of your employment."

- Discuss the problem and agree on a possible solution: "I believe you have the potential to be a productive employee. If I did not, you would be gone. Poor performance is spelled out in the employee handbook, which can result in dismissal. The handbook was discussed with you during your first week here. I have already discussed this matter with our employment attorney. Because I believe you have potential, I will place you on a performance improvement plan or PIP. A PIP is a formal, written and signed agreement between a manager and an employee that identifies precisely why the employee's productivity is unacceptable and what acceptable performance looks like so there is no misunderstanding.[264] The objective is to improve their work performance. The PIP also contains manager/employee agreed-upon, measurable objectives to improve performance within a prescribed timeline. I will prepare the PIP and discuss it with our employment attorney. Then we will meet again soon and jointly agree on a plan to improve your performance." Details on writing PIPs are found in this chapter.

- Summarize the major points: Your employee should briefly summarize the major points to avoid misunderstandings later. "So that there is no misunderstanding, please summarize the problem and our solution." The employee may stumble through it, and you may need to assist.

- Closing lines (Please end the meeting on a positive note.): "I believe that you can improve your work. I will get back to you soon to discuss your performance improvement plan." Finally, "Do you have any questions?"

- Document the meeting: Ask your witness to write a summary memo immediately after the meeting ends. If there are additional counseling meetings, please have a different witness attend each.

7. Frequent complaining or gossip that affects morale.

- Opening line options (Please begin the meeting on a positive note.): "We all need helpful feedback from time to time. I want our talk to be positive and productive." Or: "This conversation will be difficult for both of us, but we need to talk.[265]

- Overall performance line (if appropriate): "You are a solid performer, and this behavior is out of character for you."

- Define the problem: "Your frequent complaints (or gossip) are hurting morale. It must stop. This is spelled out in the employee handbook, on which you were briefed your first week here." Next, describe specific remarks, dates, times, and locations of the employee's complaints or gossip so there is no misunderstanding.

- Discussion: Listen carefully. Since you have sufficient, documented evidence, say, "You must cease your frequent complaints (or gossip) immediately. If you have a problem, you know to see me first. The employee handbook lists the consequences of frequent complaining or gossip, including dismissal. I have already discussed this case with our employment attorney. If you make any further inappropriate remarks, you will be dismissed."

- Summarize the major points: Your employee should briefly summarize the major points to avoid misunderstandings later. "So that there is no misunderstanding, please summarize the problem and our solution." The employee may stumble through it, and you may need to assist.

- Closing lines (Please end the meeting on a positive note.): "Your work performance has always been satisfactory (or outstanding).” Or: “I know you can continue to be an important asset to the organization. We would not be having this conversation if I did not, and you would already be gone.” Finally, “Do you have any questions?”

- Document the meeting: Ask your witness to write a summary memo immediately after the meeting ends. If there are additional counseling meetings, please have a different witness attend each.

8. Bad attitude toward the organization or coworkers.

- Opening line options (Please begin the meeting on a positive note.): “We all need helpful feedback from time to time. I want our talk to be positive and productive.” Or: “This conversation will be difficult for both of us, but we need to talk.[266]

- Overall performance line (if appropriate): “You are a solid performer.”

- Define the problem: “Your bad attitude is affecting the morale of our office. With you, everything is negative. We spend many of our waking hours together, and we need to be positive and respectful of others.” Be specific on as many of the “bad attitude” remarks as you have documented in writing.

- Discussion: I would like to understand why you have a bad attitude about the organization (or your coworkers.) Listen carefully. Since you have sufficient written evidence, say: “I need you to show a more positive attitude at work and stop your bad attitude remarks immediately. Our employee handbook spells out the consequences, which include dismissal. I have already discussed this with our employment attorney. If you make any further inappropriate remarks, you will be dismissed.”

- Summarize the major points: Ask your employee to summarize the major points to avoid misunderstandings later. “So that there is no misunderstanding, please summarize the problem and our solution.” The employee may stumble through it, and you may need to assist.

- Closing lines (Please end the meeting on a positive note.): "Your work performance has always been satisfactory. I know you can continue to be an important asset to the organization. We would not be having this conversation if I did not, and you would already be gone." Finally, "Do you have any questions?"

- Document the meeting: Ask your witness to write a summary memo immediately after the meeting ends. If there are additional counseling meetings, please have a different witness attend each.

Notify the unions, if required.

- For bargaining unit employees, contact your employee labor relations staff to keep unions appraised of all performance and disciplinary issues. Please remember that managers do not deal directly with unions, even if a union representative works for you.

- The union may have a representative attend any counseling meeting. Additionally, you should notify the equal employment opportunity officer; the senior HR officer; the chief inclusion, diversity, equity, and accessibility officer; the labor attorney, and the employment attorney as early as possible. Remember that problem employees will tell their version of the story and bend the facts to put themselves in the best possible light. Cognitive bias causes us to better remember the first information we receive about a situation.[267] Therefore, you are wise to speak to these offices first. Years ago, a friend put this idea succinctly in one sentence. "Those who speak first....speak the truth."

Dismissing (Firing) an Employee

- Firing an employee is your last option when all other options have failed.

- There is a difference between dismissing employees and laying them off. The focus of this section is to discuss dismissing employees. Employees are always dismissed for cause. Employees may be laid off because of a company reorganization or a reduction in the workload.

- **In all cases, before dismissing any employee, check with an employment attorney to ensure you have sufficient justification and documentation for the dismissal. You must also discuss your draft counseling remarks with this attorney. In addition, please provide the attorney with copies of all previous counseling documents, performance improvement plans, witness statements, physician assessments, police reports, and any other documents that deal with the employee's behavior and performance throughout their time with the organization.**

- **When firing an employee, I plan as though I expect a lawsuit to result. This is one of the most challenging management tasks. That is why I strongly urge you to consult a labor attorney with questions on labor-management agreements and an employment attorney for all other questions dealing with counseling, disciplining, and dismissing employees to ensure everything goes smoothly. The cost of an attorney's advice is always far less than the cost of an error that results in the loss of a lawsuit.**

- Discuss the proposed dismissal with the HR staff, the employment attorney, and the EEO office staff. If a union represents the employee, please also notify the union through your employee and labor relations staff.

- There are a number of justifications for dismissing an employee. Here is a partial list: theft, violence, substance abuse, insubordination, misconduct including fraud, criminal behavior, bullying, etc.[268]

- Create a termination checklist with the following items. This checklist is activated once there is an agreement between the manager, the employment attorney, the labor attorney (if a union represents the employee), and an HR representative that the employee must be fired.

- The soon-to-be terminated employee's manager should prepare remarks for the termination meeting.

- The employment attorney reviews, revises if needed, and approves these remarks.

- The HR administrator overseeing the termination should prepare the termination letter. The employment attorney must review and approve it. The termination letter should contain:

  - The employee's name and an employee number or unique identifier

  - The managers' names and duty titles

  - The final date of employment

  - The current date

  - The name of the HR administrator who is overseeing the termination and their contact information

  - When and how the employee will receive their final pay

  - Severance package information

  - Retirement fund transfers, date when benefits end, etc.

  - The company's job reference policy

  - The process for maintaining health coverage and applying for unemployment benefits[269]

  - The reason for the termination, if required. Most U.S. employees work "at will" and can be fired at any time for any reason. Of course, the reason cannot be illegal to include discrimination, retaliation, or refusing to participate in illegal activities.[270]

- The manager should practice their remarks with a peer. When firing employees, be prepared for a range of responses. The most frequent responses I have received are one of these: denial, anger, bargaining, depression, and acceptance. Interestingly, these are the five stages of grief discussed in Dr. Elizabeth Kübler-Ross's 1969 book On Death and Dying.[271]

- The following people need to be in the room when the problem employee is notified of their dismissal: the immediate manager, an employment attorney, the labor attorney if a union represents the employee, and the HR administrator who is overseeing the termination.

- There should be a security guard posted immediately outside the room in which the termination letter will be presented.

- Termination meetings should last no more than 30 minutes.

- Here are some draft remarks for dismissing an employee. Please talk slowly and treat the employee with the utmost respect throughout the meeting. You should also show empathy. This will make the meeting go more smoothly and also reduce the possibility that the employee will retaliate later:

  - "This conversation will be difficult for both of us."[272]

  - "After much discussion with my colleagues, we agree that the best way forward for our organization is to terminate your employment."

  - Pause after this statement to see if the employee has questions or wants to talk. Please let them talk. It can be therapeutic. Ensure that you make it clear that the employee will not be rehired under any circumstances.

  - The manager will present the employee with the termination letter. Both the manager and the HR administrator will go over all items in the letter to ensure that the employee understands their options and is allowed to ask questions.

  - The HR administrator should inform the employee that he or she is available for additional questions at any time. Their contact information is in the letter.

  - The HR administrator will collect any company-owned property to include ID badges and phones that the employee brought to the meeting.

- At the end of the meeting, the manager should thank the employee for their time and give them their best wishes.

- Following the dismissal:
  - The employee should return any company-owned equipment and pick up personal items. Allow the employee to return to the office after hours; to be escorted to their desks to pick up their personal items and turn in any company-owned items they may have brought from home. There is no need to embarrass the employee in front of their peers. In this scenario, the security staff would have already gone to the employee's desk and retrieved any company-owned equipment.
  - The manager should prepare a memorandum describing the meeting, the list of attendees, and the start and stop time. It should be maintained in the HR office, and a copy should be sent to the legal staff.
  - HR should create an offboarding checklist for the dismissed employee. A member of the HR staff should go to each stop on the checklist and offboard the employee.
  - The manager should notify other employees who worked with the terminated employee that they no longer work for the organization. Under no circumstances should the manager discuss why the employee no longer works there.

- If the reason for dismissal was any illegal behavior or activity, the manager must send a letter with all relevant details to the organization's senior legal attorney to determine if any law enforcement organizations need to be notified. You are addressing this letter to the senior attorney because this may not be the responsibility of the employment attorney.

- You need to find out why the employee did not work out. Did the hiring official not do a reference check or background check? This is an expensive lesson, so you need to learn from it.

- Organizations should have a written policy on dismissing employees. It should contain all the guidance on this subject above. This policy should be reviewed by the Policy Review Committee at least annually. Please see Section 4.6, Policies. Procedures, and Checklists for more information.

ILLUSTRATIVE STORY

In my experience, employees who think they are about to be fired will often sabotage their work by erasing or copying their online work files. Check with your IT staff to ensure that all their files are backed up and cannot be copied or erased by the employee.

ILLUSTRATIVE STORY

At one organization, managers turned to the employment attorney for help firing underperforming employees. The employment attorney immediately reviewed these employees' most recent annual performance evaluations, which were almost always rated "satisfactory" or higher. This made dismissing the employees difficult. The employment attorney chose to "bribe" underperforming employees to leave by offering them 60 days of salary and to sign an agreement not to sue the organization for wrongful dismissal.

- If you are considering firing an employee, ensure that the infraction meets the legal standard for dismissal.

ILLUSTRATIVE STORY

At one organization, one of the employees was fired for having a large amount of pornography on their company computer. The organization's employment attorney reviewing the case was outraged and recommended immediate dismissal. The fired employee filed a lawsuit for wrongful dismissal. The union agreement stated that the employee should have been warned instead of dismissed for the first such infraction. The organization paid back pay and legal fees to settle the claim.

ILLUSTRATIVE STORY

New employee Duane was well-liked but unable to complete most of his entry-level tasks satisfactorily. His boss, Kimberly, worked for several months, without success, to improve Duane's skills. Kimberly also asked the HR staff if there was another job open in the organization that Duane might be good at. Unfortunately, there were none at that time. As Duane approached the end of his probationary period, Kimberly met with her boss to discuss the next steps. Kimberly acknowledged that Duane was unable to do his work satisfactorily. The obvious next step was to fire Duane, but Kimberly dreaded the meeting. Kimberly's boss worked with her on a script to cover the key points and chose to attend the meeting as a witness. She was worried that Kimberly would have difficulty with the meeting. During the meeting, Duane and Kimberly both burst into tears. Kimberly had difficulty speaking her few lines. Within weeks of this meeting, Kimberly left the organization. Dismissing an employee during their probationary period is the easiest dismissal possible. If you find it difficult to fire an employee when doing so is appropriate, maybe being a manager is not for you.

A final thought on dealing with problem employees:

- When firing an employee, it should not surprise them if you have followed the guidance in this chapter.

2.8 EXIT INTERVIEWS

Employees are every organization's most valuable resource. Finding out why employees quit and how an organization must change is critical for survival. An exit interview process gives you continual answers to these questions.[273] Effective managers know exit interviews are another low-cost management initiative providing vital information to improve recruiting, retention, and survival.

> **Definition of exit interview process:** A process that includes a meeting or meetings between each departing employee and a management representative or representatives, or information collected from an online survey, to learn why each employee is leaving and how to use this information to identify problems and collect other actionable information to improve recruiting, retention, and survival. Effective managers ensure appropriate action is taken on all concerns raised in exit interviews.

- The primary reason that people quit:
  - Historically, managers, not money, are the primary reason employees remain or quit.[274] One survey shows that 57% of employees leave because of their boss, and another 32% are seriously considering leaving for the same reason.[275] Yikes! Hiring effective managers is another no-cost way to attract and retain the best employees.
  - During the COVID-19 pandemic, the Great Resignation resulted in a significant increase in staff turnover in the United States. We now know that at least 65% of these job switchers ended up dissatisfied with their new job situations.[276] Effective managers know that a robust exit interview process will reduce turnover by finding and fixing the causes of employee attrition.

- Benefits of exit interviews:
  - Knowing why your employees quit is the key to understanding how to optimize employee retention.
  - Exit interviews allow organizations to learn how to improve, ensure departing employees feel good about their contribution, and encourage some employees to remain with the organization under different circumstances.[277] There is no other way to acquire this vital information.
  - Online exit interviews can elicit more candid feedback and are inexpensive and easy to manage, but follow-up is needed to increase participation rates.[278] Just program your HR software to automatically send online exit interviews via email at the appropriate times listed in Exit Interview Steps table below. HR personnel will need to follow up with each person who does not complete the exit interview within a few days of sending it.
  - It is important to understand why some employees choose to not speak up during their exit interview and share the reasons for their departure. These employees often fear losing future networking or job endorsements and are cautious not to burn any bridges. At the same time, departing employees are more forthcoming than those still in their jobs.[279] Former employees are also more candid several months after their employment ends.[280] Details are in this table.

Exit Interviews Steps

Type of Employee	Method of Exit Interview	When	Interviewers
Low-skilled blue-collar employee Entry-level white-collar worker	In order of preference 1. Online[1] 2. Face-to-face[2] 3. Video conference 4. Telephone	**1st interview** Halfway between the announcement and departure **2nd interview** 3–6 months after the employee departs[3]	Online HR staff[4] Outside consultant[4] Second-line manager (the employee's boss's boss)[5] Never the immediate boss[5]

(continued)

Exit Interviews Steps *(continued)*

Highly skilled blue-collar employees Senior, non-management employees Managers	In order of preference 1. Online[1] 2. Face-to-face[2] 3. Video conference 4. Telephone	**1st interview** Halfway between the announcement and departure **2nd interview** 3–6 months after the employee departs[3] Please ask whether they want an online survey or to talk with a trained exit interview counselor	**1st interview** HR staff[4] Outside consultant[4] Second-line manager (the employee's boss's boss)[5] Never the immediate boss[5] **2nd interview** HR staff[4] Outside consultant[4] Never the immediate boss[5] Second- or third-line manager*
High-potential employees Executives	Let them choose from the exit interview menu.[6]	Let them choose from the exit interview menu.[6]	Let them choose from the exit interview menu.[6]

[1] Online exit interviews can provide more candid feedback, but follow-up is needed to increase participation rates.

[2] Interviewees prefer F2F interviews over videoconferencing. Greg J. Sears et al., "A Comparative Assessment of Videoconference and Face-to-Face Employment Interviews," *Management Decision* 51, no. 8 (2013): pp. 1733-1752.

[3] Many managers feel that a second exit interview three to six months after the first one will get more forthright answers than the initial interview. Offering a second opportunity to complete an exit interview will increase the participation rate. Everett Spain and Boris Groysberg, "Making Exit Interviews Count: This underused practice can be a powerful tool for retention," *Harvard Business Review*, April 2016, https://hbr.org/2016/04/making-exit-interviews-count.

[4] An HR staff member or outside consultant with exit interview training who is familiar with the organization's HR policies.

[5] The immediate boss should never be allowed to conduct exit interviews on their direct reports. This will help ensure that the interviewee feels comfortable should their immediate boss be one of the reasons they are leaving. As discussed elsewhere in this book, the immediate boss is often why employees leave.

[6] An exit interview menu is available for executives and high-potential employees. It allows them to choose the interviewer (CEO, COO, member of the board of directors, outside consultant, etc.), location, time, and method (face-to-face, video conference, or phone). Recommend two exit interviews and conduct the second one three to six months after the executive or high-potential employee departs.

- Exit interview actions
  - Instructions for interviewers:
    - All exit interviewers should be trained and familiar with the organization's HR policies.

- **Document each exit interview and follow up on individual concerns or complaints. If, for example, a departing employee reports any illegal activity, immediately report this in writing to your employment attorney to initiate an investigation. For more severe offenses, organizations may be required to contact local law enforcement. Please consult an employment attorney with questions.**

- Employees can decline to participate in an exit interview. There should be no adverse consequences for their decision.

- Begin by thanking departing employees for their contributions to the organization. Thank them again as you end the exit interview.[281]

- Reassure departing employees that their identifying information will be removed from any comments they make in the exit interview unless they report anything illegal. This ensures the confidentiality of the process, making the departing employees feel safe and respected.[282]

- Use the same exit interview questions for all departing employees.

- Exit interview questions should be open-ended and allow departing employees an opportunity to provide detailed responses. Additionally, the departing employees should be offered an opportunity to speak to an external consultant or HR staff member with exit interview training who can conduct a face-to-face exit interview. The interviewer should be well-versed in the organization's HR policies. The interviewee's immediate boss should never conduct exit interviews, as they may be the reason the employee is leaving. Finally, the Exit Interview Steps table on the preceding page recommends two exit interview opportunities for each departing employee to increase the participation rate. Typical exit interview questions:

  - Please tell me why you are leaving.[283]

- □ Is there anything that we can do better?[284]

- □ Would you recommend us to a friend? If not, why?[285]

- □ How would you describe our organization's culture?[286]

- □ Were you satisfied with your managers?[287]

- □ What needs to change for you to return here?[288]

- □ Were you given clear objectives?[289]

- □ Did you receive adequate coaching and mentoring?[290]

- □ Do you have any additional comments?[291]

- □ For online exit interviews: Would you like to speak to a trained exit interviewer?

- ○ Instructions for senior management:

  - ▪ Make retention an organizational priority.

  - ▪ Review exit interview summaries, assess recommendations, and ensure that action is taken to resolve each recommendation.

- ○ Instructions for the HR office:

  - ▪ Use the same exit interview questions for all interviewers and online exit interviews. This will help you find trends more efficiently.

  - ▪ Consolidate the exit interview information, identify trends, develop recommendations, and update senior management at least quarterly.

  - ▪ Fix any problems that can be resolved at the HR level.

  - ▪ Look for best practices in preparing, conducting, and assessing exit interviews.

  - ▪ HR should consider the following questions when reviewing the exit interview results:

    - □ Do any comments require immediate referral to the legal staff?

    - □ Do any issues or recommendations need immediate attention?

- Why are people leaving? What issues can be fixed in HR? Which issues need to be forwarded to the appropriate office for action?

- Are we finding candidates who have the right experience and skills? Is our job advertising effective?

- Was our onboarding effective?

- Are there any organization policies that need updating?

- Do we have any staff members who need additional training?

ILLUSTRATIVE STORY

A new, dynamic manager substantially revised the exit interview process at one organization. Within a few months of implementing the new process, the exit interviews clearly showed why people were leaving and what needed to change. The organization's senior managers said they were not interested in reading the results.

How can you motivate people to complete exit interviews? Give them money? Let us look at a study on selfless donations. Dr. Richard Titmuss, a British sociologist, speculated that paying people to donate blood would actually reduce the donations.[292] Two economists decided to experiment to find out whether Titmuss was correct. The experimenters determined that adding a financial incentive did indeed reduce blood donations by almost half. People are demotivated when being offered money to do something they consider altruistic. The largest blood donation response was by people who gave their blood freely, and who could choose to give the fee to a charity.[293] Based on this study, you can and should encourage people leaving an organization to complete an exit interview. If an employee completes an exit interview, a monetary amount, say $100, would be given to a registered charity of the employee's choosing, in their name. Yes, you should pay them another $100 if they complete a second interview. Many managers feel that a second exit interview three to six months after the first one will get more forthright answers than the initial interview.[294] Please ask the charities to send a thank you note to those completing the exit interviews. We want to ensure that they know the money was donated in their name.

A final thought on exit interviews:

- Exit interviews are only effective if organizations use the valuable information they provide. Research shows that only 15% of departing employees completed an exit interview.[295] Incentivizing those who have not completed an exit interview is essential.

CHAPTER 3
Effective Managers at Work

"If you light a lamp for someone else, it will also brighten your path."[296]—The Buddha, founder of Buddhism, 6th or 5th century BCE

3.1 YOUR FIRST WEEKS AT A NEW JOB

An International Institute for Management Development survey found that beginning a new job is among the most challenging and stressful events in managers' professional lives. Quite often, how well they do in the first few months indicates how well they will perform in their new roles long-term.[297] For a successful start, this chapter contains all the steps you must accomplish and the order in which you must do them.

- As an incoming manager, make as few changes as possible during the first 60 days. If you make changes before 60 days, your employees may see you as ready to change things before fully understanding all the consequences. You are also wise if you get the advice of stakeholders, i.e., employees and customers, before making important decisions. Please see Section 3.4, Decision-Making, for more information.

- **What to do in the first weeks as an incoming manager**
  - Before your first day of work at your new job:
    - Do as much onboarding online as possible. These days, onboarding paperwork and briefings are often online for new employees to complete before their first day of work. Millennials and Gen Zers expect visual onboarding and training as they grew up watching YouTube and are visual generations.

- Review any material that your new organization sends. In my 45 years as a manager, I never received any material in advance of starting a job, but this needs to change. Please send your new employees, especially managers, job-related information so that their transition will be easier. Specific documents are listed below. For additional information to send new employees, please see the form, Job-Related Information for Your Successor, in the Appendix.

- Study the organization's website to understand how it wishes to appear to the public. This even includes the type of clothing they prefer so that you can dress appropriately for your first day. Mark Twain had this to say about the importance of clothes: "Clothes make the man. Naked people have little or no influence on society."[298]

- Study their strategic plan and annual reports and determine what strategic goals and objectives you and your staff members will be supporting.

- Call your new office and ask if your predecessor left transition information. If not, call your new boss and ask permission to contact your predecessor to discuss upcoming deadlines or projects. You should ask permission to ensure that there is no reason your new boss does not want you to talk to your predecessor. When speaking with your predecessor, ask questions from the checklist titled Job-Related Information for Your Successor in the Appendix.

- Ask for a copy of your predecessor's performance objectives and accomplishments during the past three years.

- Ask for documents that show whether these performance objectives were achieved.

- Ask for a list of your direct reports, peers, and key customers.

- Ask your new staff members to arrange for you to meet with your boss on your first day. Then ask for your staff to arrange individual meetings your first week with your direct reports, peers, and key customers. This is also the order in which you should meet with them. Further, ask your staff to arrange a second meeting with your boss after you have spoken with your direct reports, peers, and key customers. Finally, ask your staff to schedule meetings with the senior HR officer; the employee labor manager; the equal employment opportunity officer; the chief inclusion, diversity, equity, and accessibility officer; the labor attorney; and the employment attorney to find out if your office has any current or past issues you should know about.

- Ask for an organizational chart showing where your staff members and you fit into the larger organization.

- Ask for your boss's performance measurements so that you know what their priorities are. Your boss's priorities are your priorities.

- Please ask that these documents above be sent by email or overnight mail as soon as you have accepted the job. You need to get up to speed as quickly as possible.

○ Onboarding your first day at the office.

- Senior managers are often onboarded in their own offices. If possible, onboard along with other new employees so that you understand HR's onboarding process. You will benefit from having the same experience as your employees. Your staff will also be impressed that you want to see how everyone else is brought on board. Follow up with a note to the HR director about your onboarding experience. Mention by name those that were exceptional. Please ask the HR director to thank everyone involved on your behalf. A handwritten thank-you note is best. If you have suggestions to improve the onboarding process, schedule a separate meeting with the HR director.

○ Meet your new boss first.

- Study any online material so you will know your boss's background and perhaps find what you have in common. The company website may have background information on managers.

- Explain to your boss that you will meet your direct reports, peers, and key customers in your first week. Following these visits, you will meet with your boss a second time. Ask your boss if there is anyone else you should meet with during the first week, such as your boss's boss. If you do meet with your boss's boss, it should only be an opportunity to meet and exchange pleasantries. You will want to research their background, i.e., schools, former jobs, etc., so you can talk about things you have in common. Do not start a discussion with your boss's boss about your new job. Your immediate boss will not appreciate you discussing anything about your job that they have not heard first.

- Show your boss your organization's current objectives and how they support strategic objectives. Ask if your boss has suggestions for improving your team's objectives.

- Ask your boss about their current priorities. Your boss's priorities are your priorities. Ask, "How can I help you starting today?"

- Ask how your boss likes to receive information (face-to-face meetings, telephone calls, written reports, emails, text messages, etc.).[299]

○ Meet individually with each of your direct reports to discuss the questions below. Please provide these questions to your direct reports in writing as far in advance as possible and ask them to provide the answers in writing so that you don't have to take notes furiously. You can go over their answers together. Please ask about their families and interests outside of work, too.

- "Please tell me about yourself."

- "How often did you meet with my predecessor? How often should we meet? Of course, we should meet at least weekly for our coaching meetings."

- "What are the performance measurements for your office, and how often did you provide updates to my predecessor? Can you suggest any improvements to any of them?" It is too early to change these at your first meeting. Remember, no changes for the first 60 days, please.

- "Besides performance measurements, what regular updates did you give to my predecessor? Can you suggest any improvements?"

- "Do you know which high-level performance measurement updates my predecessor regularly gave my boss? If not, can you recommend which performance measurements I should brief my boss on?" Hint: Your most important performance measurements support your strategic plan goals and objectives. For more information, see Section 3.2, Now That You're Settled In.

- "Do you jointly own any objectives with other offices inside or outside the organization? If so, what are they, and do you have any suggestions to improve them? Are the offices you share objectives with doing their share of the work?"

- "Do you have any recommendations for improving anything in your office or the organization?"

- "Are there any employee problems I should know about? Please do not put this information in the response answers. When we meet face-to-face, please brief me from notes or memory."

- "Are there any operational problems I should know about?"

- "Do you have any important deadlines coming up soon that I should know about?"

- "Please put a note on each category of correspondence that I review, sign, or forward. Let me know if I should continue to review and approve these documents or delegate any of them to you and why." You want to keep your employees' notes and observations on delegating work. Wait to delegate responsibilities until you have been at the organization for 60 days or more.

- "I am scheduled to meet individually with my peers in the next week or so. Are there any individuals or offices that I should thank on your behalf and why? Be generous."

- "I am scheduled to meet individually with our key customers in the next week or so. Is there anything I need to know about before I speak to any of them? Please give me a few important facts about each of our key customers, including the volume of the goods and services we provide them and the state of our relationship. Are there any individuals or offices that I should thank on your behalf and why? Be generous."

- "Were you able to take all your vacation days this year? If not, we will work together to find a way for you to take all your well-deserved time off this year. There will be no exception to this rule." Then smile.

- "I suspect that some of you may be interested in knowing my management style. I follow the guidance in this book. It tells me to do everything I can to make you successful. I promise you I will do exactly that." Then, hand them a copy of this book.

- After these meetings, write a handwritten note to each, thanking them for their time and great advice.

○ Meet individually with each of your peers (those on the same organizational level as you) with the following comments or questions:

- "Please tell me about yourself."

- Pass along any thanks from your staff for individuals or offices who have been particularly helpful.

- "How much do our offices deal with each other? If our offices jointly share any objectives, what are they, and are we doing our part to your satisfaction?"

- "Are there any objectives or obstacles we can help you with?"

- "What do we do well? What can we improve?"

- ■ "Do we need to meet regularly, or should we play it by ear for now?"
- ■ After these meetings, write a handwritten note to each, thanking them for their time and great advice.
- ○ Meet individually with your key customers with the following comments or questions:
  - ■ "Please tell me about yourself."
  - ■ Pass along any thanks from your staff for individuals or offices who have been particularly helpful.
  - ■ "What do we do well, and what can we do better?"
  - ■ "Are we meeting your expectations?"
  - ■ "How often should we meet? At regular intervals, as needed, or both?"
  - ■ After these meetings, write a handwritten note to each, thanking them for their time and great advice.
- ○ Meet with your boss for a second time. This meeting should follow your meetings with your direct reports, peers, and key customers. After reviewing your organization's objectives for the next 12 months, please leave a copy with your boss. Ask your boss, when they have time, to let you know if anything needs changing or modifying. Finally, tell your boss anything from your introductory meetings that you should bring to their attention. Do not write a thank-you note to your boss.
- ○ Within your first two to three weeks on the job, meet with the senior HR officer; the employee labor manager; the equal employment opportunity officer; the chief inclusion, diversity, equity, and accessibility officer; the labor attorney; and the employment attorney to find out if your office has any current or past issues you should know about. Do not expect those offices to come to talk to you. You must take the initiative. If you sense that there are morale issues in your team, please contact your HR staff to conduct an office climate survey. This is the best way to assess your employees' morale,

attitudes, level of teamwork, level of trust, appropriate recognition and appreciation given, etc.

- ○ Schedule time to walk around and introduce yourself informally to your employees and get to know them. Meeting your employees where they work is the least stressful for them. When meeting your staff members for the first time, please tell them you are honored to join such an outstanding team.

ILLUSTRATIVE STORY

On my first days at nearly every new job, employees quickly approached me with requests. Here are two examples of their requests. At one job, a direct report requested additional staff. At another job, someone asked for training funds. In both cases, I sought staff advice before responding. Before approving an additional employee, I asked the HR office for a workload analysis. Their report said that this office had too many staff members, and I could safely reduce its staff by one, which I did. At my second job, a direct report requested additional training funds to attend a course on the opposite coast. There was a similar course available in our metropolitan area. Since the total cost of his request (registration, travel, and hotel costs) exceeded the amount he was allocated annually, I did not approve his request but suggested he consider a locally taught course. In both cases, I explained my decision to the direct reports. In over 40 years of managing, I have found that I get the strangest requests in my first days at a new job. Direct reports ask for things that the previous boss likely did not approve. They hope to test you and get their request approved. Heads up!

Final thoughts:

- "If we did the things we are capable of, we would literally astound ourselves."[300] —Thomas Edison, American inventor

- "Let me tell you the secret that has led me to my goal. My strength lies solely in my tenacity."[301] —Louis Pasteur, French chemist and microbiologist

3.2 NOW THAT YOU'RE SETTLED IN

Your job is to make your employees successful. The more successful they are, the more successful you are.

> **Definition of performance measurement:** The process of measuring progress in achieving outcomes, showing efficiencies and effectiveness, and highlighting areas that need attention.[302]

- The objective of performance measurement is to identify and implement improvements to performance.[303]

- The most important performance measurements support your strategic plan goals and objectives. Please see Section 2.4, Performance Development, for more information. Be careful what you measure. Ask your employees and key customers to help you determine performance measurements to support your strategic plan goals and objectives. Your employees understand which measurements help them achieve their work unit's strategic objectives. Your customers know what they want. They should help drive current and future strategic objectives.

  - Additional examples of regular program updates include the sales numbers compared to your goal, customer satisfaction ratings, etc.

  - Section 2.2, Coaching and Mentoring, contains guidance on direct reports' weekly updates on performance measurements, recurring work and nonrecurring work, decision requests, and any sensitive information on employees.

  - In your first meeting with your boss, you asked them if there were any specific updates they would like to see. You decide on all additional information to discuss with your bosses. Please see Section 3.1, Your First Weeks at a New Job, for more information.

> ***ILLUSTRATIVE STORY***
>
> *At one organization, everyone reporting directly to the executive vice president was allotted 60 minutes biweekly to update her. Most chose to keep a running list of subjects in a notebook and talk informally without consulting their staff members first about topics that were important to them. Nicole decided to regularly update her boss on the performance measurements that were tied directly to strategic plan goals and objectives. She asked her staff for these updates two days before the weekly meetings with the executive vice president. This gave her time to review the material, ask questions, and prepare to brief her boss. Nicole's boss liked this format and said Nicole's updates were her favorite because they quickly covered much more important material than others did. Nicole's boss instructed all her other direct reports to create updates like Nicole's.*

- A few rules for performance measurement updates:
  - Ask employees to submit performance measurements and other updates to you electronically. You do not need to meet with your direct report in person unless either of you wants to discuss a subject in more depth. Employees' time is also valuable.
  - These electronic updates are maintained in your organization's knowledge management database.
  - These updates are excellent sources when compiling lists of employee accomplishments.

- At the end of the first 60 days at your new job, it is time to review your direct reports' notes on what types of correspondence you should delegate to them. Since your employees were already reviewing these documents, there is no workload increase if they complete them at their level. It makes your job easier, too. Not surprisingly, I have found that when asking employees to approve documents at their level, they take more care in reviewing them. A general rule is to delegate all tasks to the lowest-level team member who can accomplish them successfully.

- Set high standards for your employees. They will perform at the level expected of them. For example, if you find mistakes in reports, send them back for corrections. Their next reports will be better. For the first few reports that need work, suggest changes for improvement so that staff members know what you have in mind. You should request an electronic copy of the document using the Track Changes feature in Microsoft Word to make changes. Please do not use red ink on a paper draft to show corrections. You did not like getting these in school, and neither did your employees.

- The quality and quantity of work vary among employees. Managers are responsible for knowing the performance levels of direct reports and rewarding, counseling, or training them to improve their performance.

- Beware of overtime work. A National Institute for Occupational Safety and Health review of multiple studies concluded that working overtime, more than nine hours per day, correlated with perceived poorer worker health and increased injury rates and illnesses. When working overtime, employees feel less alert and have lower cognitive functioning, increased fatigue, increased injuries, and decreased vigilance.[304] For example, hospital nurses who work 10-hour shifts or longer experience higher levels of burnout and job dissatisfaction.[305]

- How many hours does the average American work each week? According to a Gallup survey, the average American works 47 hours weekly. That is an average of 9.4 hours per day in a five-day workweek.[306] If an employee is working at or over 50 hours per week, an effective manager needs to find out why.

- Beware of employees working long hours. A 2013 Stanford University study shows that increases in output are relatively small as hours rise beyond 50 hours a week. There are no productivity increases in working more than 55 hours per week.[307] When employees consistently work long hours, there is often a reason that is not work-related.

ILLUSTRATIVE STORY

At one organization, an employee worked long hours to avoid interactions with a spouse with whom he had a strained relationship.

ILLUSTRATIVE STORY

At another organization, a senior manager in his 60s consistently worked long hours. Frank had been diagnosed with major depressive disorder as a young man. He explained that when he was focusing on his work, he was not depressed. This is a typical coping mechanism among people with severe depression.

ILLUSTRATIVE STORY

At one organization, a senior manager, Christopher, occasionally worked late to meet short deadlines. Every time he did this, there was an employee, Steve, in a nearby office who was always working. Christopher mentioned to Steve's boss that it appeared Steve was consistently working very long hours. Steve's boss told Christopher confidentially that Steve's wife and only child had been killed in a car accident a year earlier. Steve wanted to spend minimum time in his empty house, so he chose to keep busy at work. He was receiving therapy to deal with his loss.

ILLUSTRATIVE STORY

I once hired an attorney to help me with a complex tax issue. I quickly noticed that I sometimes received emails from him late at night or early in the morning. He was working far more than 50 hours per week. He was working so many hours that he was sleep- deprived. At one point, I received an email from him with advice I knew was incorrect. I fired him. People who bill customers by the hour and work more than 50 hours per week are less than fully productive but make more money at their customers' expense.

ILLUSTRATIVE STORY

Of course, some people feel that working more than 50 hours per week will be seen more favorably by the organization's senior management. Unfortunately, many managers do not understand that 50 hours per week is the maximum that anyone can be fully productive at their jobs.

ILLUSTRATIVE STORY

Some companies even demand that their workers put in very long hours. Elon Musk bought Twitter, now known as X, in October 2022 and immediately fired half the staff. He then told the remaining staff that they must work long, intense hours or quit.[308] If employees are at the office longer than 50 hours per week, they will merely spread out their work to fill the time at the office. In this example, Musk has accomplished nothing except to alienate his X employees. In the time since Musk bought X, the value of the company has decreased by 80% (at the time of this writing).[309]

ILLUSTRATIVE STORY

Japanese workers traditionally work long hours to show devotion and hard work. Of course, the guideline that 50 hours per week is the most in which workers can be fully productive applies to Japanese workers, too. As a result, I sent the following letter to former Japanese Prime Minister Yoshihide Suga in September 2021. It is abbreviated but contains all the key points.

Prime Minister Suga
2-3-1 Nagata-chō, Chiyoda-ku,
Tokyo 100–8968, Japan
September 5, 2021

Dear Prime Minister Suga,

I wish to share with you a suggestion that I hope might assist the Japanese people. I am writing a book on management and read a 2013 Stanford University study that concludes that workers can only be fully effective for a maximum of 50 hours per week.

Japanese labor laws require that employees work a maximum of 8 hours a day or 40 hours a week. Despite the law, Japanese workers work some of the longest hours in the world. Many Japanese companies require employees to work at least 80 additional hours per month longer than the legal limit. This adds up to a total of 60 hours per week minimum. Thus, many Japanese workers work at least ten hours per week longer than the Stanford study shows they can be effective. This is a big waste of time and talent.

A 2017 Gallup poll shows that a mere 6% of Japanese employees are actively engaged in their work, a staggering 71% are "not engaged," and 23% are "actively disengaged."

Microsoft employees in Japan have adopted the 4-day workweek, and their productivity jumped 40%.

In the post-COVID-19 world, employees have more leverage over hours and benefits. Companies offering perks like telework, coaching, and professional development will attract the best employees. Japanese companies are reluctant to reduce hours. If the Japanese government financially incentivizes Japanese companies to reduce hours, a few companies will take advantage of the offer. When these trend leaders begin to attract the best employees, other companies will follow suit or lose their best employees. Use employees to leverage large-scale change.

Reducing Japanese working hours to at or below 50 hours per week will reasonably result in the following:

- Worker morale will improve, and stress will decrease.

> - Worker engagement will improve. They will care about their work and do all they can to do the best work possible.
>
> - The Japanese economy will expand.
>
> - The Japanese workers will use their extra hours off to help reverse their declining birth rate.
>
> I greatly admire the Japanese people and hope that the conclusions of these studies and my suggestion can help reduce Japanese workers' hours.
>
> Sincerely and respectfully,
> Garry W. Stanberry

- In 2023, the German gross domestic product (GDP) per person was $52,745 yearly, and Japan's GDP per person was only $33,8341. German workers are far more productive per person and work far fewer hours than Japanese workers.[310]

- Never speak ill of your predecessor. For one thing, you will look petty. Also, there are often employees who like their former boss. Though this advice might seem obvious, I have seen too many new bosses making inappropriate comments about their predecessors. Their message, in effect, is, "Thank goodness I am here to fix all the problems my predecessor left me." If you speak of your predecessor at all, say something nice.

ILLUSTRATIVE STORY

A departing manager prepared a binder for his successor. The detailed information in the binder included responses to the Job-Related Information for Your Successor form in the Appendix. The incoming and departing managers met to review the binder's contents in depth. When the former manager spoke with a former direct report months later, the direct report remarked, "The new boss has publicly said several times what a great job you did in preparing him for his new job. He says you prepared him for success."

- Train and prepare your successors. All organizations experience turnover. How you prepare for that inevitability is important. Instruct departing employees to complete the Job-Related Information for Your Successor form in the Appendix to help their replacements get a good start.

3.3 COMMUNICATION

Effective managers do more listening than talking. Earnestly listen. When your employee, peer, boss, union official, or customer finishes talking, please acknowledge that you understand what they said and any actions you plan to take. Always finish by saying thank you with a smile. Follow up on any of their requests, suggestions, or concerns. Put their requests, suggestions, or concerns on your To-Do list so you can track and prioritize them. (Please see Section 4.11, Time Management, for more information.)

- A study published by the Oxford University Press states that face-to-face communication is the best communication method to make people feel less lonely and more connected. This is followed by voice calls, which make people feel more connected only. Video calls and texting were less connecting than face-to-face or voice calls. Finally, emails and social media did not decrease loneliness nor promote connectedness.[311] Face-to-face communication triggers the release of oxytocin, which causes a positive emotional response[312] that facilitates trust and attachment.[313]

- In a Korn Ferry survey, 55% of millennial bosses responded that online messaging is their customary way to communicate with their direct reports, then emails at 28%, and only 14% said they prefer to communicate face-to-face. In sharp contrast, employees said they would like their millennial bosses to talk to them more face-to-face. How bosses communicate with their staff helps drive organizational culture.[314] That makes your weekly coaching sessions even more important. Please see Section 2.2, Coaching and Mentoring, for more information. Get out from behind your desk and talk to your direct reports face-to-face as often as you can.

- Types of communication.
  - Video chat. This allows face-to-face meetings of participants anywhere in the world. It includes FaceTime, Microsoft Teams, Zoom, and WhatsApp, etc.

- ○ Instant messaging (IM) allows users to send links, photos, texts, and videos. IM tools include text messages, WhatsApp, Slack, WeChat, Google Chat, Microsoft Teams, and Facebook Messenger. IM is quicker than emails, but everyone should use one of these tools exclusively for it to work most effectively. IM is not suitable for formal communication or extensive group discussions.

- ○ Phone calls. One of my former bosses had a communication rule. If she could not resolve an issue in three emails or texts, she arranged a phone call or face-to-face meeting. Communication etiquette continues to evolve. No one uses voicemail, and you should text to arrange a call.

- ○ Emails

  - Emails are the millennial boss's second most preferred method of communication after online messaging. Emails allow space for much more text than IMs.

  - Many people look first at where their name is in the email "to" field. They are happy if their name is near the top; if they are near the end, they are not.[315] How do we fix this? List email addresses in the "to" and "cc" fields in alphabetical order or by seniority. People are sensitive to being last on an addressee list unless it is in alphabetical or ranking order.

  - Here is an open request to Microsoft CEO, Mr. Satya Nadella:

> Dear Mr. Nadella, Please create MS Office options to sort "to" and "cc" addresses alphabetically or randomly. Please indicate on the "to" and "cc" lines whether the names are sorted alphabetically or randomly so people will absolutely know how the addresses were machine-sorted. The first thing many look at in emails is the "to" field. If they are listed first, they are happy. People wonder if they are listed last as an afterthought. Thank you for

> your consideration of this request. It will save much anxiety and cost nothing. Mary Parker Follet would call this a win-win. Thank you. I hope you are having a fun week! Sincerely and respectfully, Garry.

- There are two types of emails. The email's subject line should state whether a response is required/requested or is for their information only. Examples:

> Subject: Info: Hiring freeze is in effect immediately.
>
> Subject: Reply requested: Corporate Inquiry on Business Travel/Response due July 28, 5:00 p.m. EST.

- Greetings and closings
  - Millennials and Gen Zers expect some formality in emails. For example, if a millennial or Gen Zer begins an email with "Dear Ms. Jones," they expect a similar greeting in the reply regardless of the seniority of the recipient. If you forget to add greetings and closings, many millennials and Gen Zers will see your emails as disrespectful.
    - Next, add a closing sentence such as: "I hope that you are enjoying your week" or "Hope you have a relaxing weekend."
    - End the email with Thanks, Best wishes, Regards, Sincerely yours, etc., and then your first name only.[316]
- Body of the emails
  - The first sentence of each email should summarize the email. Here is an example when you want a response from the email recipient: "Our corporate budget office asks that you provide to Brigit Smith, by July 28, a list of your travel destinations, dates, and estimated expenses

scheduled through the end of our fiscal year (December 31st)."

- ☐ Always be concise and use the smallest words possible.

- ☐ Use the fewest number of words possible. "I would have written a shorter letter, but I did not have the time."[317] —Blaise Pascal (1623–1662), French philosopher and mathematician

- ☐ Keep your emails upbeat.

- ☐ When writing emails, letters, and reports, I often consider the following words to ask myself whether I have left anything out: who, what, when, where, why, and how.

- ☐ Program your computer to include your signature block on each email and use a conservative font like Arial, Aptos, or Times New Roman in font size 12. Use the same font and font size throughout your emails. Use only black for the text color.

- ☐ Your signature block should include your name, title, office street address, office phone number, fax number, cell number, and your organization's quiet hours and time zone.

- ☐ Use your company, not your personal, email account for business correspondence.

- ■ More thoughts on emails

  - ☐ Think before you hit the "send" button: "How will this look if I read it in *The New York Times, The Harvard Lampoon*, or if it is used as evidence in a lawsuit?"

  - ☐ Proofread your email. Use spell-check.

  - ☐ The last task before sending an email is adding email addresses in the "to" and "cc" fields. Then, sort the addresses using the RANDOM or ALPHABETICAL options. (Thanks, Mr. Nadella!)

  - ☐ Hit the "send" button.

- The pandemic drove more telework and more meetings. A July 2020 study of over three million workers in North America, Europe, and the Middle East was conducted to assess the impact of COVID-19 on employees' digital communications patterns (email, phone calls, video conferencing, etc.). The study found significant increases in the average number of meetings, but the duration of these meetings declined, resulting in 11.5% less time in meetings overall. Also, since the pandemic began, the average workday has lengthened by 48.5 minutes.[318] That cancels out the commuting time savings for those who telework at home. Please ensure that none of your employees works more than 50 hours per week and that you schedule the fewest number of meetings possible.

- Emails outside of work hours: All emails should be sent only during regular business hours. You owe it to your employees to only send emails within work hours.

ILLUSTRATIVE STORY

The internal communication flow was slow at a software development company with over 1,000 employees because employees could not quickly tell which emails needed answers. Managers created an organization-wide email response system. All emails that required a response were sent to the "response-required" employee. This employee sent out the response-required emails with "RESPONSE DUE: Month/Day/Year" in the subject line along with the subject. This employee also ensured that the replies were received on time. In only a few weeks, employees complimented the management team because they spent less time searching to determine which emails required responses.

- Face-to-face communication: What do you do when you absolutely need a response from someone? You are 34 times more effective in getting your answer by asking face-to-face rather than emailing.[319] As we learned in Section 3.7, Flexible Work Arrangements (also Workplace Flexibilities), interpersonal interactions release oxytocin, a neuropeptide that facilitates trust and attachment.[320]

- Albert Einstein was a wonderful role model in many ways. He spoke to everyone the same way, regardless of their position.[321]

A final thought on communication:

- I find that the higher I move up in organizations, the more I rely on writing. Since we are wisely scheduling the fewest possible number of meetings, writing becomes even more important and is a permanent, retrievable record. As an example, even if a staff member misses a meeting, the written minutes will always be available. Your written words are an important part of your organization's knowledge management system.

3.4 DECISION-MAKING

Difficult decisions tend to have negative consequences for every alternative. The way to make the best decisions is to involve staff and customers in the decision-making process. Your staff and customers have unique perspectives that can contribute to better decisions. Your staff members will give their best efforts to make it work if they are part of the decision-making process and must live with the decision. And your customers know what they want.

The best way to deal with problems is to prevent them from occurring. If they do occur, it is crucial to address them as soon as possible. A motivated and engaged staff will prevent and identify problems and suggest ways to resolve them.

A 2018 McKinsey Global Survey states that only 20% of survey respondents felt that their organization was proficient at decision-making.[322] In my experience, most managers make decisions without consulting their employees and customers.

Definition of the decision-making process (abridged): The process of making a decision that best resolves the problem and achieves the optimal outcome.

Definition of the decision-making process (unabridged): The process of making a decision by first defining the problem and desired outcome, identifying decision criteria and allocating weight to each, identifying alternative solutions and evaluating each, choosing the best solution that resolves the problem and achieves the optimal outcome, developing an implementation schedule, measuring progress toward implementing the solution, implementing the best solution, and measuring the ongoing effectiveness of the solution or until the outcome is achieved.

- The 23 detailed steps in the decision-making process are below, along with two examples.
  - The first example immediately below is a one-time task, so it requires all 23 decision-making steps.
  - In the second example below, the task is recurring, so fewer steps are needed.

The Decision-Making Process with an Example
This is a one-time task, so it requires all 23 decision-making steps.

Step #	Definition	Example
1	The manager determines if the task needs to be done at all.	Yes, the information technology (IT) help desk speed and accuracy are below the national average. The manager wants to explore all the options to find a better solution.
2	The manager determines whether they have the authority to delegate the task.	Yes, the manager is the chief of the Office of Administrative Services and oversees the IT help desk.
3	The manager defines the problem and the desired outcome.	**Problem:** Our help desk speed and accuracy are continually rated below the national average of 4.7. This is on a scale of 1–5 (5 being the highest.) **Desired outcome:** Improve both the speed and accuracy of IT help desk customer satisfaction scores from 4.1 to a score of 4.7 or higher on a scale of 1–5 (5 being the highest).
4	The manager selects the most qualified direct report to accomplish the task.	The chief of Administrative Services appoints the direct report that is responsible for managing the IT help desk.
5	The manager provides the direct report with any information that may influence the selection of decision criteria or an option to consider.	In this example, the manager informs the direct report to consider outsourcing the contracting help desk responsibilities to one of several national help desk companies. Independent surveys show that this is likely to improve the speed and accuracy of responses because commercial help desks operate on a high volume and have fewer overhead costs per unit of work.
6	The manager instructs the direct report to select members of their decision-making team. The direct report and the decision-making team may further refine the problem and desired outcome.	**Members of the decision-making team:** **1.** The employees who will implement this change. **2.** Customers, in this example, are all employees because everyone receives IT services. To ensure your customers are represented, choose two employees who are IT savvy. In this example, the decision-making team is satisfied with the manager's definition of the problem and the desired outcome.

(continued)

The Decision-Making Process with an Example *(continued)*
This is a one-time task, so it requires all 23 decision-making steps.

Step #	Definition	Example
7	The manager and direct report determine if this task has any relationship to other tasks that may create conflicts. The manager may ask the decision-making team for advice.	In this example, there are none.
8	The manager and direct report decide if there are adequate resources available. The manager may ask the decision-making team for advice.	Yes, adequate resources are available in this example.
9	The manager and direct report decide if any additional training is needed. The manager may ask the decision-making team for advice.	No additional training is needed in this example.
10	The manager tells the direct report how much empowerment the direct report will have in completing the task.	The manager tells the direct report that she will have maximum empowerment to complete the task. This means that the direct report will update the manager during their weekly coaching meetings, or more frequently as she deems appropriate, so there is no need for the manager to look over her shoulder.
11	The manager delegates authority to the direct report for task completion.	The manager delegates authority and the direct report accepts authority to complete task.
12	The manager and direct report decide whether to put the above steps in writing and initial the agreement.	The manager and direct report put their agreement in writing and initial it so there will be no misunderstanding later.
13	The direct report and decision-making team identify the decision criteria.	**1.** Improve the speed of resolving IT problems. **2.** Improve the accuracy in resolving IT problems.
14	The direct report and decision making team allocate weight to each decision criterion.	Speed is measured on a scale of 7–10 in half-point increments (10 being the highest). Accuracy is measured on a scale of 7–10 in half-point increments (10 being the highest).

(continued)

The Decision-Making Process with an Example *(continued)*
This is a one-time task, so it requires all 23 decision-making steps.

Step #	Definition	Example
15	The direct report and decision-making team identify alternative solutions.	**Option 1:** Introduce AI to assist with basic IT help desk questions. **Option 2:** Assess current help desk staff for weaknesses and train them. **Option 3:** Contract out help desk work.
16	The direct report and the decision-making team evaluate alternative solutions, weighing the pros and cons of each based on the decision criteria.	**Option 1** **Pros:** AI can successfully assist with basic questions and improve speed and accuracy. **Cons:** AI works well for basic questions but cannot answer more complex ones at present. **Option 1 team score:** The team scored option 8.0 for speed and 7.5 for accuracy. **Option 2** **Pros:** Training will help improve the score, but it is unknown if this will achieve the 4.7 goal. **Cons:** Previous attempts at training staff improved speed and accuracy but did not improve the score to 4.7 or better. **Option 2 team score:** The team scored this option 7.5 for speed and 7.5 for accuracy. **Option 3** **Pros:** Based on an independent market survey, contracting help desk responsibilities to one of several national help desk companies is likely to improve the speed and accuracy scores to achieve the goal of 4.7 or higher. **Pros:** The overall cost will be less because commercial help desks operate on a high volume and have fewer overhead costs per unit of work. **Option 3 team score:** The team scored this option 9 for speed and 9 for accuracy.
17	The direct report and the decision-making team choose the best solution that will resolve the problem and achieve the optimal outcome.	**Option 3.** Contracting the help desk work is most likely to achieve the desired overall speed and accuracy scores of 4.7 or higher. In addition, this solution will also reduce costs.

(continued)

The Decision-Making Process with an Example *(continued)*
This is a one-time task, so it requires all 23 decision-making steps.

Step #	Definition	Example
18	The direct report briefs the manager on the decision criteria and the best solution chosen. The manager can modify or approve the best solution.	In this example, the manager gratefully accepts the recommendation of the direct report and the decision-making team.
19	The direct report, the decision-making team, and the implementation team will develop a preliminary work plan schedule and an implementation plan schedule with objectives and milestones as needed.	January 3—The contracting office sends out requests for bids. March 1—The contracting office, with representatives of staff and customers, selects the IT help desk contractor that best meets their requirements. April 15—Implementation help desk contract date.
20	The direct report appoints a qualified staff member to oversee the measurement of progress toward completing the preliminary work plan schedule.	The preliminary work schedule includes: January 3—The contracting office sends out requests for bids. March 1—The contracting office, with representatives of staff and customers, selects the IT help desk contractor that best meets their requirements.
21	The direct report and the implementation team will execute the implementation plan schedule.	April 15—In this example, the implementation is merely to activate the new help desk contract on the date the manager chooses, with advice from all divisions.
22	The direct report appoints a qualified staff member to oversee the measurement of progress to ensure the desired performance objectives and outcome are achieved on time and on budget.	Continuously monitor the IT help desk speed and accuracy ratings to ensure they meet the desired performance level. In this example, an independent help desk performance tracking contractor will provide a weekly report on speed and accuracy.
23	The manager follows up to ensure the task is ongoing satisfactorily and accomplished on time and on budget.	In this example, the task is ongoing. The direct report will update the manager at their weekly coaching meeting. The manager is on distribution for contractor updates to ensure that the speed and accuracy of the help desk remain within the standard of 4.7 or higher.

Examining the Steps in the Decision-Making Process in More Detail

Step 1: The manager determines whether the task needs to be done at all.

- Organizations are dynamic, and tasks are subject to change or may no longer be necessary. Also, effective managers do not rely exclusively on direct reports to assess whether a task is no longer needed. In my experience, this is the most overlooked step.

Step 2: The manager determines whether they have the authority to delegate the task.

- Was this task formally given to you in your job description? Was it verbally given to you by your boss? Or did you assume responsibility for the task over time? Discuss with your boss if it is not clear.

Step 3: The manager defines the problem and the desired outcome.

- Defining the problem and the desired outcome is the most important step in the decision-making process. It is the foundation upon which all other decision-making steps rest.

- In Step 5 below, the manager instructs the direct report to select members of their decision-making team. This team may further refine the problem and desired outcome.

- How do you achieve the desired outcome? By creating measurable objectives and milestones that are a roadmap to your desired outcome. In Step 19 below, the direct report, the decision-making team, and the implementation team will develop an implementation plan schedule with measurable objectives and milestones.

Step 4: The manager selects the most qualified direct report to accomplish the task.

- Often, the direct report chosen is responsible for the area in which the task resides. There are occasions in which the managers can choose from two or more direct reports. In this case, the manager should consider their position, experience, judgment, and technical, professional, and people skills. Tasks can also be given to a high-value employee as a learning experience.

Step 5: The manager provides the direct report with any information that may influence the selection of decision criteria or an option to consider.

- The manager works at a higher level and has a broader view of the environment in which the task will be accomplished.

Step 6: The manager instructs the direct report to select members of their decision-making team. The direct report and the decision-making team may further refine the problem and desired outcome.

- The decision-making team will be the people who should be actively involved in each step of the decision-making process because they have an interest in this decision. They are likely the employees who will implement the decision and customers who must live with the outcome. These two groups should be well represented as important decision-making team members throughout the decision-making process. Each sees each step from a unique perspective, and their joint involvement will most likely result in a better outcome. Your employees and customers who have a direct interest in the decision will understand the pros and cons of each option. Involving employees will also help them be more engaged. Your customers will also have a better understanding if there are any delays.

- Once the decision-making team is selected, they should be given the opportunity to further refine the problem and the desired outcome. If they want to recommend any changes, they must notify the manager as soon as possible. While the manager gives as much empowerment as possible, they must approve any recommended changes. The manager may be aware of circumstances in which the suggested changes will not work. The direct report empowers each member of the decision-making team to reconvene the group to revisit any step or to suggest changes at any time.

- The ideal size of a decision-making group is seven. The decision-making effectiveness of the group is reduced by 10% for each additional member.[323]

Step 7: The manager and direct report determine whether this task has any relationship to other tasks that may create conflicts. The manager may ask the decision-making team for advice.

- The relationship between this task and others can change before the task is completed.

Step 8: The manager and direct report decide whether there are adequate resources available. The manager may ask the decision-making team for advice.

- The need for additional resources can change before the task is completed. Unexpected expenses or scheduling conflicts may arise.

Step 9: The manager and direct report decide whether any additional training is needed. The manager may ask the decision-making team for advice.

- This can be formal training or on-the-job training.

Step 10: The manager informs the direct report about the level of empowerment or self-direction they will have in completing the task.

- Effective managers give direct reports maximum empowerment, as people want as much control over their lives and jobs as possible. The direct report will update the manager during their weekly coaching meetings or more often if required.

Step 11: The manager delegates authority to the direct report for task completion.

- Both the manager and the direct report share responsibility for its completion.

Step 12: The manager and direct report decide whether to put the above steps in writing and initial the agreement.

- When in doubt, create a written agreement so there will be no misunderstanding later.

- This document is uploaded into the organization's information management system as a permanent record.

- The manager should add the milestone dates to their To-Do list. Please see Section 4.11, Time Management, for more information. Suppose the direct report forgets to provide an update to the manager during their coaching meeting. In that case, the manager will see it on their To-Do list and ask about the status.

Step 13: The direct report and decision-making team identify the decision criteria.

- There are many decision criteria to choose from. Here are some that are typical:
  - Cost-effectiveness
  - Return on investment
  - Safety
  - Effectiveness (the degree to which a product or service successfully produces a desired result).
  - Overall cost
  - Ease of implementation
  - Ease of modification/scalability/flexibility
  - Risk levels. Please see Section 4.8, Risk Management, for more information.
  - Customer satisfaction. Please see Chapter 8, Excite Your Customers.
  - Sustainability. If your customers demand earth-friendly products or services, your criteria should include sustainability.

Step 14: The direct report and decision-making team allocate weight to each decision criterion.

- Use a scale of 7–10 in half-point increments, with 7 being the lowest and 10 the highest score.

Step 15: The direct report and the decision-making team identify alternative solutions.

Step 16: The direct report and the decision-making team evaluate alternative solutions, weighing the pros and cons of each based on the decision criteria.

- For more complex decisions, you may need outside help. For example, when choosing software, you are wise to contract with one of several companies that specialize in helping companies choose the best software that meets their requirements. You are unlikely to have that type of expertise on staff. Your staff will still need to identify what they want the software to do. For more information, please see Section 2.1, Hire and Retain Great Employees.

Step 17: The direct report and the decision-making team choose the best solution that will resolve the problem and achieve the optimal outcome.

Step 18: The direct report briefs the manager on the decision criteria and the best solution chosen. The manager can modify or approve the best solution.

- The manager may have knowledge that may alter the solution recommended by the direct report and the decision-making team.

- Managers should always remember to say thank you to the direct report and the decision-making team for their work.

Step 19: The direct report, the decision-making team, and the implementation team will develop a preliminary work plan schedule and an implementation plan schedule with objectives and milestones as needed.

- Preliminary work plan schedule. This includes any activities that precede the beginning of work to achieve the objectives. This may include designing, planning, creating cost estimates, arranging for contractors to assist with implementation, ordering raw materials, requesting permits, conducting surveys, etc.

- Implementation plan schedule. This includes all the steps to achieve both the objectives and milestones and the desired outcome.

Step 20: The direct report appoints a qualified staff member to oversee the measurement of progress toward completing the preliminary work plan schedule.

- Managers receive updates on progress toward completing the preliminary work plan schedule weekly at the coaching meeting with their direct report or more frequently as needed.

- While the direct report has delegated authority to a qualified employee to measure progress toward implementing the preliminary work schedule, the direct report is responsible for ensuring that the measurements are done correctly and on time.

Step 21: The direct report and the implementation team will execute the implementation plan schedule.

- The direct report and the implementation team share responsibility for the successful completion of all tasks.

- The manager and direct report should add the milestone dates to their To-Do lists. Please see Section 4.11, Time Management, for more information. Suppose the direct report forgets to provide an update to the manager during their coaching meeting. In that case, the manager will see it on their To-Do list and ask about the status.

Step 22: The direct report appoints a qualified staff member to oversee the measurement of progress to ensure the desired performance objectives and outcome are achieved on time and on budget.

Step 23: The manager follows up to ensure the task is accomplished or remains ongoing satisfactorily.

- The manager should be given updates on completing this task and others in their weekly coaching meetings or more often as needed. Please see Section 2.2, Coaching and Mentoring, and Section 3.2, Now That You're Settled In.

- The manager, direct report, and the implementation team share responsibility for the successful completion of each task.

The Decision-Making Process with an Example
This task recurs annually; not all steps in the decision-making process are necessary

Step #	Definition	Example
1	The manager determines whether the task needs to be done at all.	Yes, the annual report to stockholders is an annual requirement.
2	The manager determines whether they have the authority to delegate the task.	Yes, the Office of Administrative Services has completed this report for several years.
3	The manager defines the problem and the desired outcome.	Problem: none, in this example. Desired outcome: Create an annual report for stockholders and publish it on or before March 1. The format should be similar to the format used in previous years.
4	The manager selects the most qualified direct report to accomplish the task.	The chief of Administrative Services appoints a new direct report to do this task who has the skills and judgment to complete it.
5	The manager provides the direct report with any information that may influence the selection of decision criteria or an option to consider.	In this case, the manager had no information to provide.
6	The manager instructs the direct report to select members of their decision-making team. The direct report and the decision-making team may further refine the problem and desired outcome.	In this example, there is no problem to define. The direct report and decision-making team may consider changes to the annual report's format and content.
7	The manager and direct report determine if this task has any relationship to other tasks that may create conflicts. The manager may ask the decision-making team for advice.	None, in this example.

(continued)

The Decision-Making Process with an Example *(continued)*
This task recurs annually; not all steps in the decision-making process are necessary

Step #	Definition	Example
8	The manager and direct report decide if there are adequate resources available. The manager may ask the decision-making team for advice.	Yes, adequate resources are available in this example.
9	The manager and direct report decide if any additional training is needed. The manager may ask the decision-making team for advice.	Yes, in this example, the direct report responsible for completing the task is new. This person can receive on-the-job training from the person who completed last year's report.
10	The manager tells the direct report how empowered they will be in completing the task.	The manager tells the direct report that they will have maximum empowerment to complete the task. This means that the direct report will update the manager during their weekly coaching meetings, or more frequently as they deem appropriate, so there is no need for the manager to look over their shoulder.
11	The manager delegates authority to the direct report for task completion.	The manager delegates authority and the direct report accepts authority to complete task. Both the manager and direct report share responsibility for the task completion.
12	The manager and direct report decide whether to put the above steps in writing and initial the agreement.	In this example, the manager and direct report agree that there is no need for a formal agreement.
13	The direct report and decision-making team identify the decision criteria.	In this example, this step is not needed.
14	The direct report and decision-making team allocate weight to each decision criterion.	In this example, this step is not needed.
15	The direct report and decision-making team identify alternative solutions.	In this example, this step is not needed.

(continued)

The Decision-Making Process with an Example *(continued)*
This task recurs annually; not all steps in the decision-making process are necessary

Step #	Definition	Example
16	The direct report and the decision-making team evaluate alternative solutions, weighing the pros and cons of each based on the decision criteria.	In this example, this step is not needed.
17	The direct report and the decision-making team choose the best solution that will resolve the problem and achieve the optimal outcome.	In this example, this step is not needed.
18	The direct report briefs the manager on the decision criteria and the best solution chosen. The manager can modify or approve the best solution.	In this example, the manager has nothing to modify or approve.
19	The direct report, the decision-making team, and the implementation team will develop a preliminary work plan schedule and an implementation plan schedule with objectives and milestones as needed.	In this example, there is no need for a preliminary work plan schedule. The direct report, the decision-making team, and implementation team created the following implementation plan schedule. Dec 20: Request division reports. Jan 15: Receive division reports. Jan 31: Complete the draft annual report. Feb 7: Legal review of the draft report. Feb 14: Complete the editing, formatting, artwork, and photos. Feb 26: Executive staff will review/ approve the draft. Mar 1: Publish online on or before this date.
20	The direct report appoints a qualified staff member to oversee the measurement of progress toward completing the preliminary work plan schedule.	This appointee will determine whether they are on track with the implementation dates above.

(continued)

The Decision-Making Process with an Example *(continued)*
This task recurs annually; not all steps in the decision-making process are necessary

Step #	Definition	Example
21	The direct report and the implementation team will execute the implementation plan schedule.	In this example, the solution is to publish the annual report on or before March 1.
22	The direct report appoints a qualified staff member to oversee the measurement of progress to ensure the desired performance objectives and outcome are achieved on time and on budget.	In this example, the direct report appoints a qualified staff member to oversee the measurement of progress to ensure the annual report is published on or before March 1 and it is on budget.
23	The manager follows up to ensure the task is ongoing satisfactorily and accomplished on time and on budget.	She put this task on her To-Do list. The manager should be given updates on completing this task and others in their weekly coaching meetings or more frequently as needed.

Next, we can examine the steps in the decision-making process in more detail.

Step 1: The manager determines whether the task needs to be done at all.

- Organizations are dynamic, and tasks are subject to change or may no longer be necessary. Also, effective managers do not rely exclusively on direct reports to assess whether a task is no longer needed. In my experience, this is the most overlooked step.

Step 2: The manager determines whether they have the authority to delegate the task.

- Was this task formally given to you in your job description? Was it verbally given to you by your boss? Or did you assume responsibility for the task over time? Discuss this with your boss if it is not clear.

- If your office owns a recurring task like this, consider creating a policy so you do not need to recreate the steps each year.

Step 3: The manager defines the problem and the desired outcome.

- Defining the problem and the desired outcome is the most important step in the decision-making process. It is the foundation upon which all other decision-making steps rest.

- In this example, there is no problem to define.

- In Step 5 below, the manager instructs the direct report to select members of his/her decision-making team. This team may further refine the problem and desired outcome.

- How do you plan to achieve the desired outcome? By creating measurable objectives and milestones that is a roadmap to your desired outcome. In Step 19 below, the direct report and the implementation team will develop an implementation plan schedule with measurable objectives and milestones.

Step 4: The manager selects the most qualified direct report to accomplish the task.

- Often, the direct report chosen is responsible for the area in which the task resides. There are occasions in which the managers can choose from two or more direct reports. In this case, the manager should consider their position, experience, judgment, and technical, professional, and people skills. Tasks can also be given to a high-value employee as a learning experience.

Step 5: The manager provides the direct report with any information that may influence the selection of decision criteria or an option to consider.

- The manager works at a higher level and has a broader view of the environment in which the task will be accomplished.

Step 6: The manager instructs the direct report to select members of their decision-making team. The direct report and the decision-making team may further refine the problem and desired outcome.

- In this example, the decision-making team might include a representative from the accounting and finance office. This representative may recommend additional data to include in the annual report in response to customers' requests.

- The decision-making team will be the people who should be actively involved in each step of the decision-making process because they have an interest in this decision. They are likely the employees who will implement the decision and customers who must live with the outcome. These two groups should be well represented as important decision-making team members throughout the decision-making process. Each sees each step from a unique perspective, and their joint involvement will most likely result in a better outcome. Your employees and customers who have a direct interest in the decision will understand the pros and cons of each option. Involving employees will also help them be more engaged. Your customers will also have a better understanding if there are any delays.

- Once the decision-making team is selected, they should be given the opportunity to further refine the problem and the desired outcome. If they want to recommend any changes, they must notify the manager as soon as possible. While the manager offers as much empowerment as possible, they must approve any recommended changes. The manager may be aware of circumstances in which the suggested changes will not work. The direct report empowers each member of the decision-making team to reconvene the group to revisit any step or to suggest changes at any time.

- The manager may ask the decision-making team for advice. The ideal size of a decision-making group is seven. The decision-making effectiveness of the group is reduced by 10% for each additional member.[324]

Step 7: The manager and direct report determine if this task has any relationship to other tasks. The manager may ask the decision-making team for advice.

- The relationship between this task and others can change before the task is completed.

Step 8: The manager and direct report decide if there are adequate resources available. The manager may ask the decision-making team for advice.

- The need for additional resources can change before the task is completed. Unexpected expenses or scheduling conflicts may arise.

Step 9: The manager and direct report decide if any additional training is needed. The manager may ask the decision-making team for advice.

- Yes, in this example, the direct report responsible for completing the task is new. This person can receive on-the-job training from the person who completed last year's report.
- This can be formal training or on-the-job training.

Step 10: Level of empowerment. The manager informs the direct report about the level of empowerment or self-direction they will have in completing the task.

- Effective managers give direct reports maximum empowerment, as people want as much control over their lives and jobs as possible. The direct report will update the manager during their weekly coaching meetings or more often if required.

Step 11: The manager delegates authority to the direct report for task completion.

- Both the manager and the direct report share responsibility for its completion.

Step 12: The manager and direct report decide whether to put the above steps in writing and initial the agreement.

- When in doubt, create a written agreement so there will be no misunderstanding later.
- This document is uploaded into the organization's information management system as a permanent record.

- The manager should add the milestone dates to their To-Do list. Please see Section 4.11, Time Management, for more information. Suppose the direct report forgets to provide an update to the manager during their coaching meeting. In that case, the manager will see it on their To-Do list and ask about the status.

Step 13: The direct report and decision-making team identify the decision criteria.

- In this example, this step is not needed.

Step 14: The direct report and decision-making team allocate weight to each decision criterion.

- In this example, this step is not needed.

Step 15: The direct report and decision-making team identify alternative solutions.

- In this example, this step is not needed.

Step 16: The direct report and the decision-making team evaluate alternative solutions, weighing the pros and cons of each based on the decision criteria.

- In this example, this step is not needed.

Step 17: The direct report and the decision-making team choose the best solution that will resolve the problem and achieve the optimal outcome.

- In this example, this step is not needed.

Step 18: The direct report briefs the manager on the decision criteria and the best solution chosen. The manager can modify or approve the best solution.

- The manager may have knowledge that may alter the solution recommended by the direct report and the decision-making team.

Step 19: The direct report, the decision-making team, and the implementation team will develop a preliminary work plan schedule and an implementation plan schedule with objectives and milestones as needed. They are:

- Preliminary work plan schedule. Includes all activities that precede the beginning of work to achieve the objectives. This may include designing, planning, creating cost estimates, arranging for contractors to assist with implementation, ordering raw materials, requesting permits, conducting surveys, etc.

- Implementation plan schedule. This includes all the steps to achieve both the objectives and milestones and the desired outcome.

Step 20: The direct report appoints a qualified staff member to oversee the measurement of progress toward completing the preliminary work plan schedule.

- Managers receive updates on progress toward completing the preliminary work plan schedule weekly at the coaching meeting with their direct report or more frequently as needed.

- While the direct report has delegated authority to a qualified employee to measure progress toward implementing the preliminary work schedule, the direct report is responsible for ensuring that the measurements are done correctly and on time.

Step 21: The direct report and the implementation team will execute the implementation plan schedule.

- The direct report and the implementation team share responsibility for the successful completion of all tasks.

- The manager and the direct report should put all major tasks like this on their To-Do lists.

Step 22: The direct report appoints a qualified staff member to oversee the measurement of progress to ensure the desired performance objectives and outcome are achieved on time and on budget.

- The manager and direct report will get updates at their weekly coaching meetings or more often as needed.

Step 23: The manager follows up to ensure the task is ongoing satisfactorily and accomplished on time and on budget. The manager should be given updates on completing this task and others in their weekly coaching meetings. Please see Section 2.2, Coaching and Mentoring, and Section 3.2, Now That You're Settled In.

- The manager, direct report, and the implementation team share responsibility for the successful completion of each task.

Final thoughts on the decision-making process:

- "No decision is, in itself, a decision."[325] —William James, American philosopher and psychologist (1842–1910)

- "Patience is also a form of action."[326] —Auguste Rodin, French sculptor (1840–1917)

- "We didn't make these decisions in a vacuum. We sat down and met with the people [employees]. It was the staff that really influenced how we made a lot of those decisions."[327] —Michael Johnson, CEO of Boys & Girls Clubs of Dane County, Madison, Wisconsin

  - I want to work for Michael Johnson. He gets it!

3.5 DELEGATION AND EMPOWERMENT

Delegation and empowerment have the same meanings but are used in different contexts. Both deal with the degree of autonomy or self-direction that managers give their employees to complete a task. Both delegation and empowerment span the complete continuum from giving no autonomy to giving maximum autonomy.

> **Definition of delegation and empowerment:** A management process of transferring the authority to complete a task to another person, generally a direct report.

- In common usage today, empowering employees means allowing them to complete tasks with minimum oversight, permitting them to use their judgment as much as possible (giving them autonomy).

- In all cases, when a manager delegates authority to complete a task, whether there is no autonomy or complete autonomy, the manager and the direct report share responsibility for completing the task.

- Effective managers ensure that those responsible for completing tasks have adequate resources and training to complete tasks successfully.

- The direct report may have employees working for them to help complete this task.

- Other delegation and empowerment considerations:

  - In an Institute for Corporate Productivity and HR.com survey, half of the companies asked were concerned about employees' delegation skills, and only 28% of these companies offered delegation training.[328]

  - Delegation is sometimes called the art of sharing responsibility. While there certainly is an art to delegating, there are also concrete steps to delegate successfully. The two tables in the previous section both serve as examples of delegation and empowerment. In both examples, the level of empowerment is addressed in Step 10.

○ There must be trust between the manager and the direct report. In giving direct reports additional responsibilities, you should trust them to finish the jobs without looking over their shoulders. In turn, the employee needs to trust you to provide the resources, training, and the good top cover and stay out of the way.[329] There are two definitions of top cover. To distinguish them, I will call them *good top cover* and *bad top cover*. Managers provide good top cover when they ensure that no one outside their immediate organization interferes with their employees or their work. If, for example, a worker makes a mistake, a good boss will take responsibility for the error and shield the employee from outside criticism. Bad top cover is when one of your employees knows someone or is related to someone higher in the organization than you. The employee can take advantage of this, deal directly with their friend or family member, and bypass you. This can be very disruptive and damage morale.

ILLUSTRATIVE STORY

In one organization, a senior manager was a personal friend of the CEO. This manager, Regina, constantly reminded everyone of this relationship. She chose one employee with whom she spent far too much time. This favored employee recognized his unique status and began yelling at other employees when he did not get his way. When another senior manager complained to Regina's boss, he was told that because of Regina's relationship with the CEO, there was nothing he could do. The problem ended when the CEO learned of his friend's misbehavior through a letter sent anonymously.

- Effective managers are comfortable with delegating. Some managers have difficulty delegating, which shows a lack of confidence in their employees or a fear of losing control.

- Some managers pull previously delegated work back to their level. This is the opposite of delegating and empowering. Managers must delegate decisions to the lowest level team member who can do the work effectively.

- New managers should proactively assess their workload and consider whether they can delegate or eliminate any tasks. For a detailed guide on this process, please refer to Section 3.1, Your First Weeks at a New Job, and Section 3.2, Now That You're Settled In.

- Managers should determine which work to delegate to direct reports versus which to do themselves.

  - Delegate as much work as possible. You will be busy with all the work you cannot delegate, including coaching, mentoring, training, planning, scheduling, budgeting, coordinating, communicating, directing, reviewing work, counseling, hiring, and firing.

    Determine what work to delegate when you are new to a job. As discussed in Section 3.1, Your First Weeks at a New Job, you should ask your direct reports to put a note on each type of document that requires your signature. The note should recommend whether you need to continue reviewing and signing each type of document or whether any of them can be delegated to direct reports. In your initial discussions with direct reports, discuss whether they have enough resources. It is important to wait at least 60 days before deciding which tasks to delegate, as this period allows you to gain a comprehensive understanding of the work. Your direct reports' notes will help you decide what work you should delegate. Your choices for each type of document are to continue reviewing and signing them, delegate authority to sign them, or eliminate them.

ILLUSTRATIVE STORY

At her new job, a senior manager felt she was signing too many documents, so after 60 days, she delegated final approval authority on most of them to various direct reports. It was clear that her predecessor had trouble delegating. The previous manager spent too much time reviewing and signing documents and not enough time planning, coaching, mentoring, etc. Again, let me emphasize that managers should delegate as much work as possible.

A final thought on empowerment:

- A major survey of senior managers worldwide shows that managers must empower staff and share a vision and values to succeed.[330]

3.6 EMPLOYEE ENGAGEMENT

The three key measures of your organization's overall performance are employee engagement, cash flow, and customer satisfaction. No organization will be successful in the long run without an engaged workforce.[331] Engaged employees improve organizational outcomes. Effective managers understand the importance of employee engagement and follow the guidance in this section.

> **Definition of thriving at work (very or fully engaged workers):** Employees who do their best at work, enjoy their work, and are team players.[332]

- World's employees who thrive at work: 23%[333]

- U.S. employees who thrive at work: 34%[334]

> **Definition of quiet quitting (doing the minimum work required):** Employees who only do the minimum work required and are mentally detached from their jobs.[335]

- World's employees who are quiet quitters: 59%[336]

- U.S. employees who are quiet quitters: 50%[337]

> **Definition of loud quitting (actively disengaged):** Employees who harm the organization and undermine managers and goals.[338]

- World's employees who are loud quitters: 18%[339]

- U.S. employees who are loud quitters: 16%[340]

- These statistics should encourage you to hire employees who demonstrate engagement in their current jobs. It just takes a few phone calls to check the candidate's references. Please see Section 2.1, Hire and Retain Great Employees, for more information.

- Managers are the primary players in creating a positive work environment. They drive 70% of a team's engagement.[341]

- Ways that managers can influence employee engagement:

  - Make your new employees feel welcome as soon as they formally accept the job in writing. Schedule a Zoom call with the new employee as soon as possible so their boss and co-workers can welcome them aboard. Building relationships early helps create a bond that will pay great dividends when they work together as a team. A meta-analysis of 32 studies shows that teamwork positively influences productivity.[342] Please see Section 2.1, Hire and Retain Great Employees, for more information.

  - Have meaningful conversations and provide worthwhile feedback with your direct reports at least weekly. A 2024 Gallup report states that 80% of employees who received worthwhile feedback in the past seven days are very engaged. This high level of engagement applies to all workers regardless of the number of days they telework. These conversations should last between 15 and 30 minutes weekly, which makes them ideal for your coaching meetings.[343]

  - Managers provide recognition and appreciation to their direct reports for progress in achieving jointly agreed-upon goals, objectives, and milestones during weekly coaching meetings. For more information, please see Section 2.2, Coaching and Mentoring, for more information. A Gallup analysis of 4 million employees worldwide across more than 30 industries shows that employees who regularly receive *praise* and *recognition* are more productive and engaged and less likely to leave.[344] After recognizing an employee for a successful accomplishment (recognition), please remember to add a heartfelt thank you (appreciation). Thank you. For more information, please see Section 3.8, Motivation, Recognition, and Appreciation.

  - Engage your direct reports through effective performance development, a management action that grows employees through future-focused coaching, allows the creation and tracking of mutually agreed upon performance expectations that include goals and objectives that align with the organization's goals and objectives, establishes employee accountability for results, and gives each employee autonomy.[345] For more information, please see Section 2.4, Performance Development.

- Managers should offer mentoring advice on career development, job skills development, employee engagement, management skills development, networking, and more. For more information, please see Section 2.2, Coaching and Mentoring. According to a 2019 LinkedIn survey, 94% of survey responders said they would happily remain at an organization that helped them develop their careers.[346] If your direct report is in the accounting field and you are not, you should help your direct report find someone in the accounting field who can serve as their mentor in such areas as job skills development, networking, etc.

- Empower your direct reports. Give them every opportunity to control as much of their jobs, schedules, location of work, and hours of work as possible. For more information on employee empowerment, please see Section 3.5, Delegation and Empowerment.

- Ensure that all employees are doing consequential work and understand their work units' objectives, how they are linked to the organization's objectives, and their role in successfully achieving these objectives. Ensure that employees are given training. Talk with employees often about engagement, both individually in your coaching meetings and in groups. Provide good top cover so your employees will not be distracted.[347]

- Treat your direct reports like partners. Employees of all ages who see their immediate boss as a partner are much happier with their lives. In terms of life satisfaction, it equals more than doubling their income for middle-aged workers.[348] Effective managers know that working closely with their direct reports costs nothing but improves their morale, performance, recruiting, and retention. Please see Chapter 6:

Partner with Your Bosses (Okay, You're the Junior Partner) for more information.

- Allow direct reports to use their strengths. Organizations with the highest engagement rates have managers who focus on their employees' strengths. Gallup has identified 34 of the most common strengths (talents) and developed an assessment tool, CliftonStrengths Assessment (formerly StrengthsFinder Assessment) to help individuals find theirs. Gallup research shows that employees who use their strengths daily have a six times greater likelihood of being engaged at work and three times more likely to say they have an excellent quality of life.[349] This management initiative costs nothing but improves employee recruitment, retention, and productivity. The book *Strengthfinder 2.0* from Gallup: Discover Your CliftonStrengths contains a unique code that allows readers to take the CliftonStrengths Assessment online. The unique code is valid for one use only. Please be careful if you're buying this book used, as the unique code may have already been used.

  - I highly recommend you take the CliftonStrengths Assessment. You might be surprised by the results. I wish I had taken it sooner. More than 90% of Fortune 500 companies use it, and more than 33 million people worldwide have taken it to find their natural talents. Gallup is a highly respected multinational analytics and advisory company.[350]

- Listen to your direct reports. Employees want to be heard, not ignored. Ignored employees tend to be less engaged.[351] This is another important reason for weekly coaching meetings with your direct reports. Please see Section 2.2, Coaching and Mentoring, for more information.

- Managers drive engagement by using every tool in this book.

- Measuring employee engagement
  - Include engagement questions in your employee annual surveys and pulse surveys. In 2019, 74% of organizations

measured engagement annually with large-scale surveys. This percentage of those conducting annual surveys is dropping in favor of more frequent, smaller pulse surveys designed to take a much more frequent "pulse" of the organization. These are done with greater frequency, fewer questions, and a subset of employees. Ensure that the organization's senior management is informed of the survey results. Results are aggregated and analyzed over time. Some organizations now use social analytics tools to assess work patterns and relationships between people to look for engagement trends. Other organizations use focus groups.[352] The most crucial part of employee engagement surveys is doing something with the results. Effective managers identify these problems as soon as possible and do something about them.

○ Another helpful measure is tracking how many current employees are referring new employees to work in your organization. More referrals bode well for employee retention, engagement, and loyalty.

A final thought on employee engagement:

ILLUSTRATIVE STORY

At one organization, the senior managers discouraged telework. One smirked and said, "No telework on my watch." Despite this, one manager of a large office strongly encouraged telework. In that office, 76% of the staff teleworked at least one day each week. This office was highly productive and received the top score on the organization's engagement survey year after year. Employees said that telework improved their work-life balance and made them more engaged. Interestingly, the organization's senior management never asked the division chief of the top-scoring office how they continually achieved the top score.

3.7 FLEXIBLE WORK ARRANGEMENTS (ALSO WORKPLACE FLEXIBILITIES)

Flexible work arrangements go well beyond telework. To attract and retain employees in today's very competitive labor market, organizations need to personalize work arrangements for each employee so that employees can have control over as many aspects of their jobs as possible. Each employee has their own ideas on the best work-life balance for them; what it takes for them to have good physical and emotional health; how, when, and where they want to arrange their work schedule; and how best to accommodate important family responsibilities such as caring for children or family members with disabilities. These flexible work arrangements not only give employees control over many aspects of their jobs but improve their quality of life. Obviously, managers cannot give their direct reports everything they want in terms of flexible work arrangements. However, you can work with them to give them as much flexibility as possible while achieving your organization's goals and objectives. It will always be clear to them how much you are working to help. There is no cost to give employees flexible work arrangements that allow them maximum flexibility while still achieving your organization's goals and objectives, but the results are priceless.[353]

> **Definition of flexible work arrangements (workplace flexibilities):** Managers and employees mutually agree on how, where, and when work gets done.[354] This includes all the options discussed in this Section, such as telework, job sharing, flextime, etc.

- Flexibility in scheduling work hours

> **Definition of flextime:** Employees have flexibility around when they can begin and end work. This can include "core hours" during which staff must be in the office. Core hours might be, for example, Tuesday through Thursday, from 10:00 a.m. to 2:00 p.m., Eastern Time.[355] This allows time for face-to-face meetings and face-to-face collaboration that sparks creativity and generates new ideas better than meeting virtually.[356]

ILLUSTRATIVE STORY

Samantha told her boss, David, that she planned to work at the office from 10:00 a.m. to 7:00 p.m. Tuesday through Thursday and work from home on Mondays and Fridays. These hours fit within David's rule on flextime, which requires that all employees be in the office from Tuesday through Thursday from at least 10:00 a.m. to 3:00 p.m. Additionally, all employees would put in at least 20 hours per week in the office. Samantha's parents were elderly and not in good health. With these work hours, Samantha was able to prepare a good breakfast for her parents and ensure that they took all their medication on time.

Definition of compressed schedules: Schedules where employees work a traditional 35 to 40 hours in less than five workdays, e.g., 10 hours a day, four days a week (40 hours).[357]

- Many countries are testing four-day workweek pilot programs. Belgium has reduced its workweek to four days but retains the 40-hour schedule and gave workers the right to ignore their bosses after regular work hours.[358]

- Australia is the latest country to pass a "right to disconnect" law. This law protects workers' rights to disconnect completely during non-duty hours.[359] Effective managers do not need to wait until legislation is passed that restricts them from contacting workers after working hours. Just do not send emails or make phone calls after work hours unless their job description requires them to respond to urgent matters like being a doctor-on-call. Ask yourself: Do you like to receive routine phone calls or emails after working hours?

- In 2022, 61 United Kingdom companies participated in a trial of the four-day workweek. After the one-year trial, 89% of those companies continued to use the four-day workweek, half the companies had reduced turnover, and

32% had improved recruitment. The four-day workweek is another no-cost initiative that improves job satisfaction, reduces burnout, improves workers' physical and mental health, and improves work-life balance.[360] Effective managers recognize that introducing a four-day workweek greatly improves employees' schedules and costs nothing.

Definition of shift work: Employees work outside standard working hours. This allows organizations, for example, to operate 24 hours a day, including hospitals, police and fire departments, some manufacturing operations, etc.[361] There is a cost to working beyond nine hours per day. Hospital nurses who traditionally work twelve-hour shifts experience higher levels of burnout and job dissatisfaction.[362]

- Flexibility in the number of hours worked

Definition of part-time/reduced hours: Employees who customarily work fewer than 35 hours per week. These employees often work for small companies that do not need full-time employees.[363]

Definition of part-year/seasonal work: Employees customarily work a specific number of months per year, such as ski resort workers who only work during snow season or tax preparers who work during tax season.[364]

Definition of a transition period, part-time: Employees who gradually return to full-time work, for example, following a significant health issue. [365]

ILLUSTRATIVE STORY

At one organization, an employee underwent major surgery with a long recuperation time. After several weeks of prescribed bed rest, she began working part time at home and increased her hours as her strength and endurance returned.

> **Definition of job-sharing:** When two or more employees share one job. Each employee works part time.[366]

ILLUSTRATIVE STORY

At one organization, a married couple split the duties of one budget position supporting a staff of about 200. The staff agreed that the couple did the job very well.

- Flexibility in work locations

> **Definition of telework, telecommuting, or remote work(place):**
> An organization-approved work agreement in which eligible employees can voluntarily work from a location other than their office. Such sites include the employee's home, a client's office or factory, a satellite office, a neighborhood work center, a local coffee shop, etc.[367]

- The COVID-19 pandemic has transformed the workplace forever. For many white-collar workers, the workplace is evolving toward a permanent hybrid arrangement of part in-office and part telework that improves employee productivity, work-life balance, recruitment, retention, and quality of life. Ms. Follett (discussed in Chapter 1) would call this a win-win for managers and employees.

- Benefits of telework

  - A 2022 survey by Owl Labs and Global Workplace Analytics shows that 66% of survey responders would look for a new job if working from home was taken away, and 39% would quit. A significant 62% feel they are more productive working from home.[368] However, employees cannot work exclusively at home and collaborate with others to create new ideas. When your employees work at the office, their face-to-face collaboration sparks creativity that generates new ideas better than meeting virtually.[369]

- Allowing telework improves employee productivity, work-life balance, recruitment, retention, and quality of life.

- Employees who are raising children will have more family time and fewer childcare expenses.

> **ILLUSTRATIVE STORY**
> *A large national insurer encourages employees who deal directly with customers to work from home. In my dealings with them, I would sometimes hear a dog bark or a baby crying in the background. On one occasion, I suggested to the employee that she take a couple of minutes to change or feed the crying baby. She thanked me and did just that.*

- Employees who care for elderly parents or an ill family member are often stressed. With our aging population, about one-third of U.S. adults are now caregivers.[370] While some states will pay people to be caregivers,[371] working from home allows the caregivers, whether paid or not, to get more done. Caregiving for a family member can be rewarding but often stressful. Allowing these employees to work from home reduces their stress.

- Those who telework save money on transportation costs, have more free time, and are easier to recruit.

- Organizations save money on building purchases and leases. Organizations that own their buildings will also save money on utility costs.

- Employees who move from high-cost-of-living areas to low-cost-of-living areas may receive lower salaries. For example, employees moving from Silicon Valley to a rural town will have much lower living expenses. Many employees are often happy to trade some salary for no commute and more free time.

> **ILLUSTRATIVE STORY**
> *A couple worked in the IT field in San Francisco. They both worked long hours, and having children seemed impossible. During the COVID-19 pandemic, all employees were asked to telework full time. The couple immediately moved to a coastal town in Delaware and were happy to take a small cut in salary. The new location was far less stressful, and the couple had their first child. When the pandemic ended, their company ordered all employees to return to work in the San Francisco office. The couple found another company that had a more lenient telework policy. They now work in Europe, have two children, and are living happily ever after.*

- ☐ Telework is earth-friendly. Less commuting means fewer carbon emissions, and by working remotely, you are contributing to a healthier planet.

- ☐ Employees are more productive at home because they have no stressful and time-consuming commutes.

- ☐ Teleworkers have far fewer interruptions. Employees who work in an office are often interrupted. A University of California study shows that interrupted people take between 8 to 25 minutes to recover from an interruption. The shorter recovery time is for simpler tasks, and the longer time is for more complex tasks. The interruption could be as short as two seconds. These workers make up for interruptions by working faster and experiencing more effort, frustration, stress, and time pressure.[372]

- ■ Drawbacks to telework

  - ☐ A 2023 Gallup survey shows that remote work can result in less networking and relationship-building, fewer professional development opportunities, less recognition,[373] and less creativity that requires face-to-face collaboration. Most new ideas tend to come from face-to-face collaboration and not by meeting virtually.[374] Effective managers ensure that all employees receive the same professional development and recognition regardless of the number of days per week they telework.

- Telework can have a downside when employees choose which days they work at the office and often do not overlap with the right people to allow face-to-face collaboration. To address this, some organizations use AI to determine which employees will work on the same days.

- Most employees and employers disagree on how much telework is right. Telework became an important management tool because of the COVID-19 pandemic. In many cases, employees were directed to work from home. Since employees have experienced telework, a World Economic Forum study shows that 65% of those who work remotely said they would prefer never to return to their office.[375] Contrasting this, research by WTW shows that more than 67% of companies worldwide have policies that mandate employees work in the office a minimum number of days per week.[376] McKinsey & Company research shows that working in the office more than 50% of the time does not lead to better outcomes. They conclude that working together at the same location about half the time is the "hybrid sweet spot."[377] Of course, organizations must use AI to determine which employees will work on the same day.

- Some companies are reevaluating the benefits of telework.

ILLUSTRATIVE STORY

In May 2022, the CEO of Tesla and SpaceX, Elon Musk, ordered all his employees to work not less than 40 hours per week in the office. In an email, Musk told his employees that if they did not work from the office, he would conclude that they no longer wish to work for Tesla or SpaceX.[378] In the time since Musk bought X, the value of the company has decreased by 71% (at the time of this writing).[379]

ILLUSTRATIVE STORY

Apple CEO Tim Cook directed staff in the San Francisco Bay Area to return to the office (RTO) three days a week starting September 5, 2022. Cook said he wanted to continue the face-to-face teamwork that drives innovation and creativity. Very quickly, some Apple employees signed a petition disagreeing with this order to return to work because they felt happier and more productive working from home.[380] By March 2023, Mr. Cook threatened to take administrative action against Apple employees who were not working in the office at least three days per week.[381] How did the RTO mandate by Apple and others work out? Many senior top talent quit, per a May 2024 study by the University of Chicago and the University of Michigan.[382] By contrast, Microsoft allowed each team manager to control their own telework policy.[383]

- A 2024 examination of a sample of RTO mandates by the University of Pittsburgh finds that these mandates did not improve their financial performance or stock market valuations, but they notably reduced employee job satisfaction.[384] Ouch.

- Economists predict the worldwide shortage of workers may stretch into decades. The declining birth rate and aging populations of most major economies drive this.[385] Given these constraints, organizations worldwide are wise to attract and retain employees by offering flexible work arrangements such as telework. If organizations have restrictive flexible work arrangements, your best employees will be the first to leave for organizations that allow it. Flexible work arrangements are now an expectation.

□ Some companies are finding new ways to increase face-to-face interactions that lead to creativity, increased productivity, and improved morale.

- Management at Google's Googleplex headquarters in Mountain View, California, promotes the "casual collisions of the workforce." A total of 8,000 employees work in 65 connected buildings. In addition, there are 960 micro-kitchens, 19 cafés, and various other opportunities for workers to cross paths with others. People have a strong preference for face-to-face interactions. Studies show that employees are significantly more likely to share ideas if they work near each other than in another room, building, or country. Interestingly, Googleplex has 123 employees per building, close to the Dunbar limit of 150 people.[386] Dr. Robin Dunbar is a British psychologist and anthropologist. His research suggests that we can have meaningful relationships involving trust and obligation with no more than 150 people. He cites an interesting example. After his ascent to the throne in 1066, King William commissioned a summary of his kingdom—the Domesday Book. This book shows that in 1086, most English villages did not exceed 150 people. In the 18th century, a similar survey was conducted, and the average village population was still below 150 people. There were more villages in the 1700s than in 1086, but the average village size remained the same.[387]

- A significant study of 10 call centers with 25,000 employees revealed that simultaneous breaks led to increased social interaction. This interaction not only boosted performance by 8% and employee satisfaction by 10% but also enhanced the weakest team's performance by 20%. The release of oxytocin, a neuropeptide that fosters trust and attachment, underscores the irreplaceable nature of face-to-face interactions in the workplace.[388]

- Here is a win-win telework plan that will make workers and managers happy. It is based on what we know about the proven benefits of face-to-face collaboration and the worker's desire for telework to improve their work-life balance. Since face-to-face collaboration has significant creative benefits, we can schedule employees, for example, to work in the office five business days per month and telework the rest of the time. Yes, this plan involves less than 50% of the time spent in the office, as recommended by McKinsey & Company. Please keep reading, as there is a suggestion below on how to effectively create additional face-to-face time without increasing the number of days at the office. These five days per month in the office allow in-office time for collaboration and pleases employees, who can live anywhere they want as long as they pay the commuting costs. Since companies will need far less office space, only about 25%, you can convert some of the remaining 75% into hotel-like rooms to house the employees for five days per month at the office. The National Conference Center at Leesburg, Virginia, has an intelligent design that maximizes employee collaboration. The hotel room-like spaces are deliberately small and spartan to encourage people to relax and talk in the evenings in open areas. This is a perfect environment for discussing work and generating new ideas. Of course, employees should be discouraged from talking about politics, religion, the Dallas Cowboys, or the Green Bay Packers. Sorry, but families cannot be invited because the evening discussions would never involve discussing work. Employee resource groups should be encouraged to meet in the evenings, too. The atmosphere should be relaxed, with minimum noise, so even extreme introverts will feel comfortable. Organizations can also build cafeterias in some newly available building space to encourage employees to remain and eat their meals together, creating more collaboration time. The in-house meals are free, and employees can pay for any meals at local restaurants. The staff should be divided into four groups, one for each week of the month. The division of the staff into four groups should be based on the offices that work closely together. For example, the operations staff should have the same telework schedule. Employees should be fully involved in deciding which offices should have the same telework schedule. AI can assist with this scheduling. The divisions that work the same week can change from month to month. For example, as organizations approach the end of their fiscal years, the planning and budget staff may want to meet face-to-face with every division to plan for the coming year. Please allow your staff to make as many decisions as possible. Employees will be happy because they are only working five days per month in the office and can live anywhere they want. Employers should be happy because the five days per month with the informal and relaxed evening hours will allow sufficient time for face-to-face collaboration. This schedule will improve productivity, morale, recruitment, retention, and your bottom line.

ILLUSTRATIVE STORY

The results of a National Bureau of Economic Research randomized control trial of hybrid workers show that working from home (WFH) two days per week reduced attrition by 33% and increased job satisfaction. The findings also showed that hybrid WFH generally benefits firms and employees, but it is frequently underappreciated in advance, primarily by managers.[389]

ILLUSTRATIVE STORY

How much telework is too much? When hiring a budget officer for a large division, the interview panel chose a highly qualified candidate working elsewhere in the organization. Before James accepted the job, he asked his potential new boss, Lauren, if she would allow him to continue to telework three days per week. Lauren knew that James was an introvert in addition to having a long commute. He found the noise of the office disruptive, and it kept him from doing his best work. Lauren replied that James could telework five days a week if he could get all his work done effectively there. James accepted the job and began teleworking three days per week. After a few months, he was familiar with the workload and everyone he regularly worked with. James then began teleworking four days per week. His work ethic and productivity were outstanding. James's response time was as quick as if he were sitting in his office. He also managed a staff of seven. He could effectively manage them from his telework location. James had his team on speed dial, and his staff had him on speed dial.

ILLUSTRATIVE STORY

What can you do when a manager needs to telework to write without interruptions but feels she must be in the office to manage her staff? At one organization, a middle manager, Amber, was revising a travel policy. It was the organization's most complex policy due to overlapping federal employee travel laws. After several months, Amber's boss, Ryan, asked her how she was doing with the travel policy. Although she only worked on the policy as time permitted, she replied that the revision was 85% complete. A month later, Amber felt the travel policy was 95% complete. A few weeks later, Ryan asked again about completing the travel policy. Amber said she was back to only 85% complete because of a new law requiring her to rewrite some policy sections. Ryan suggested that she consider teleworking to complete the policy. Amber replied that, as a manager, she needed to be at the office to manage her staff. Ryan suggested with a smile that if she tried teleworking for only one day and it did not work for her, he would never recommend it again. This was exactly the incentive that Amber needed to try it. Following her one day of teleworking, Ryan was eager to learn how things went. Amber replied, "I could only work six and a half hours and had a splitting head-ache, so I had to quit early." Ryan responded, "I cannot tell if your teleworking was successful. Did you make any progress?" Amber said she had accomplished more in revising the policy in one day than in the previous two months. She forgot to wear her glasses and got a headache from eyestrain. Amber began teleworking every Thursday for the next few years. Just before her retirement years later, Amber was telework-ing twice a week. Teleworking enabled a better quality of life, providing Amber with a more balanced work-life schedule. While teleworking, Amber was always available to her staff, customers, and bosses.

> ***ILLUSTRATIVE STORY***
>
> *In one organization, an employee, Joseph, was awaiting an organ transplant. His doctor recommended that he be allowed to work from home full time because his immune system could become compromised in an office. Joseph was very productive working from home. The manager did not mention his condition to other employees for privacy reasons. However, Joseph chose to inform his colleagues. Joseph said that he missed the interactions of working in the office, but the support he received from his colleagues made his teleworking experience more positive.*

Definition of quiet vacationing: Employees taking time off without telling their boss or requesting personal time off.

- According to a Harris Poll, about 40% of millennials have taken time off without telling their boss.[390] Sadly, another Harris poll shows that 80% of American workers feel pressured to be available to respond at any time.[391] Effective managers ensure that each employee takes all their vacation days every year. No exceptions. If employees take their vacation/PTO, they will be less stressed and will consistently do more and better-quality work. This manager's action improves recruitment, retention, and work-life balance and costs nothing. Using all PTO every year is a win-win for employers and employees.

A final thought:

- Richard Branson, the cofounder of the Virgin Group, advocates for telework. He believes in giving employees the freedom to work wherever they choose, trusting in their drive and expertise to perform well regardless of their work location.[392]

3.8 MOTIVATION, RECOGNITION, AND APPRECIATION

Most organizations are unaware of the research and understanding about what motivates people. They still use outdated ideas that often do the opposite of motivating people.[393] Effective managers can improve motivation, productivity, morale, retention, and the bottom line at no cost by following the guidance in this section.

> **Definition of motivation:** The willingness to achieve.

- Motivation can be seen as a continuum from very positive to very negative. Positive motivation can inspire employees to achieve objectives. Negative or no motivation can cause employees to do little to no work or worse.

- Employees who work with their bosses to create their own objectives are more motivated to achieve them. Please see Section 2.2, Coaching and Mentoring, for more information. Incentivizing employees by giving them "if-then" rewards to achieve goals can demotivate them because it requires them to give up some of their autonomy.[394]

- People wish to have autonomy (self-direction), mastery (continuous improvement), and purpose (doing something that matters, doing it well, and being part of something bigger than themselves).[395] Giving employees autonomy, mastery, and purpose improves their motivation, productivity, morale, retention, and bottom line at no cost.

  - Daniel H. Pink's *Drive: The Surprising Truth About What Motivates Us* (Riverhead Books, 2009) is a *New York Times* bestseller and essential reading on motivation. It is an eye-opener.

- There are over 20 studies that show that people who get monetary rewards perform less well than those who receive no award. What researchers have learned is that training and goal-setting are far more effective in improving productivity than pay-for-performance.[396] Effective managers know the best way to grow employees is through future-focused coaching that creates mutually agreed-upon performance expectations to include goals and objectives that align with the organization's goals and objectives, establishes employee accountability for results, and gives employees autonomy.[397] Performance development improves recruitment, retention, productivity, and engagement. Please see Section 2.4, Performance Development, for more information.

> **Definition of recognition:** Positive words for good results such as an accomplishment.[398]
>
> **Definition of appreciation:** The focus is on the person, not the accomplishment. Appreciation involves acknowledging the talents, abilities, or good qualities of someone even if they did their best but failed.[399]

○ An example of recognition: "You did a great job on the report."

○ An example of recognition and appreciation is: "You did a great job on the report. Thank you very much for all your effort!"

○ How important is it to say thank you? A UC Berkeley study shows that workers are 23% more productive when they are given recognition and 43% more productive when given recognition and appreciation.[400] All it takes is a well-timed thank you when it is appropriate.

○ Mike Robbins has an excellent TED Talk on appreciation at https://www.youtube.com/watch?v=a3wX8nmvlZ0. At 12:43, you will hear Mike say that there is empirical evidence that when one person expresses appreciation to another, and it is received, the serotonin levels (which create a sense of satisfaction, happiness, and optimism) in both people are raised. Appreciation makes us feel better.[401] Thanks, Mike!

○ Recognize above-average performance for a specific accomplishment as soon as possible. Please be sure to add a thank you. Go out of your way if you need to ensure it is timely. On the other hand, flattering employees without real achievements often has a negative effect.

> **Definition of peer-to-peer recognition:** Employees recognizing the accomplishments of their coworkers.

- In a Boston Consulting Group study, 200,000 participants ranked "appreciation for your work" as the top factor for job happiness.[402]

- Peer-to-peer recognition increases positive emotions and well-being and improves relationships.[403] A 2016 Globoforce and Society for Human Resource Management study shows that peer-to-peer recognition improves employee engagement and makes employees happier with their work.[404]

- Gallup recommends that recognition should be given within seven days.[405] Recognition should also be genuine, very specific, and given publicly. Consider appointing some influential workers to model peer-to-peer recognition, such as online recognition, thank-you notes, shout-outs during recognition and awards meetings, etc.[406] Encourage your staff to be creative. Please remember that recognition can be for individuals and groups.

- "Gratitude is not only the greatest of all virtues, but the parent of all others."[407]—Marcus Tullius Cicero (106–43 BCE), Roman statesman and philosopher

- Team vs. individual recognition awards

  - A meta-analysis of 32 studies shows that teamwork positively influences productivity.[408] Recognize everyone who helped achieve a goal or objective, not just the most visible employees. Place copies of recognition awards in employees' HR records and add these achievements to your employees' semi-annual summaries. Please see Section 2.4, Performance Development, for more information on the semi-annual summary of achievements.

  - A study published in the *Harvard Business Review* reveals that recognizing the top performer in a team also improves the performance of the team members.[409]

- ○ You can give more than one type of recognition for the same achievement. Be creative and tailor your recognition to the individual.

  - Organizations should give their employees the same, or slightly higher, salaries than people in other organizations (i.e., the 60th percentile of each job type). Avoid cash awards. One study found that gifts were more motivating than cash.[410]

  - Some common ways to provide recognition and appreciation are listed below and are roughly in order from the least significant to the most significant. These can be either individual or team recognition awards. Be creative.

    - □ Send handwritten notes. Expressing thanks is beneficial for both the recipients and the expressers. Research shows managers are sometimes reluctant to send written thanks because they are concerned it will make the recipient feel awkward. These concerns are overestimated, and the benefits to the recipient are underestimated. Once the letter is written, the writer will feel positive emotions, too.[411]

      ILLUSTRATIVE STORY

      I often use a fountain pen to write thank-you notes. A fountain pen requires the user to draw ink from an ink bottle into the pen's internal reservoir. Luminaries like Leonardo da Vinci have used fountain pens since the 15th century. Ballpoint pens replaced fountain pens beginning in the early 1960s. Writing with a fountain pen is fun and makes beautiful thank-you notes. Years ago, I ran into a former employee at an airport. We had not seen each other for over 10 years. He fondly mentioned the handwritten thank-you note I gave him and said he still had it. Fountain pens are tactile and are welcome in an age when everything is machine-made. Fountain pens make you slow down and enjoy the experience of writing. Recipients also appreciate handwritten notes. I am delighted to report that fountain pens are making a comeback, thanks to millennials, Gen Zs, and Gen As! Thanks!

- Send laudatory emails and copy as many people as possible, including senior staff. Please remember to always include the words thank you.

- Offer verbal recognition and appreciation in a group setting. Smile with both your eyes and your mouth. If you smile with your mouth only, it will seem fake, and people will notice. Check out your smile in the mirror, and you will see what I mean.

- Read positive customer reviews at meetings or gatherings with a big smile. Please remember to always include the words thank you.

- Have employees post recognition and appreciation of fellow employees on their organization's intranet. Encourage everyone to include a thank you with these posts.

- Post pictures of high-achieving employees and groups prominently on your organization's website. Group pictures are preferred. If you hang pictures of high-achieving employees and groups in one of your buildings, you end up feeling like you can never remove them. You can also continuously rotate pictures on a computer screen in a prominent place like a lobby.

- Take employees to lunch. Remember to include recognition and appreciation.

- Offer an afternoon or day off. Some introverts will prefer time off to public recognition. Please ask them what they prefer. Remember to say thank you.

- Write letters of appreciation to present at a gathering of employees and place a copy in the recipients' HR files.

- Present certificates of appreciation at meetings and place a copy in the recipients' HR files.

- ☐ Provide training opportunities such as extra career development or training outside their disciplines. Allow the employees to choose the training.

- ☐ Provide opportunities to shadow a boss for a day or more. Employees can attend all meetings with their bosses and see how they respond to questions and deal with people.

- ☐ Offer additional challenging responsibilities that support the employee's career development goals. This can include special projects outside their normal work area.

- ☐ Provide opportunities to lead workgroups. Remember to recognize and thank them for their accomplishments which inspired you to give them this opportunity.

- ☐ Give temporary assignments outside their current organizations. Remember to recognize and thank them for their accomplishments which inspired you to give them this opportunity.

- ☐ Give pay raises while remaining in the same job. Remember to recognize and thank them for their accomplishments which inspired you to give them this opportunity.

- ☐ Give promotions that include additional responsibilities and higher pay. Remember to recognize and thank them for their accomplishments which inspired you to give them this opportunity.

- ☐ Offer verbal recognition and appreciation (thanks), such as during a coaching meeting. Look for at least one accomplishment to recognize and thank each direct report during each weekly coaching meeting. A 2024 Gallup report states that 80% of employees who received worthwhile feedback in the past seven days are very engaged.[412] This feedback to your direct reports should include recognition and appreciation for the objectives they have made progress in completing successfully since your coaching meeting the previous week. This high level of engagement applies to all workers regardless of the number of days they telework. These conversations should last between 15 and 30 minutes weekly and include discussing their progress toward achieving their objectives, which makes them ideal for your coaching meetings.[413] This weekly recognition and appreciation is the most effective way to improve employee engagement, retention, and motivation. And it costs nothing.

   ○ Nontraditional recognitions/rewards:

   ▪ Fruit baskets delivered to employees' homes.

   ▪ Achievement summaries sent to hometown newspapers.

   ▪ Present your overachievers with copies of this book.

- Keeping top performers. Create a professional development plan for each top performer with their help. Challenge them with stretch assignments that they help you choose. Assign a senior executive as a mentor or coach and hold the executive accountable if your top performer leaves. Ensure that you compensate them above others with lesser potential. Also, deal with problem employees immediately, or your top performers will quit. Please see Section 2.7, Problem Employees, for more information.[414]

ILLUSTRATIVE STORY

At one organization, a senior manager persuaded other senior managers to transition primarily from individual awards to group and individual awards. With group and individual awards, a far greater percentage of the staff was recognized. The employees felt this was better and fairer.

ILLUSTRATIVE STORY

A senior manager gave each employee 5% of their salary as a yearly performance bonus. This became an expectation.

ILLUSTRATIVE STORY

At one organization, the awards committee had a modest cash budget. The CEO decided to give large individual cash awards to those who worked closest to him. He wanted to give nearly half the award money to six or eight employees out of more than 1,000 employees. The awards committee unanimously disagreed with him. They argued that others on the staff had done as much or more but did not have the same visibility as those who worked directly with him. The CEO could override the board's decision. However, he reluctantly agreed with the board's recommendation. Unfortunately, the CEO had already told his chosen six or eight people that they were getting large cash awards. These six or eight employees pressured the CEO for an explanation. The CEO blamed the awards committee chairperson and did not renew her contract.

ILLUSTRATIVE STORY

The Department of Defense's Joint Forces Staff College prepares officers for their most senior positions. This college does not have distinguished graduates, which reduces competition and improves cooperation. Attendees work in groups of 12 officers and create and accomplish challenging goals as a team.

- Bosses sometimes get recognition too. Receiving an award as a manager can be awkward because, in most cases, the staff almost always contributed to your success. If you are notified that you are receiving recognition, you might recommend a group award for your team instead. If your boss insists on presenting a tribute to you in a public setting, I suggest saying something like this: "Thank you for this recognition, but the honor must go exclusively to my staff who did all the work. I am delighted to accept this award on their behalf. I will place the award in our break room (or conference room or wherever it is suitable) to remind everyone of their outstanding work. I extend a heartfelt thank you to my staff for all they did to earn this award. You are all awesome!"

- When something goes wrong, do not look for someone to blame; find the cause of the problem. The error will be fixed sooner if you focus on the correction. Just because you are not looking for someone to blame does not mean you should not discuss it. Assessing the problem is a good learning opportunity. Determine what went wrong and how to avoid this problem in the future.

Final thoughts on appreciation:

- "When a man does all he can, though it succeeds not well, blame not him who did it."[415] —George Washington, 1st President of the United States

- "The deepest principle in human nature is the craving to be appreciated."[416] —William James, American philosopher (1842–1910)

- "People ask for criticism, but they only want praise."[417] —W. Somerset Maugham, writer

3.9 OFFICE SOCIAL EVENTS

As a manager, you should actively champion all your organization's social events. Social events boost morale, build friendships, and improve employee engagement. They also foster positive relations with your employees.[418]

- Advice for managers at all office social events:

  - Attend as many of your office social events as you can. If you cannot attend, it had better be for a good reason, such as being out of town on business or attending a funeral. Also, apologize to your staff and explain why you cannot attend.

  - Show up to office parties a few minutes early. This will allow you to thank the party organizers in person. Also, thank them publicly during the event. It is even better if you can describe what each organizer did when thanking them publicly. Finally, send each organizer a handwritten thank-you note as soon after the event as possible.

  - Since you are already there a few minutes early, you can greet people, especially your employees, as they arrive. I always stand near the entrance door at office parties as people arrive. This makes it easier to ensure you greet everyone. If you miss speaking to anyone, apologize the next time you see them.

  - During the party, you can ask your employees about family, vacation or holiday plans, sports, interests, or hobbies. Avoid discussing religion, politics, gossip, the New York Yankees, or the Boston Red Sox. Also, avoid office subjects unless it is to briefly acknowledge an employee's recent major accomplishment.

  - Drink alcohol sparingly, if at all. Alcohol-free (and marijuana-free) parties are best. Serving alcohol or marijuana may be subject to local, state, or federal regulation.

  - If alcohol and marijuana are available, ensure that attendees get home safely. Give employees rides home or arrange for designated drivers. Remember that the liability is yours if someone has been drinking too much or ingested hallucinogens and has an accident on their way home.

- ○ Discourage gift-giving. There will likely be people who cannot afford to participate. Besides, have you ever received an office gift that you actually wanted?

- ○ Be friendly with your employees, but do not be their friend. For example, managers should never have lunch with any employees or do any activities together outside of work unless they are company-sponsored events. Finally, managers should not attend any events in any employee's home unless everyone in the office is invited.

- Additional advice for managers at office potlucks:

  - ○ Managers should bring the entrées to potlucks. As I mentioned before, if you cannot attend, it had better be for a good reason. In that case, drop off an entrée in advance or arrange to have it delivered.

  - ○ Be aware that some employees may find it financially challenging to bring food. Party organizers should state that anyone wishing to bring a food item may do so and leave it at that.

  - ○ Please try to accommodate employees with dietary or religious food restrictions. You may need to buy specific food for them. Please ask them if you are unsure what they would like and ask them about the best place to buy the food. You may think you are buying the correct food that meets, for example, religious food restrictions. Still, if it is not certified as halal or kosher, then it will not meet these rigorous religious food restriction requirements.

ILLUSTRATIVE STORY

At one organization, an office had a Cinco de Mayo luncheon hosted by the senior staff. The senior staff paid for all the ingredients and prepared and served the food. It was so much fun that they did it again the following year. Within a couple of years, all the offices throughout the corporation were involved.

- Organizations or managers should fund social events that staff members suggest and vote on. Here are some suggestions: Cinco de Mayo luncheon (spring), picnics in the building or at a local park (summer), Halloween or Thanksgiving (fall), and holiday cookie decorating (winter). Encourage your staff to be creative in choosing events and types of food.

ILLUSTRATIVE STORY

My goal at all social events is to talk with everyone individually. At one organization, all our social activities centered around food. The senior staff paid for the entrées. They also cooked and served the food. Other employees could bring food if they wanted to. One of the employees played a mix of music. People got up to get food, play silly games with equally silly prizes, or chat with others. These events usually took most of the afternoon. I began at one of the round tables and asked if I could join them. There were always empty places as others were wandering around socializing. I slowly went around the table and asked everyone about their summer or holiday plans. Everyone was happy to tell me where they were going. I said something positive about each person's plans. When I finished at a table, I moved to the next until I had been around the entire room. If people brought food items, I tried all of them. I love homemade food and always find something nice to say about each one. I avoid being a food judge, so I do not upset anyone by choosing one person's cookies over someone else's pie for the top prize. If I am gently prodded to be a food judge, I give everyone's entries first place and smile.

3.10 ORGANIZATIONAL CULTURE

> **Definition of organizational culture:** An organization's attitudes (from positive to negative), beliefs (accepted as facts), norms (usual and typical behaviors), practices (processes being followed), and values (guiding principles), which influence behavior and have a profound effect on success and happiness.[419]

- Effective managers can positively influence an organization's culture, which improves recruiting, retention, productivity, and your bottom line at no cost.

- Columbia Business School and Duke University's Fuqua School of Business surveyed nearly 2,000 CEOs and CFOs on organizational culture. Results: 92% said culture was important in their organizations, but only 15% said their organization's culture was where it should be.[420] Effective managers can positively influence their organizational culture by following the guidance below.

- How do you create a great organizational culture?

  - A Society for Human Resources Management survey identified *respectful* treatment as the top contributor to employee satisfaction.[421] Effective managers are models of respectful treatment, setting the standards of behavior for others.

  - Hire respectful and engaged people. For more information, please see Section 2.1, Hire and Retain Great Employees, and Section 3.6, Employee Engagement. Hiring respectful and engaged employees is another gentle reminder to screen applicants carefully during the hiring process. Please do not overlook the background and reference checks.

  - Engage employees. Please see Section 3.6, Employee Engagement, for more information.

  - Empower employees. Please see Section 3.5, Delegation and Empowerment, for more information.

  - Motivate employees through effective performance development. For more information, please see Section 2.4, Performance Development.

○ Offer meaningful learning opportunities. Please see Section 2.3, Training, for more information.

○ Help your direct reports develop their own solutions to job-related issues through your skillful listening and insightful questions. This helps them create their own path forward and makes them more committed to success. For more information, please see Section 2.2, Coaching and Mentoring.

○ Offer mentoring advice on career development, communication skills, management skills, networking, work-life balance, etc. For more information, please see Section 2.2, Coaching and Mentoring. Mentees can have more than one mentor at the same time. If your direct report needs mentoring advice that you cannot provide, effective managers help their direct reports find someone with the right background.

○ Provide motivation, recognition, and sincere appreciation. For more information, please see Section 3.8, Motivation, Recognition, and Appreciation.

○ Effective managers model good behavior. For more information, please see Section 9.1, What It Takes to Be the Best Manager Possible.

○ Encourage your staff to create and participate in ERGs. For more information, please see Section 2.5, Inclusion, Diversity, Equity, and Accessibility.

ILLUSTRATIVE STORY

The collapse of Credit Suisse, a global investment bank, sent shock waves through stock markets worldwide in March 2023. Weak financial and risk controls gave rise to a risk culture that allowed investment officers to seek higher returns that also come with higher risks. This risk culture led to aggressive risk-taking. Additionally, Credit Suisse was known for a toxic culture, which also contributed to the banking giant's collapse.[422]

A final thought on organizational culture:

• As Richard Branson, cofounder of the Virgin Group, says, great company culture is no more than treating others as you would like to be treated.[423]

3.11 STRATEGIC PLANNING

"People should not be unfamiliar with strategy. Those that understand it will survive. Those that do not will perish."[424] —Sun Tzu (544–496 BCE), *The Art of War*

> **Definition of strategic planning:** A dynamic process to create actionable and measurable objectives that show how the organization plans to differentiate within its marketplace and create sustainable value.
>
> **Definition of the strategic plan:** A dynamic written action plan that defines how an organization differentiates within its marketplace and plans to create sustainable value. The strategic plan includes actionable and measurable objectives. It explains how the organization plans to achieve its objectives that influence decision-making on overall resource allocation and hiring, guides organizational divisions to cooperate, and ensures that all significant decisions support the general strategic direction.[425]
>
> **Definition of strategic planning models:** Various tools that assist organizations in creating a strategic plan with actionable and measurable objectives that show how it will differentiate within its marketplace and create sustainable value. These tools assist planners with various aspects of creating a strategic plan, including the difficulty of bridging the gap between developing a strategy and implementing it day-to-day.[426]

- Considerations when creating and implementing your strategy.
  - In *The Economist's* survey of 500 senior executives, 90% reported that their organizations do not achieve their strategic goals because of poor implementation. And 59% of respondents acknowledged that their organizations have difficulty bridging the gap between developing a strategy and implementing it day-to-day.[427] Your strategic plan should contain actionable and measurable objectives explaining how your organization plans to achieve its objectives.
  - Strategy in corporate America gets far less attention than it should. Research reported in the *Harvard Business Review* reveals that 85% of senior managers dedicate under an hour to strategy monthly, half allocate no time at all, and only 5% of employees have a basic understanding of their organization's

strategy. This is an epic fail. Your employees are the people closest to your customers, and they shouldn't know the least of anyone about their organization's strategy. Effective managers ensure that all employees understand their work units' objectives, how they are linked to the organization's strategic objectives, and their role in successfully achieving them.[428]

- A Booz & Company online assessment of more than 125,000 employees from 1,000 organizations in more than 50 countries shows that the number one attribute of companies that successfully execute strategy is ensuring employees know what actions and decisions theirs are.[429] The status of completing these actions and decisions should be a recurring discussion topic in coaching meetings. For more information, please see Section 2.2, Coaching and Mentoring.

- Where do you begin the strategic planning process? This process begins with your vision statement, which is a high-level summary of what the organization wants to achieve. For more information, please see Section 4.4, Mission, Vision, and Values Statements. Next, evaluate several strategic planning models and use those that best meet your needs. Some of the most commonly used ones are, in alphabetical order, the Balanced Scorecard, Blue Ocean, gap analysis, PEST analysis, Porter's five forces, and SWOT analysis. These are defined below.

> **Definition of the Balanced Scorecard:** A strategic planning and management framework tool that augments traditional financial measurements, that show past performance, with non-financial measurements that power planned performance, including 1) expressing the organization's strategy and vision into actionable and measurable objectives; 2) ensuring that individual work units' objectives are linked to the organization's objectives and everyone in the organization understands their role in successfully achieving them; 3) creating three- to five-year stretch objectives with customer input; continually revising internal processes, and growth and learning, to ensure that people, procedures, and systems are continually assessed for gaps such as the need for reskilling, upskilling, new technology, revising procedures, etc.; and 4) most importantly, providing managers with feedback on progress toward achieving the objectives that allow them to make adjustments or even major changes to the strategic objectives.[430]

- ○ The Balanced Scorecard is only successful if organizations dedicate appropriate resources and training, and it is effectively implemented and sustained.[431] The Balanced Scorecard quickly became a vital strategic planning and management framework tool when it was created by Robert Kaplan and David Norton in 1992. It continues to evolve and become even more effective.

- ○ For those developing strategic plans, *The Balanced Scorecard: Translating Strategy Into Action* (Harvard Business REview Press, 1996) is a must-read.

Definition of Blue Ocean: A blue ocean is an uncontested market niche.

- ○ Lefty's, an online company providing products for left-handed people, is currently considered a blue ocean.

- ○ When one or more new companies begin offering products for left-handed people, this market niche becomes a red ocean. Red oceans have varying degrees of competition, encouraging organizations to create unique products or services with little or no competition. W. Chan Kim and Renée Mauborgne coined the terms "red ocean" and "blue ocean" in 2015.[432]

  ILLUSTRATIVE STORY

  In 2009, the taxi industry had not changed in over a century. Uber created a then uncontested market niche by hiring drivers to use their own cars to offer on-demand rides using the Uber mobile app.[433] Next on the horizon, the relatively new ride-sharing industry will be upended with the use of driverless robotaxis. The robotaxis will all be owned by corporations and will no longer rely on drivers using their cars for on-demand rides.

Definition of gap analysis: A process that was originally designed to identify gaps in biological diversity or biodiversity. The term gap analysis has expanded to now include identifying gaps in organizational strategies.

- ○ In the case of biodiversity, the entire ecosystem is assessed for gaps in flora and fauna. These gaps are filled with new acquisitions or changes in the management of flora and fauna. J. Michael Scott developed the gap analysis at the University of Idaho in the early 1980s.[434]

ILLUSTRATIVE STORY

The COVID-19 pandemic disrupted manufacturing worldwide. Often, insufficient parts were delivered to the manufacturing sites to maintain production. In many cases, the bottlenecks at ports were causing delays in the timely delivery of parts. Manufacturers did gap analyses to identify the specific parts shortages, where they were made, and determine how to remedy this problem. Many manufacturers chose to increase stockpiles of parts and look for suppliers closer to the manufacturing sites.

Definition of the PEST (political, economic, sociocultural, and technological) analysis model: This analysis allows organizations to examine these four factors in their business environment to determine potential impacts. The PEST model helps organizations understand their marketplace so they can tailor their strategy toward creating sustainable value.

- Political considerations include changes to laws, regulations, tariffs, taxes, etc.

- Economic considerations include the impact of rising inflation, global competition, exchange rates, etc.

- Sociocultural considerations include changes in demographics, consumer tastes, etc.

- Technological considerations include changes driven by AI, robotics, etc. This model is often used jointly with a SWOT Analysis.

- The PEST analysis model was developed by Harvard professor Francis Aguilar in 1967.[435]

- PEST has expanded to now include legal and environmental considerations. PEST became PESTLE.

  - Legal considerations include changes in labor laws, consumer laws, trade laws, etc.

  - Environmental considerations include climate change, increasing emphasis on sustainability, energy costs, etc.[436]

> **Definition of SWOT analysis:** Strengths, Weaknesses, Opportunities, and Threats. A SWOT analysis helps organizations identify their competitive advantages: strengths (S) and opportunities (O). The analysis also determines organizational vulnerabilities: weaknesses (W) and threats (T).

- A SWOT analysis must be done at regular intervals because the organization's strengths, weaknesses, opportunities, and threats will change over time. A SWOT analysis assists planners in creating and updating their strategic plans.[437] SWOT analysis helps organizations get a clearer picture of how they should differentiate themselves from their competitors to create sustainable value. Robert Franklin Stewart, Lockheed Martin's senior long-range planner, created the SWOT analysis in 1960.[438]

> **Definition of Porter's Five Forces:** Identifies and analyzes five sources of competition within a market.[439] The following table defines the Five Forces and shows an example.

Porter's Five Forces with an Example

	The Five Forces[440]	**The Five Forces Using the U.S. Auto Industry as an Example**
1	The competition within your market	For decades, the U.S. auto industry made large, gas-guzzling cars. Entering this market was difficult because of the high startup costs.
2	The threat of new competitors	a. Beginning in the 1970s, Japanese cars upended the U.S. auto industry. These cars were smaller, more efficient, and more reliable than U.S.-made autos. b. The industry was upended again in the early 2000s when electric vehicles (EVs) were introduced.
3	The threat of substitute products or services being introduced	a. Metro systems b. High-speed trains c. Ride-sharing services d. Car-sharing clubs
4	The customer's bargaining power	The customer's bargaining power increases with the introduction of each new non-auto transportation system or the expansion of existing ones.
5	The supplier's bargaining power	The supplier's ability to acquire costly, rare-earth metals directly affects the long-range health of EVs. Batteries need lithium and cobalt, and magnets in motors need neodymium or samarium. Manufacturers are researching how to build EVs without using these rare-earth metals.

○ Porter's Five Forces was developed by Michael E. Porter of the Harvard Business School in 1979.[441]

ILLUSTRATIVE STORY
A boutique clothing brand faced difficulties due to the lack of a clear strategy. Designers developed collections based on personal preferences rather than customer demand, and marketing efforts were uncoordinated across different platforms. Important information about target customers and seasonal trends was incomplete or inconsistent. As a result, inventory did not match demand, and many items remained unsold, damaging the brand's reputation and revenue.

Final thoughts on strategy:

- "Strategy without tactics is the slowest road to victory. Tactics without strategy is the noise before defeat."[442] Sun Tzu (544–496 BCE), *The Art of War.*

- Without a strategic plan, your organization is rudderless.

How Do Managers Track Progress in Completing Their Objectives?

Definition of key performance indicator (KPI): A quantifiable measurement that shows progress toward achieving strategic objectives within predetermined time frames.[443]

- KPIs can be built using the SMART objectives model in Section 2.2, Coaching and Mentoring.

- Performance measurement charts

  ○ Here are some common performance measurement examples: gross and net profit margin, rate of return, customer satisfaction and retention, employee turnover rate, employee engagement rate, revenue per employee, and percentage of customers who are "Very" or "Extremely" satisfied.

- ○ Performance measurement example #1: IT help desk customer service score.

  - ▪ Our help desk speed and accuracy are continually rated below the national average of 4.7 on a scale of 1–5 (5 being the highest rating). After considering several options, we have decided to contract out our IT help desk work to a national help desk company. Based on a market survey, contracting help desk responsibilities to one of several national help desk companies is likely to improve the speed and accuracy scores to achieve or exceed the goal of 4.7.

  - ▪ The overall cost to the organization is expected to be less because commercial help desks operate at a high volume and have fewer overhead costs per unit of work.

  - ▪ In this example, the effective date for switching from our in-house help desk to the national help desk company is March 1.

  - ▪ This is a lagging indicator since it does not identify future trends.

Performance Measurement Chart[444]

Measure	IT Help Desk Customer Service Scores
Target	Objective: Improve speed and accuracy scores from 4.1 to 4.7 or higher on a scale of 1(low)–5 (high).
Data Source	Rating reports provided by an independent help desk performance tracking contractor.
Frequency of Reporting	Weekly
Owner	The Office of Administrative Services

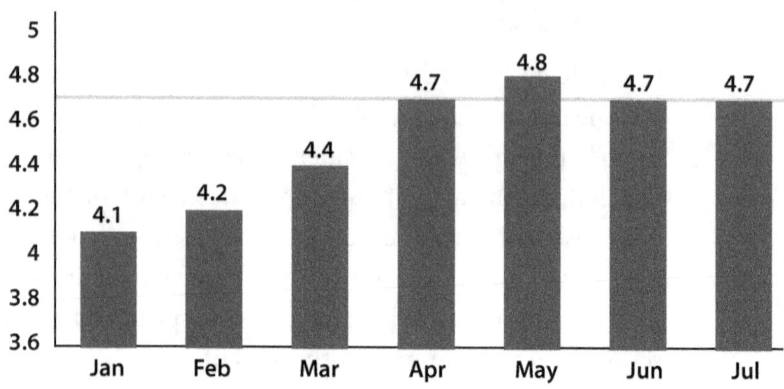

○ Performance measurement example #2: Safety training to reduce work injuries.

- Our manufacturing division has seen an increase in work-related injuries. There were 2.8 million work-related injuries in the U.S. in 2022.[445] A study published in *The Ergonomics Open Journal* shows that safety training reduces work-related injuries.[446]

- This is a leading indicator since safety training will influence the future number of injuries.

- In this example, safety training began in December 2023.

Performance Measurement Chart[447]
Safety Training Impact on Reducing Work-Related Injuries

Measure	Reduce the number of work-related injuries.
Target	15% reduction in work-related injuries within three months following completion of safety training
Source	The Office of Safety
Frequency	Monthly
Owner	The Office of Safety

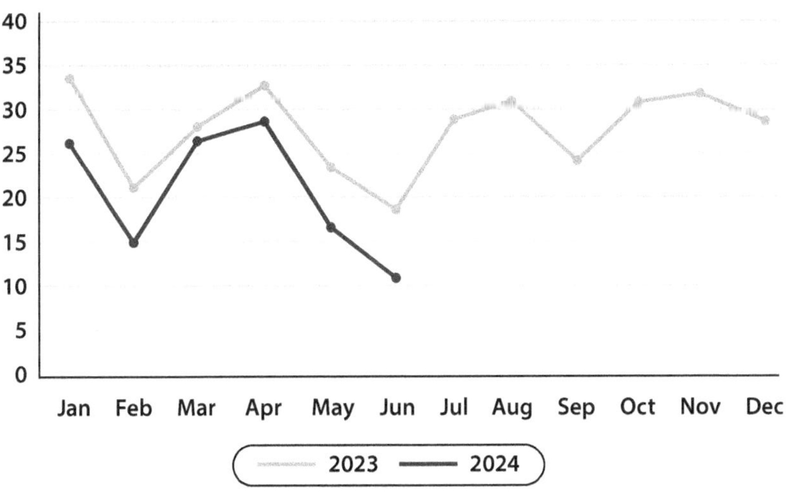

Final thoughts on measurements:

- "Most people use statistics the way a drunkard uses a lamp post, more for support than illumination."[448] —Mark Twain (1835–1910), American writer and humorist

- "Not everything that can be counted counts, and not everything that counts can be counted."[449] —Albert Einstein (1879–1955), theoretical physicist

CHAPTER 4

Use All These Manager's Tools

"Everyone thinks of changing the world, but no one thinks of changing himself."[450]

—Leo Tolstoy, Russian writer, philosopher, social activist

Change yourself. Becoming an effective manager seems daunting until you read the guidance in these 40 compact sections, which contain information that is concise, quickly understood, and ready to apply immediately.

4.1 EMPLOYEE HANDBOOK

> **Definition of an employee handbook:** A management-written collection of organizational documents that includes information about the organization, such as its history, mission, vision, and values; the organization's policies, procedures, and checklists; a summary of benefits; applicable federal, state, and local labor laws that state the legal obligations of the employer; workers' rights;[451] and other relevant information. Some organizations put handbooks on their websites, and others print them. Either way, they are legal documents.

- Subjects to consider for your handbook include:
  - A warm welcome letter from your CEO.[452]
  - References and web links to all federal, state, and local employment laws that apply to your organization. The U.S. Department of Labor's website, http://www.dol.gov, contains all federal labor laws.
  - Policies and procedures. Some policies to consider adding to your employee handbook are ethics, conflicts of interest, disciplinary procedures, complaints or grievances, harass-

ment, leaves of absence, safety, overtime pay, vacation, working conditions, confidential information, drug and alcohol, workplace violence, employee counseling (with a statement that managers must have a witness present when counseling employees), and HR (including a policy that requires that HR be notified of sexual relationships between managers and employees). For more information on sexual relationships between managers and their employees, please see Chapter 10, How to Build the Best Organization Possible. To remain current, policies, procedures, and checklists should be reviewed at prescribed intervals to determine whether they need to be revised. For more information, please see Section 4.6, Policies, Procedures, and Checklists.

- Please provide the "why" on work rules. For example, employees aren't allowed to speak to any media members. The public affairs office communicates with the media to ensure a coordinated message reaches the public.

- The handbook should contain a statement that all policies are subject to change over time.

  ○ A summary of benefits only. These benefits change over time. Direct employees to HR with specific questions.

  ○ A statement about the union, if any, and its right to negotiate changes in conditions of employment.

  ○ A statement that the handbook is not a contract or any promise about continued employment.

  ○ A statement that the handbook supersedes any previous guidance.

- Other considerations for the handbook include:

  ○ Policies should be written so employees can understand them. Avoid legal jargon.

  ○ The handbook should be approved by unions, if required.

- o When creating your employee handbook, an attorney should review everything before it is placed online. If any material needs to be updated, remove it from your website as soon as possible. Only replace the outdated material after an attorney familiar with the subject has reviewed and approved the revision.

- o The handbook should be reviewed and acknowledged in writing by each employee during onboarding.

- o Requirements for items that should be included in employee handbooks will vary by location and industry.

- There are several free employee handbook templates online found at these websites:

  - o Society for Human Resource Management (SHRM) (free to SHRM members)[453]

  - o Indeed (free)[454]

  - o FormSwift (free)[455]

  - o Rocket Lawyer (free)[456]

  - o Several additional free templates are available for creating an employee handbook for your organization. Just search for "employee handbook free template" in your search engine.

- Creative handbooks can help engage, educate, and entertain employees. Valve Corporation, a game developer, has an employee handbook that went viral. It is informative and entertaining.[457]

4.2 KNOWLEDGE MANAGEMENT

Knowledge is only beneficial if it can be easily created, shared, used, and managed effectively for its intended purpose.[458] Knowledge includes your organization's intellectual property, strategic planning documents, contracts, proprietary software, performance measurements, internally created training courses, policies, procedures, checklists, meeting minutes, and workers' knowledge and experience, among other forms of knowledge.

> **Definition of knowledge management (KM):** "Knowledge management is the process of creating, sharing, using, and managing the knowledge and information of an organization."[459] —John P. Girard, Ph.D., and JoAnn Girard, thought leaders in knowledge management

- The Girards created this definition using the most frequently used words from 100 definitions of knowledge management (*knowledge, organization, process, information, use, share, create,* and *manage*).[460]

- They used knowledge management to create a definition of knowledge management. Brilliant!

- Your organization's knowledge management can be a competitive advantage.[461] We are bombarded daily with vast amounts of information. With all this "noise," organizations must know how to get precise information to those in need quickly and easily.[462]

- Benefits of knowledge management:

  - Improves problem-solving, decision-making, innovation, productivity, and customer satisfaction; facilitates knowledge preservation; reduces knowledge loss due to staff turnover; and helps avoid reinventing the wheel.[463]

  - Manages the organization's intellectual capital, increases learning and knowledge sharing, improves collaboration, allows best practices to be passed on, and leverages the knowledge and experience of employees.[464]

ILLUSTRATIVE STORY

The Air Force Inspection Agency (AFIA) provides independent inspections of all Air Force units to enhance their peacetime and wartime missions. The AFIA thoroughly inspects all departments at regular intervals, including operational air squadrons, aircraft maintenance, hospitals, etc. After each inspection, inspectors craft a report that not only highlights strengths such as best practices but also pinpoints areas for improvement. These insights are quickly shared via secure video teleconference. The inspected units are then tasked with providing a written response for each deficiency and a plan with milestones to rectify each. Each inspection report is also provided to all similar Air Force units, and each is expected to ensure they comply with the latest inspection results. The AFIA's inspection database, equipped with analytical tools, identifies emerging issues and actionable information.

ILLUSTRATIVE STORY

At one organization, the computer help desk team demonstrated adaptability. They maintained a list of commonly asked questions and developed answers for each. When a question was posed, they were ready with a pre-crafted response. This list grew organically as the team encountered new questions, showcasing their ability to adapt and grow. Moreover, this list served as a valuable resource for new help desk staff members, accelerating their productivity and accuracy.

○ Data, information, knowledge, and wisdom (DIKW) and their interrelationships. DIKW can be visualized as a pyramid, with data forming the base. Each level upward is increasingly smaller and represents an increase in utility. Data, information, and knowledge are all growing exponentially.

Definition of data: A collection of unusable miscellanies.

Definition of information: Interpreted data made usable.[465]

Definition of knowledge: "Justified true belief." From Plato's Socratic dialogue on the nature of knowledge in his book *Theaetetus* (369 BCE).[466]

Definition of wisdom: The use of knowledge to advance humankind.

ILLUSTRATIVE STORY

A corporate headquarters amassed much patient data from its clinics and hospitals. This data included the number of patient encounters, types and numbers of medical procedures, etc. Their objective was to turn this data into usable information. The staff created a process to push the information to users automatically. They created thresholds that would automatically trigger alerts. For example, corporate and hospital-level staff could ask for notifications when the number of patients seen by any given medical provider dropped below a specific threshold. This information would be automatically "pushed" to those requesting it.

Definition of a knowledge management system: Software that allows users to manage, store, access, and use information effectively.

A final thought on knowledge management:

- People are the most valuable resource in every organization. The second most valuable resource is all the information each organization possesses and its ability to create, manage, share, and use it.[467]

4.3 MEETINGS

Only schedule meetings if you absolutely must. In a Harvard Business Review study, 76 companies gradually reduced meetings by 40% while increasing productivity by 71%. A related survey shows that 92% of employees found that meetings were not necessary and were too costly of their time.[468] It is maddening for employees to sit in meetings and realize that not only are they wasting their time, but they could be getting some real work done. Who is at fault for all these unnecessary and unproductive meetings? Managers. A Society for Human Resources Management study found that 84% of workers blame badly trained managers for generating needless stress and work.[469] I am inclined to think that managers are not badly trained; they are just not trained at all. The most effective managers have the fewest meetings.

- The only reasons for meetings:
  - To solve problems, make group decisions, or develop recommendations.[470] Please see Section 3.4, Decision-Making, for more information.
  - To coach or mentor. Please see Section 2.2, Coaching and Mentoring, for more information.
  - To present information face-to-face or online, such as updates to your bosses, or to conduct town hall meetings.[471] Please see Section 3.2, Now That You're Settled In, for more information.
  - To counsel problem employees. Please see Section 2.7, Problem Employees, for more information.
  - To welcome and orient new employees. Please see Section 2.1, Hire and Retain Great Employees, for more information.
  - To motivate employees, such as at award presentation meetings.[472] For more information, please see Section 3.8, Motivation, Recognition, and Appreciation.
  - To gain buy-in.[473] For more information, please see Section 9.1, What It Takes to Be the Best Manager Possible.

- For electronic brainstorming meetings to generate new ideas and problem-solve. Please see the information on electronic brainstorming meetings later in this section.

- For peers to meet regularly and informally to discuss business subjects and be social. Please see Chapter 5, Partner With Your Peers, for more information.

- To conduct employee resource group meetings. Please see Section 2.5, Inclusion, Diversity, Equity, and Accommodations for more information.

- To conduct exit interviews. Please see Section 2.8, Exit Interviews, for more information.

- One very irritating way that managers micromanage is by having too many meetings. Please do not be one of those managers.

- The chairperson is responsible for all aspects of meetings, including the following tasks.

  - Before the meeting:

    - Make a list of those you wish to invite and put a justification next to each name. The ideal size of a decision-making group is seven. The decision-making effectiveness of the group is reduced by 10% for each additional member.[474] As a chairperson, you must be careful and invite only those needed for the meeting. This saves staff time, ensures that the meetings are more productive, and helps reduce the stress of too many meetings.

    - Send an agenda to all invitees at least five business days in advance, along with any read-ahead material. Agendas should include the following:

      - Meeting attendees

      - Meeting objective(s)

      - Meeting location and dial-in link

      - Meeting start and end times. If an hour-long meeting is scheduled to begin at 2:00 p.m., please show the end time as 2:55 p.m., so attendees can get to their next activity on time.

- □ A meeting agenda that includes a list of discussion items and the amount of time allotted for each

- □ Attach any background information needed by the participants. Ask invitees to recommend additional agenda items or people to invite.

- Remind members that they can invite their experts to discuss complex agenda items or answer questions. These experts need only remain long enough to discuss or answer questions about their agenda item(s).

- If you think any agenda items may be contentious, discuss them in advance with anyone you think may have opposing views. If possible, work out differences before the meeting. People are often more reasonable one-on-one. Also, there is no time for lengthy debates during meetings.

- The COVID-19 pandemic drove a significant increase in videoconferencing, which is here to stay.[475]

- Serve coffee. According to a 2018 study published in the *Journal of Psychopharmacology*, serving coffee at meetings can increase alertness, increase involvement, and make the attendees feel better about their participation.[476]

- Appoint an attendee to take notes, help ensure that you stick to the schedule and prepare minutes after the meeting.

- □ Of course, you may have an administrative person prepare the minutes. If you do not have an administrative person, please rotate this duty among the attendees unless you want to prepare the meeting minutes yourself.

- □ Gently remind the notetaker that you will ask for a summary of the key points at the end of the meeting, including decisions, recommendations, dissenting opinions, and any action items (responses to questions or issues raised during the meeting, when these responses are due, and by whom). The chairperson should also keep track of these items to ensure nothing is overlooked when preparing the minutes.

- ▫ Some agenda items are complex, and those preparing minutes want to ensure that the minutes are as accurate as possible. The person preparing the minutes is welcome to ask presenters to send a summary of their agenda items. Meeting minutes preparers only need to review these summaries and then cut and paste them into the minutes.

- During the meeting:

  - Start all meetings precisely on time. It shows respect for the attendees who show up on time. Also, every minute you delay beginning the meeting is one less minute available for the meeting agenda items. Some attendees will have other time commitments immediately following your meeting. Finally, never start meetings unless you have enough members to vote (a "quorum").

  - Do not rely on wall clocks. They are often battery-operated and rarely accurate. Use your cell phone. It does not take long for attendees to learn that you always start meetings on time. Attendees will show up on time as a result.

  - If you are new to an organization, state at the first meeting you chair: "I will do my best to start meetings on time as I want to show my respect for your time. I recognize that your time is valuable. I need your help sticking to the agenda and the time allotted for each item. Please remind me if I am getting behind on the agenda. We all want to finish the agenda on time or earlier. Thanks." (Big smile.)

  - State the reason for the meeting if it is not recurring. Please see "The only reasons for meetings" above.

  - Remind attendees that they should not use any electronics during the meeting. One major corporation requires meeting attendees to place their electronics in a box before meetings begin to reduce distractions. Results: No one is distracted, and discussions are more productive.[477]

- When you have a question on meeting rules, consult *Robert's Rules of Order* for any questions on how to run meetings, including what constitutes a quorum, how to appoint committees, how to manage tie votes, etc. *Robert's Rules of Order* has been the gold standard for meeting rules since 1876 and was last revised in 2020.[478]

- Involve all attendees, introverts and extroverts, as time permits. This is best done by going around the room to get feedback or vote on any given issue. Be sure to address those who phone in by name. (Please avoid: "Does anyone on the phone have any comments?" Instead: "Samantha and Andrew, any thoughts you want to share?")

- Gently stop those who dominate the meeting: "Thanks, Travis, that is a good point. Let's see if anyone else has thoughts on this subject." Alternatively, "That is a good point, Travis, but it is not on our agenda, and unfortunately, we do not have time to discuss it today. Would you like me to put it on the agenda for our next meeting?"

- At the end of the meeting, the notetaker should summarize all decisions, recommendations, dissenting opinions, and action items that require a response, when responses are due, and by whom. This will ensure that there will be no debate regarding the comments or agreements later. While the notetaker is speaking, you should check their comments against your notes.

- State whether there is a need for a follow-up meeting. Of course, some meetings are recurring.

- Thank members for attending and dismiss them on time or earlier.

- If you run the meeting beyond the scheduled time (and it had better be for a darned good reason), apologize and explain why all the agenda items must be discussed in this meeting.

- After the meeting:
  - Prepare the meeting minutes as soon as possible. Include attendees' names, what office they represent, vote outcomes, decisions and recommendations, dissenting opinions, and action items that require a response, when responses is due, and by whom.
  - Ensure that the meeting minutes are sent to all attendees and those unable to attend within five business days of the meeting and ask for their suggestions for any changes.
  - The chairperson is responsible for the meeting minutes. If the meeting minutes preparer does not complete the minutes by the due date, the chairperson must prepare them.
  - File the member-approved minutes on the organization's intranet. They are an essential part of your organization's knowledge management system.

    ILLUSTRATIVE STORY

    At one organization, a senior committee member, Vicki, always had comments or questions on nearly every subject. If Ashley, a manager, was responsible for an agenda item, she approached Vicki as soon as the agenda went out, asking if she had any questions she could answer before the meeting. Vicki took advantage of Ashley's offer and started having even more questions she wanted to ask during meetings. As a result, Ashley had to invite experts with detailed knowledge of her agenda items. This was expensive and time-consuming. Ashley texted the experts a few minutes before their agenda items were discussed to reduce their time at meetings, allowing them to arrive on time without sitting through irrelevant discussions. They were free to leave after discussing their agenda items.

ILLUSTRATIVE STORY

One senior manager, Ben, a baby boomer, was accustomed to conducting regular staff meetings. Ben joined the workforce before computers and cell phones, when face-to-face meetings were more meaningful. Most of Ben's employees were millennials or Gen Zers who attended his weekly staff meetings. Ben's millennial and Gen Z staff would end up discussing old items just to have something to say. Staff consensus was that the meetings were a waste of time. As soon as Ben retired and Jessica was appointed the interim director, she canceled the weekly meetings. When the new director arrived, the weekly meetings were never discussed and did not resume.

ILLUSTRATIVE STORY

At one organization, the culture was very informal, and meetings never ended early. Meeting chairpersons often allowed discussions to continue far longer than necessary. No one complained. When a new manager arrived, she kept to the agenda and usually finished meetings ahead of schedule. Several people thanked her for the way she ran meetings. Attendees had smiles on their faces because they had more time for other tasks. These happy attendees explained that they did not want to complain, so they had gone along with the previously dragged-out meetings.

> **Definition of stand-up meetings:** Everyone stands up for the duration of the meeting.

- o Stand-up meetings are meant to go quickly.

- o Stand-up meetings tend to be "all business," as everyone wants them to be over as soon as possible.[479]

- o One study showed that stand-up meetings take 34% less time and produce the same quality decisions as sit-down meetings for small groups of five people or fewer. In stand-up meetings, attendees typically discuss nonroutine problems and meetings last 10 to 20 minutes.[480]

> **ILLUSTRATIVE STORY**
> *Joshua, a hospital chief executive officer, chaired a 15-minute stand-up meeting each morning at 8:00 a.m. with key medical staff. These meetings were limited to discussing any changes to inpatient health status overnight and often took less than the 15 minutes scheduled.*

> **ILLUSTRATIVE STORY**
> *Former Secretary of Defense Donald Rumsfeld used a standing desk throughout his career. In addition to the health benefits of standing desks, informal meetings in his office ended sooner. Those who stopped by were incentivized to say what they wanted and leave.*[481]

- The purpose of brainstorming meetings is to generate creative ideas.

  - Alex F. Osborne, the "father of brainstorming," developed the following four rules to maximize the productivity of these meetings:

    - There will be no criticism of any ideas.

    - Freewheeling ideas (or the wilder, the better) are welcome.

    - The focus is on quantity.

    - Combining and improving ideas is encouraged.[482]

  - A meta-analysis of 34 studies shows that electronic brainstorming groups produce more and better quality ideas than face-to-face brainstorming groups.[483] Sorry, Mr. Osborne.

Definition of electronic (or computer or virtual) brainstorming meetings:
Electronic brainstorming meetings combine computer technology and brainstorming rules. Members participate by typing their ideas into their computers. Their ideas immediately appear on the screens of all participants anonymously. All participants can then comment on or offer improvements to others' ideas.[484]

- ○ Advantages of electronic brainstorming:
  - ▪ Electronic brainstorming meetings of four or fewer members have no performance advantages over face-to-face meetings, but electronic brainstorming meetings with six or more participants have proven successful. As the size of these groups increases, the productivity of electronic brainstorming meetings improves.[485]
  - ▪ Since there are no distractions or interruptions, everyone can quietly concentrate and assess all the ideas.
  - ▪ Contributors are anonymous, so the fear of rejection is removed.
  - ▪ Participants can provide ideas or comments at any time, wherever they are in the world.
  - ▪ No one dominates the meetings.
- ○ Electronic brainstorming meeting suggestions for facilitators:
  - ▪ Diverse groups are more productive. Please see Section 2.5, Inclusion, Diversity, Equity, and Accessibility, for more information on the advantages of diverse groups.
  - ▪ Ensure your electronic brainstorming meetings include introverts. One of the reasons that electronic brainstorming sessions are successful is that they allow the full participation of introverts, who make up as much as half of your staff. Introverts are deep thinkers, better strategists, and can solve your most challenging problems.[486]

- Sitting for long periods at your desk increases your risk of death from cardiovascular disease and cancer. There are exercises you can do at your desk that can get your heart pumping and increase your strength. Medical websites have safe and effective exercises you can do at your desk. There is one desk exercise that has extraordinary benefits and is very easy to do called the soleus pushup. While seated and with your feet flat on the floor, lift your heels while keeping your toes on the ground. When you get to the top of its range of motion, return your heels to the floor.

Repeat. Researchers have shown that the soleus pushup speeds up metabolism and improves blood glucose levels.[487] I have highlighted this simple yet very effective exercise because you can easily do it at your desk or in meetings. Many meetings are stressful because they are unnecessary. By doing soleus pushups during meetings, you can feel a small sense of accomplishment even when the meeting is a total waste of everyone's time.

A final thought on meetings:

- The most effective managers have the fewest meetings.

4.4 MISSION, VISION, AND VALUES STATEMENTS

Mission Statements, Vision Statements, and Value Statements: Definitions & Examples

	Mission Statement: A brief, inspiring statement of an organization's primary purpose.	**Vision Statement:** A summary of what the organization wants to achieve.	**Values Statement:** An accepted set of beliefs and guiding principles, such as being socially responsible, accountable, ethical, sustainable, embracing integrity, etc.
The statements above in a few words.	Our purpose.	What we aspire to achieve.	What we believe in.
Warby Parker (online eyewear company)	"To inspire and impact the world with vision, purpose, and style."[488]	"We aim to use resources responsibly, reduce waste, and maintain a neutral carbon footprint across our operations."[489]	"Inject fun and quirkiness into everything we do. Treat others as they want to be treated. Pursue new and creative ideas. Do good. Take action. Presume positive intent. Lead with integrity. Learn. Grow. Repeat."[490]
Facebook	"To give people the power to build community and bring the world closer together."[491]	"People use Facebook to stay connected with friends and family, to discover what's going on in the world, and to share and express what matters to them."[492]	"Focus on impact. Move fast. Be bold. Be open. Build social value."[493]
Southwest Airlines	"Connect people to what's important in their lives through friendly, reliable, and low-cost air travel."[494]	"To become the world's most loved, most flown, and most profitable airline."[495]	"Pride, integrity, humility, teamwork, honesty, service with LUV, efficiency, discipline, excellence."[496]

Which of these three documents is most important? The vision statement, which states what your organization aspires to achieve, is the foundational statement for your strategic plan.

A major survey of senior managers worldwide shows that managers must empower staff and share a vision and values to succeed.[497] Please see Section 3.5, Delegation and Empowerment, for more information.

4.5 PHYSICAL WORK ENVIRONMENT

The pandemic has brought about a significant shift in the work dynamics of many white-collar employees. The emergence of the hybrid work model, which blends office and remote work, is proving to be a beneficial norm. While traditional offices will continue to exist, they are undergoing a complete transformation. This section is designed to equip you and your employees with the necessary guidance to adapt to these changes and reinvent your workspaces.

- In 2022, the Bureau of Labor Statistics' American Time Use Survey researchers found a strong link between being outdoors and mental health. Those working in agriculture and forestry have the highest self-reported happiness.[498] Not all of us can work outdoors, but office designs can increase natural light, add plants, add bird chirping sounds, and much more. This section gives you many options for designing the perfect office space and includes many recommendations that bring the outdoors in.

  - Farmers and forestry workers may have high self-reported happiness because they work outdoors. I suggest that having fewer meetings contributes to their happiness, too.

- It is a well-established fact that the physical work environment significantly impacts worker productivity, perceptions, and behavior. The most effective managers recognize the value of their employees' input in shaping the office environment. This section encourages you to seek your employees' advice on crucial factors such as office temperatures, air quality, lighting, and noise, which fosters a sense of ownership and comfort.[499]

  - Temperature

    - According to a Cornell University study, the optimal office temperature is 77 degrees Fahrenheit, and errors increase as the temperature drops.[500] In addition, an overly cold office is a significant gender issue. A study published by *The Journal of Clinical Investigation* concludes that women have a lower sedentary metabolic rate than men. This results in women producing less heat and being less comfortable in colder offices than men.[501] A study published in *Applied Ergonomics* shows that women prefer a room temperature of 77.1 degrees Fahrenheit (25 degrees Celsius), and men prefer a room temperature of 71.6 degrees Fahrenheit (22 degrees Celsius). Women feel less comfortable than men at extremes of high and low temperatures.[502] Setting the office temperature at 77 degrees Fahrenheit will reduce errors, make women more comfortable, reduce energy bills, and be earth friendly. Also, why should women need to wear sweaters at the office in the summer?

ILLUSTRATIVE STORY

At one organization, several people complained that they sat under air vents that blew cold air directly on them in the summer and warm air in the winter. A sympathetic senior manager bought some gorgeous African-made fabric and hung it over the vents to diffuse the air, solving the problem beautifully. Please see more information on the uses of fabric for decorating and soundproofing later in this section.

ILLUSTRATIVE STORY

At another organization, an enterprising facility manager, Ashley, checked to see how many employees entered the building on weekends. This was easy because building entry required employees to swipe their security badges. When Ashley learned that very few people entered the building on weekends, she turned down the air conditioning and heat to reduce energy costs. She programmed the heat and air conditioning to return to the normal temperature at 6:00 a.m. each Monday morning. The building was comfortable when the employees began arriving at 7:30 a.m.

- ○ Indoor air quality
  - ■ Carbon dioxide (CO_2) and other indoor air pollutants directly impact cognitive functioning, which means a stuffy room makes people dumber (temporarily). According to

researchers at the Lawrence Berkeley National Laboratory, results of decision-making tests were worse when concentrations of CO_2 were as low as 1,000 parts per million (ppm).[503] We have all been in stuffy conference rooms that make us drowsy (and make us feel dumber). This is a normal reaction when too much CO_2 is in the room. I recommend that organizations buy portable CO_2 detectors with alarms for each conference room. They cost about $30 each. I recommend that the carbon dioxide detectors be set to go off if the meter reaches 950 ppm. If the meter reaches this level of CO_2, improve ventilation by opening doors or windows, turning on fans, or clearing the room. If the problem persists, talk to your facility management staff about assessing the air handling system.

ILLUSTRATIVE STORY

Most air-handling ductwork is designed to conform to the original floor plan. As floor plans change and walls are moved, the air handling systems are seldom reconfigured because it is costly. As a result, many buildings have rooms that have inadequate air handling. That is why some office buildings have some rooms that are colder in the winter and warmer in the summer. Of course, if the executive offices are reconfigured, great pains are taken to ensure perfect air handing for the alphas.

- Plants
  - A study by the University of Exeter, the University of Groningen in the Netherlands, the University of Queensland, and the Australia-Cardiff University's School of Psychology concludes that employees in offices with plants are 15% more productive, happier, and more creative than those in spartan offices.[504] A Washington State University paper cites many studies that conclude that indoor plants improve our mental and physical health.[505] Houseplants improve air quality in tightly constructed buildings such as high-rise office buildings. The spider plant is the best overall at remov-

ing chemicals from the air. A NASA study concludes that spider plants will remove 95% of chemicals from the air in only 24 hours.[506]

- ○ Natural lighting
  - ▪ Numerous studies show that greater exposure to daylight (natural light) improves workers' productivity, health, sleep, and ethical behavior.[507]
  - ▪ Use windows to let in natural light. A study published in the *Journal of Clinical Sleep Medicine* concluded that natural light exposure is important for physical and mental health. Employees with more natural light exposure sleep longer and better, have more physical activity, and have a better quality of life than workers with less natural light exposure.[508] Cornell University researchers found that workers in offices with natural light have an 84% reduction in headaches, eyestrain, and blurred vision.[509]
  - ▪ Paint walls white to maximize the reflection of light.[510]
  - ▪ Install movable architectural glass walls to maintain office privacy and share natural light. Why should people who have window offices get all the natural light?
- ○ Minimize noise
  - ▪ Noise causes distractions that make us less productive. A study published in *Noise Health* concludes that noisy conditions significantly impair employee performance.[511]
  - ▪ There are many ways to reduce noise in the workplace. They are listed below. Your staff must decide on how to reduce noise. They need the opportunity to control as much of their lives as possible.
  - ▪ In one study, 54% of participants reported that they were bothered by people talking and phones ringing. This noise contributed to dissatisfaction with their jobs.[512]
    - ▫ Request that employees silence their phones and program them to flash small yellow or white lights (or wear a headset). (Yes, I know phones have red lights, but those

are too distracting. Let's encourage manufacturers to add yellow or white lights instead of red.)

- □ Also, ask employees to talk quietly. Think of your office as a library. People always talk quietly in libraries. Why can't we do the same thing in offices? If anyone talks too loudly, feel free to look at them over the top of your glasses, just like a librarian.

- □ Put "QUIET, PLEASE" signs in your offices.

- Noise levels in the workplace must meet Occupational Safety and Health Administration (OSHA) standards.[513] Effective managers set noise levels far quieter than those required.

- To reduce office noise, maximize sound-absorbing materials in ceilings, walls, and furnishings. Choose cubicle walls that have fabric instead of wood paneling. Use decorative rugs or textiles as wall decorations.

- Hang fabric banners from the ceiling 18 inches to two feet apart to absorb sound.[514]

- Consider using white noise or sound masking to make office background conversations less distracting.

> **Definition of white noise:** A constant sound that combines all audible frequencies. Some compare it to AM radio static or air handling systems airflow (heating or air conditioning).

- □ Interestingly, unwanted speech is distracting, but not necessarily noise in general. By adding more noise to a room, including white noise, you can make others' conversations less intelligible and easier to ignore.[515] A white noise sound system with volume control can be easily added to any room cheaply. An even better option is sound masking.

> **Definition of sound masking:** Sound masking creates a background sound that only matches and thus masks only human voice frequencies. It is more pleasant than white noise.

- □ Sound masking is more expensive than white noise because it requires custom design and professional installation to ensure even coverage. The location of white noise speakers is more evident than sound masking speakers.[516]

- Install carpet.

- Add plants in plant stands with fabric or other sound-absorbing panels.

- Use moveable glass walls to allow some privacy, reduce sound, and allow everyone to enjoy sunlight.

- Use moveable, sound-proof pods. Yes, they are expensive, but they end up being a bargain when your introverts are even more productive.

- Place copy and fax machines in alcoves or dedicated rooms with sound-absorbing walls and ceilings. Why do we need paper copies when electronic copies cost nothing, create no noise, and are earth-friendly? Please put a sign over the copier that says, "Do you really need paper copies? The money saved by not making paper copies is used to buy plants." If people continue to use the printers, move them to the basement. If some people continue to use the basement printers, modify your printer contract so that the repair response time is delayed for several days. Costs for printer repair contracts go down significantly when the response time is several days versus the same day.

- Select one day per week for all meetings.

- Allow employees to wear a badge or other identifier so that everyone will know that you do not want interruptions.

- Put a DO NOT DISTURB sign on your office door or cubicle wall.

- Encourage staff to come to work early to get more done without the usual interruptions.

- Telework more.

- Quiet hours? A 2013 study published in the *European Review of Applied Psychology* shows that allowing a quiet hour is effective at improving performance.[517] Let your staff decide when to have a quiet hour or more. During this time, no phone calls, meetings, or drop-bys are allowed. Please let your customers know about your quiet hours. When your quiet hour program is a big success, your customers will want to introduce quiet hours, too.

- In 1787, the cobblestone street in front of the Pennsylvania State House was covered in dirt to muffle the sound of horses' hooves, carriages, and carts. The Founding Fathers needed quiet to write the United States Constitution.[518]

- Bring nature indoors

  - An *International Journal of Environmental Health Research* study concludes that bringing nature indoors helps create healthful workplaces. Use natural sounds such as birds chirping or water rushing. Add indoor potted plants. Maximize natural light. Let outside air and sounds in. Use photographs of nature. Show nature videos with sounds on computer screens when they are not being used.[519]

  - Let people bring friendly pets to work.

    ILLUSTRATIVE STORY

    I had the privilege of serving three Air Force tours of duty in the United Kingdom. On the occasions when I visited British air bases, I always noticed that next to every desk was a bowl of water. It seems that nearly everyone brought their dogs to work every day. The dogs sat quietly at their owners' feet. I always asked about their dogs and always got a big smile and an introduction.

  - Biophilia, according to biologist Edward O. Wilson, is a genetically driven human desire to seek connections with the natural world. We all feel more relaxed when we are in nature.[520]

- Amazon's Seattle headquarters has a four-story "living wall" with over 40,000 plants. Apple's campus in Cupertino, California, has 9,000 trees. Facebook's Menlo Park headquarters has a nine-acre, green rooftop park. Microsoft's offices in Redmond, Washington, have treehouses for meetings and work.[521]

  ILLUSTRATIVE STORY

  At one organization, a large division provides services to African countries. Workers who traveled to Africa often returned with beautiful and surprisingly inexpensive African-made fabrics that they displayed on walls, hung from ceilings, and draped over furnishings. There was so much sound-absorbing fabric that this floor was the quietest in the building. It was easily the most elegant floor with all that gorgeous fabric. If you're interested, just google "African fabrics for sale." Of course, you can choose other beautiful fabrics from any region where your organization does business. Select the fabrics for your staff and let them do the decorating. Your staff will think you are an artistic genius. You can also let your staff pick out the fabrics and do the decorating. If you do this, you will lose your "artistic genius" status but improve your "great boss" status.

  - Ensure that you allow sufficient space so that each of your employees always has the solitude to do their best work. The British have a useful expression, "penny wise and pound foolish." How useful is it to save money on your floor space, like open floor plans, when your staff cannot focus, become frustrated, and then quit?

- Other considerations for office design:
  - Create the right mix of private office space, open floor plans, and communal areas such as conference rooms and social event spaces (e.g., break rooms and lunchrooms) so employees can get their work done effectively. Let your staff help design their work areas with help from professional designers. A well-designed office allows staff members to work together collaboratively and develop social cohesion, allowing the sparks of creativity to generate new ideas. New ideas often come from face-to-face collaboration.[522]

- Maximize the use of conference and office space. Use empty office space for meetings. Put a big sign on the door indicating that you are away and when you plan to return. Also, signal your office availability by entering it into the conference room/empty offices reservation software.

- Open floor plans. These save money on office space, the most significant expense for most organizations after salaries. Open floor plans also supposedly foster collaboration. However, there are substantial downsides to open floor plans, such as increased perception of excessive noise, thermal discomfort, and poor air quality. With open floor plans, employees complain more about everything except lighting.[523] Surprisingly, open floor plans decrease face-to-face communication by about 70%, with a 20% to 50% increase in emails.[524]

  ### ILLUSTRATIVE STORY

  Like countless others, one organization transitioned to open floor plans on each floor except the executive floor. The management team said it would save significant money on rent. The new cubicles had low walls so that everyone could at least enjoy the natural light. Many employees started wearing wireless earbuds. An employee there informed me that many of those wearing earbuds were not necessarily listening to music. They were wearing earbuds to signal to others not to disturb them.

- Remote work radically changes how organizations manage offices and their floor plan configurations. Gone is the traditional one-desk-per-person arrangement, replaced by fewer desks available on a first-come, first-served basis. This unassigned seating is also known as *hot desks* or *hoteling*. Whatever it is called, unassigned seating saves money on real estate and recognizes that the post-pandemic future includes remote work. Use AI to help determine which employees should work on the same day. The AI should also consider how many unassigned seats are available in each work area each day. With more companies requiring employees to return to the office, there could be times when there may not be enough unassigned seats for everyone. This represents really lousy planning or perhaps no planning at all.

○ Ergonomic chairs, with proper adjustments for posture, help reduce back strain.[525]

○ Sit-stand *and* standing desks: A 2019 University of Pittsburg assessment of 53 peer-reviewed studies concluded that workers often have less back pain when using standing desks. The top of the desk should be at elbow height so that your fingers hang down to type. Stand straight. The monitor should be positioned so that you can see the top third of the screen at eye level.[526]

ILLUSTRATIVE STORY

Sit-stand desks allow employees to lower their desks to sit down when they wish. Be sure to always offer employees electrically-operated sit-stand desks. This allows employees with limited upper body strength or other limitations to adjust their desk height easily. It will also reduce or eliminate back injuries from raising and lowering the desks. Also, buy a thick rubber mat, sometimes called an anti-fatigue mat, for each sit-stand desk you buy to reduce leg fatigue. Finally, move around a lot. You get more benefits from a standing desk when you move around and use different muscles.

▪ Here is an explanation of why sitting for long periods is particularly bad for men. According to WebMD, sitting for long periods puts pressure on the prostate gland and will ultimately inflame it.[527]

○ Social cognitive neuroscientists have discovered how the human brain responds to the social world using functional magnetic resonance imaging (fMRI). They have determined that our need for social connections is a lifelong need like warmth or food.[528]

A final thought on the physical work environment:

• When redesigning office floor plans, please consider the needs of people with disabilities. Thanks.

4.6 POLICIES, PROCEDURES, AND CHECKLISTS

Procedures and checklists train people to do multi-step or repetitive tasks effectively, help reduce errors, and orient new employees.[529] All procedures and checklists should become attached to organizational policies. This makes them accessible regardless of staff turnover and ensures they are reviewed regularly and revised as needed.

Some examples of common policies are the flexible work arrangements policy, ethics policy, workplace health and safety policy, compliance policy, and many others. The close relationship between policies, procedures, and checklists is made clear in this chart.

Policies, Procedures, and Checklists

	Policy	**Procedure**	**Checklist**
Definitions	An organization's written guidelines or rules (i.e., operations, safety, compliance, etc.).	A written list of objectives or tasks needed to carry out policies.	A written list that describes each required step, in detail, to be taken to complete a task. The steps are listed in the order they are to be accomplished.
Benefits	Spells out an organization's guidelines or rules. Provides structure for delegating decision-making.[530] Allows all employees to have the same understanding.[531] Frees management from routine decisions.[532]	Written guides on how to implement policies. Helps ensure compliance. Reduces errors.	Provides instructions to perform repetitive tasks.[533] Defines employees' roles and responsibilities in completing checklists.[534] Enables new employees to understand their jobs sooner.[535] Allows others to step in to do the job on short notice.[536] Helps ensure compliance. Reduces errors.
Who writes them	Employees who are familiar with the subject write policies.	Employees who are familiar with the subject write procedures.	Employees who are familiar with the subject write checklists.
Who approves them	Senior management reviews and approves policies, often in a policy review committee.	Procedure approval levels can be delegated by senior management.	The checklist approval level can be delegated by senior management.

(continued)

Policies, Procedures, and Checklists *(continued)*

	Policy	**Procedure**	**Checklist**
Example	Safety Policy. All employees must always follow the safety rules. These rules exist for your safety and the safety of others.	All employees requesting entry to the contamination-free rooms (cleanrooms) must be pre-authorized to enter and must always wear protective suits while in the cleanrooms. WARNING: Failure to follow the cleanroom checklist may result in contamination of experiments, exposure to pathogens, and disciplinary action.	Steps to allow access to cleanrooms (abbreviated for this example):[537] 1. Get pre-approval to enter a cleanroom in building 17, room 403. 2. Read and understand the cleanroom protocol. 3. Take a shower. 4. Do not wear cosmetics, perfumes, or colognes in a cleanroom. 5. Stow personal items. 6. Put on your cleanroom gear in the correct order. 7. Pass through the air shower and adhesive floormat upon entry. 8. After exiting the cleanroom, remove your gear in the opposite order than when putting it on.
Tracking numbers	Safety Policy (#35)	Cleanroom Guidance (#35.1)	Cleanroom Access Checklist (#35.1.1)

- Where do you file written policies, procedures, and checklists so they are always available regardless of staff turnover? Formally attach procedures and checklists to their corresponding policies and maintain them on your organization's intranet site and in your employee handbook. To remain current, policies, procedures, and checklists should be reviewed at prescribed intervals. The policy review committee oversees the review process. The frequency of reviews varies depending on the type of document. Most policies, along with their attachments, are reviewed annually.[538] Maintaining such records so they can always be retrievable is called "memorializing" them.

- How to revise policies
  - For policies that are undergoing their annual or periodic review, the policy review committee sends each policy to all offices with a deadline to respond. Often at the annual policy reviews, no changes are suggested.

  - When recommended policy changes are forwarded to the policy review committee, the committee administrative staff consolidates all suggestions in a single document using Track Changes. Minor changes can be sent to all offices for consideration and response. For more complicated changes, the policy review committee should invite representatives of the affected offices to meet in a conference room. They will be revising the copy with the tracked changes. The chair, usually a senior representative of the office most affected by the policy, begins with the first recommended change and asks, "Does anyone have any suggested changes to the first sentence." Then, "Does anyone have any suggested changes to the second sentence?" The chair continues until everyone has considered all the recommended changes. The revised policy is then sent to the policy review committee for review and approval consideration. I have found that it is not effective to send the revised draft policy back to the affected offices numerous times with each set of changes until there are no more changes. After one or two reviews, I no longer get any changes. That is because most reviewers have given up and are no longer reviewing the changes of others. To revise more complicated recommendations effectively, all affected offices need to be in the same room and jointly review each recommended change together.

ILLUSTRATIVE STORY

Recently, my tax attorney recommended that I create a small business for tax purposes. After creating a limited liability company (LLC), my next step was to open a company checking account. I made an appointment with a small business banking representative at a national bank where I have a personal checking account. I showed up on time and completed and signed several forms. I also wrote a check for $25,000 from a personal checking account to deposit into my new company checking account. At 4:00 p.m., the bank closed, and employees began leaving. My small business banking representative hurriedly finished up with me, and I was out by 4:20 p.m. A few weeks later, I noticed that my $25,000 check had been cashed, but I was unsure whether the money was in my new account. I tried calling the representative who set up the account, without success. I then called the bank's national customer service number and asked my question. After speaking to three offices, customer service referred me to their fraud office. After some time, a fraud office auditor assured me that the money was in my new account, but no one had added it to my main menu screen so I could see it. The auditor referred me to their small business office to add the new business account to my existing online accounts. This was the office I contacted first. All this unnecessary effort was because the original bank representative forgot to add a screen so I could see my company account online. If he had used a simple checklist, he would have known he was overlooking one of the steps. As a result, he inconvenienced me and several people at his corporate office.

ILLUSTRATIVE STORY

At one organization, a wise and experienced senior manager reminded employees each year to prepare for the "silly season." This refers to the summer months when most employees take their vacation days. Employees often make mistakes during this time because they are doing unfamiliar jobs for employees who are away. Procedures and checklists ensure that those filling in can make informed decisions and avoid mistakes. Most employees take fewer vacation days than they earn because they are concerned that mistakes made while away could cost them their jobs. Organizations with detailed procedures and checklists will make far fewer mistakes when staff members are away. This will encourage employees to take their well-deserved time off. Managers who oversee the creation of robust procedures and checklists will reduce errors, improve retention, and make employees and their families happy at no cost.

4.7 CONTINUOUS PROCESS IMPROVEMENT

Definition of continuous process improvement: An ongoing analytical process that improves processes, products, and services.[120]

ILLUSTRATIVE STORY

A small business delivers its manufactured parts directly to factories that produce finished products. In one instance, the truck driver arrived at the destination and discovered he was at a large office building. After calling his dispatcher, they quickly realized that the delivery address was not the factory but the corporate headquarters. The solution was to update the delivery checklist so that it required the dispatcher to confirm the delivery address before the driver departed.

- Before improving a process, you need to define each step involved. All processes can be broken into steps. The majority of people are visual learners. Creating a flow diagram is the best way to visualize the process steps, including decision points, delays, flow directions, etc., and their relationships. Typical symbols used to create flow diagrams are shown in Diagram 1 on the following page. Process steps are shown using these symbols.

Diagram 1. Process Flow Diagram Symbols.

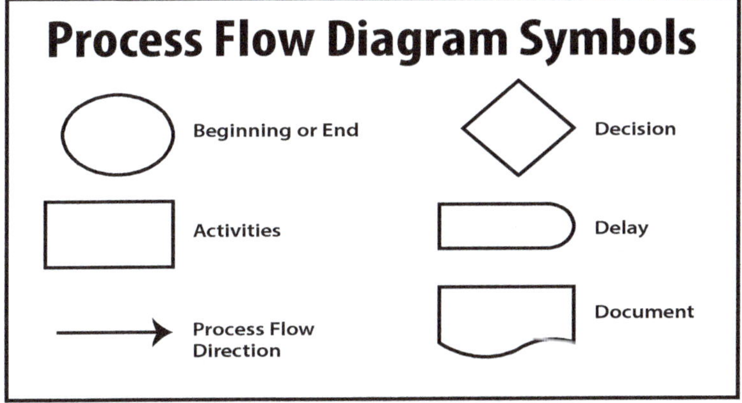

Below is a sample flow diagram.

Diagram 2. Sample Flow Diagram.

Options to Get to Work

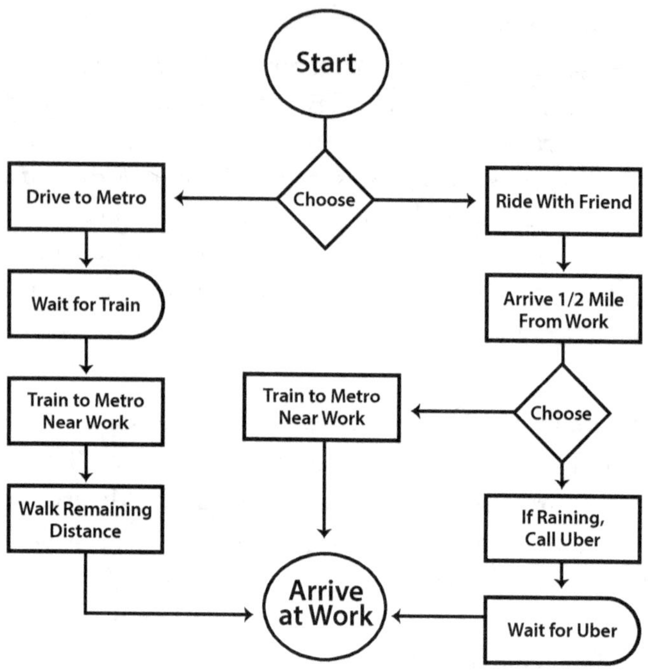

- How would you improve the sample process shown in Diagram 2? You could create additional options for going to work by bus or bicycle.

- A process flow diagram is a valuable tool that can help you improve any process by increasing your understanding of the flow of information, people, and resources.

- Once you see the steps, look for ways to improve your processes. Your process improvement efforts must have an objective, such as reducing costs or time.

- Every Fortune 500 company uses Six Sigma for process improvements in both the manufacturing and service industries. The objective of Six Sigma is to achieve error-free performance using proven quality techniques and principles. Numerous books and courses are available to learn more about Six Sigma.[540]

ILLUSTRATIVE STORY
One organization was losing highly qualified applicants because it was not hiring people quickly. Olivia, a senior manager, asked an analyst to build a flow diagram showing the steps in the hiring process. (These 14 hiring steps are highlighted in Section 2.1, Hire and Retain Great Employees.) Next, they used readily available HR data to measure how many days each step took. Once the diagram was populated with the number of days each step took, it was evident that the hiring managers took far too long to 1) review the applications; 2) determine which candidates to interview; 3) conduct the interviews; and 4) select the best candidate. Olivia spoke with several hiring managers and learned they were putting off hiring because it was not a priority. She told them that candidates apply for multiple jobs and almost always take the first offer. The company's hiring delays resulted in the best candidates being hired by other organizations. This encouraged the hiring managers to make hiring a priority.

Definition of the value chain (VC): A value chain includes all the steps involved in creating a product or service from the idea stage to the creation and use of the goods or services to recycling after use.[541]

- The five primary VC activities are inbound logistics, operations, outbound logistics, marketing and sales, and service, and four secondary activities include company infrastructure, procurement, HR management, and technology management. All nine VC activities are defined below, along with an example.[542]

- A VC analysis is a method to assess your nine activities holistically to show dependencies, linkages, and inefficiencies, allowing you to improve your competitive advantage by reducing costs and making your product or service unique to maximize value. Please see Section 3.11, Strategic Planning, for more information on differentiating your goods or services.[543]

The Value Chain's Five Primary Activities with an Example

Primary activities[544]	Definitions[545]	Example: Manufacturing athletic shoes
Inbound Logistics	Includes obtaining and storing raw materials until needed.	Obtain canvas, dyes, rubber, eyelets, etc., and store them until needed.
Operations	Includes converting raw materials into finished goods.	Manufacture tennis shoes.
Outbound Logistics	Includes warehousing and distributing finished goods to consumers.	Deliver tennis shoes to retailers and sell them direct to consumers online.
Marketing & Sales	Includes sales, advertising, and pricing.	Advertise your tennis shoes to your target market.
Service	Includes installation, training, maintenance, repair, and after-sale services/returns.	Handle returns.

- There are also four VC secondary or support activities.

The Value Chain's Five Secondary Activities with an Example

Secondary or support activity[546]	This activity consists of:[547]	The manufacturing of athletic shoes example continued from above
Company Infrastructure	Management, legal, finance, etc.	The company's employees support all five activities and four secondary activities.
Procurement	Acquiring raw materials, infrastructure, etc.	Procurement of raw materials, supplies, machinery, buildings, etc.
HR management	Hiring, training, retaining	The complete range of HR functions to hire, train, and retain all the staff needed to support all five primary and four secondary activities.
Technology development	Research and development, IT management	The most important research question: What professional athletes can we afford to pay to endorse our athletic shoes?

The value chain was developed by Michael E. Porter and explained in his book *Competitive Advantage: Creating and Sustaining Superior Performance* (Free Press, 1998). This book is an indispensable guide for creating and maintaining a competitive advantage.[548]

A final thought on process improvement:

- "When it is obvious that the goals cannot be reached, do not adjust the goals; adjust the action steps."[549] —Confucius, Chinese philosopher (551–479 BCE)

4.8 RISK MANAGEMENT

> **Definition of risk management:** The ongoing process of identifying, evaluating, and controlling all risks associated with each threat and deciding whether to accept, avoid, reduce, or transfer the risk associated with each.[550]

- Risk management program responsibilities must be assigned to a single office or committee managed by the chief, risk officer. All offices are responsible for identifying and submitting risk concerns to the office or committee responsible for risk management. The risk management office or committee will evaluate these risks and make recommendations to senior leaders or other appropriate offices on whether to accept, avoid, reduce, or transfer each risk.

- Risk management is a versatile tool that applies to many areas of a business. Businesses are exposed to a wide range of risks, including internal ones like illness or death of a business owner, theft, fraud, significant equipment downtime, IT loss or downtime, and external ones such as market changes, rent increases, changes in laws, extreme weather events, etc. While managers can better control internal risks, external risks are more challenging to manage.[551] Without a risk management office or committee, there is an increased likelihood that one or more of these risks will be overlooked.

- There should be a risk management policy defining the process by which risks are managed. Please see Section 4.6, Policies, Procedures, and Checklists, for more information.

- Ways to mitigate risk:
  - Risk acceptance (passive and active).

> **Definition of passive risk acceptance:** Your organization chooses to accept certain risks and does not create a contIngency plan to respond if the risk occurs. This is for minor losses that will not significantly impact the organization's overall health.

> **Definition of active risk acceptance:** Your organization sets aside contingency funds to be used in the event that risk occurs.[552]

- Risk avoidance.

> **Definition of risk avoidance:** Your organization chooses to completely avoid certain risks.[553]

- Example: Your organization chooses to no longer do business in countries where the U.S. Department of State has posted travel advisory levels of "reconsider travel" or "do not travel." As of March 1, 2024:

  - Iceland was in the State Department Travel Advisory Level 1: Exercise Normal Precautions.

  - United Arab Emirates was in the State Department Travel Advisory Level 2: Exercise Increased Precautions.

  - Pakistan was in the State Department Travel Advisory Level 3: Reconsider Travel.

  - Russia was in the State Department Travel Advisory Level 4: Do Not Travel.[554]

- Risk Reduction

> **Definition of risk reduction:** a systematic process to proactively identify, evaluate and reduce risks.[555]

- According to a Kaiser Family Foundation survey, organizations with more than 1,000 employees are more likely to self-insure for health plans. These organizations pay medical claims directly.[556]

- Risk Transfer

> **Definition of risk transfer:** Your organization chooses to shift the risk by either buying an insurance policy or contractually agreeing to a hold-harmless clause.[557]

ILLUSTRATIVE STORY

The COVID-19 pandemic disrupted supply chain management, resulting in worldwide productivity losses. Assembly lines will stop if manufacturing parts are not available when needed. How do industries address this risk? In its May 2020 survey, McKinsey & Company learned that just over 75% of respondents planned to increase the inventory of critical products, increase sources of raw materials, and diversify supply bases by buying the parts locally or regionally. By Q2 of 2021, 92% said they had done this. McKinsey learned that, to the contrary, companies took tepid steps to diversify their supply bases and buy parts locally or regionally but did begin increasing parts inventories. Long-term supply chain management risks remain. The fix requires companies to seek suppliers to build components closer to manufacturing sites.[558]

ILLUSTRATIVE STORY

Taiwan makes most of the world's most advanced semiconductors. It is an independent country but was part of China before 1949. China wants Taiwan back. If China takes Taiwan by force, the microchip factories will either be confiscated or destroyed. Either way, there would be a significant disruption to manufacturing worldwide. Congress authorized $53 billion to fund microchip building in the U.S. (risk reduction).[559]

ILLUSTRATIVE STORY

ABC Inc. shipped computers to employees working in developing countries. Customarily, ABC did not buy the insurance and instead relied on self-insuring (risk acceptance). When the company began to have a high theft rate of computers shipped to three specific countries, ABC chose to start insuring computer shipments to these three countries (risk transfer). The decision was a good one. The thefts continued, and the insurance cost was less than replacing the stolen computers. ABC further reduced its costs by instructing employees traveling to these countries to add computers to their baggage. The additional baggage cost was less than shipping and insuring the computers.

ILLUSTRATIVE STORY

In April 2023, the First Republic Bank failed because it did not manage risks effectively. The bank bought too many long-term assets, such as government securities and mortgages, when interest rates were low (risk acceptance). With rising interest rates, First Republic earned lower interest than its competition. As a result, its clients began moving their money out to seek higher returns elsewhere, and the bank failed.[560]

Final thought on risk management:

- The first objective of organizations is to survive. Regularly assessing internal and external risks and determining whether to accept, avoid, reduce, or transfer risks are important management responsibilities.

4.9 SPAN OF CONTROL

> **Definition of the span of control:** The optimal number of people that can report directly to a manager while continuing satisfactory levels of productivity.[561]

- Of course, these direct reports can also have people reporting to them. Effective managers can determine the optimal span of control. This section will tell you how.

- What is the ideal number of direct reports that managers can effectively manage? It depends. Employees have become much more independent, so managers can manage more employees.[562]

- Middle management continues to shrink. Studies show that U.S. company managers have an average of 9.7 direct reports, increasing to 11.4 at large companies.[563]

- Many factors influence the span of control. Managers can manage more staff:

  - When managers are effective

  - When turnover is low

  - When tasks are more recurring

  - When employees have more experience[564]

  - When managers hire, develop, and retain great employees. Please see Chapter 2, Hire, Develop, and Retain a Great Team, for more information.

  - When managers direct the creation of policies, procedures, and checklists. Procedures and checklists train people to do multi-step or repetitive tasks effectively, help reduce errors, and orient new employees.[565] All procedures and checklists should become attached to organizational policies. This makes them accessible regardless of staff turnover and ensures they are reviewed regularly and revised as needed. Please see Section 4.6, Policies, Procedures, and Checklists, for more information.

- When managers grow employees through future-focused coaching. This facilitates the creation and tracking of mutually agreed-upon performance expectations to include goals and objectives that align with the organization's goals and objectives. It also establishes employee accountability for results and gives each employee autonomy.[566] Please see Section 2.2, Coaching and Mentoring, and Section 2.4, Performance Development, for more information.

- When managers mentor employees and arrange for other managers to mentor employees in areas in which they have no experience. Please see Section 2.2, Coaching and Mentoring, for more information.

- When managers ensure employees are offered training so each can learn and grow. Please see Section 2.3, Training, for more information.

- When managers create an organizational culture that embraces inclusion, diversity, equity, and accessibility. Groups with dissimilar backgrounds challenge each other to do their best. Please see Section 2.5, Inclusion, Diversity, Equity, and Accessibility, for more information.

- When managers address any inappropriate behavior by problem employees as soon as possible. Please see Section 2.7, Problem Employees, for more information.

- When managers empower employees. Empowering your employees makes them more independent and requires less of your time to oversee their work—a win-win. Please see Section 3.5, Delegation and Empowerment, for more information on empowerment.

- When managers give employees maximum flexibility on their work arrangements like telework and flexible hours. Please see Section 3.7, Flexible Work Arrangements (also Work Flexibilities), for more information.

- When managers motivate, recognize, and appreciate their employees. Please see Section 3.8, Motivation, Recognition, and Appreciation, for more information.

- When managers ensure that their employees understand their work units' objectives, how they are linked to the organization's strategic objectives, and their role in successfully achieving them. Please see Section 3.11, Strategic Planning, for more information.

- When managers create a physical environment in which all employees, including introverts, extroverts, and people with disabilities, can do their best work. Please see Section 2.6, Introverts and Extroverts, and Section 4.5, Physical Work Environment, for more information.

- When organizations institute quiet hours. A 2013 study published in the *European Review of Applied Psychology* shows that allowing a quiet hour is effective in improving performance.[567] If the staff is more productive, the same work can be done by fewer employees.

- When managers treat their direct reports like partners. Please see Chapter 6: Partner with Your Bosses (Okay, You're the Junior Partner) for information on employees' critical relationships with their bosses.

- When organizations offer all the low- to no-cost options for improving recruiting, morale, retention, and productivity identified in Chapter 10, How to Build the Best Organization Possible.

- When managers do everything possible to make their employees successful by using every tool in this book.

- What other factors should you consider in determining how many direct reports a manager can effectively handle?

  - Are any of your employees working more than 50 hours per week? No one is fully effective if they work more than 50 hours per week.[568]

  - Do your employees need more staff, training, or technology?

    - Ask HR for a workload analysis if it appears that more staff is needed. Please see Section 2.1, Hire and Retain Great Employees.

- Look for training opportunities for employees that will increase their productivity. Ask them if they can make training recommendations for themselves and others.

- Ask your staff if they can recommend technology to reduce work hours.

○ Are some of your employees more effective than others? Coach and train the slower ones and reward the effective ones.

○ Do any of your employees appear stressed? Regularly ask your direct reports at your coaching meetings if they can handle the workload. They will likely not tell you; you need to ask regularly. Please see Section 2.2, Coaching and Mentoring, for more information.

○ Do any of your managers have trouble delegating? For more information on delegation, please see Section 3.5, Delegation and Empowerment.

ILLUSTRATIVE STORY

Taking the ratio of managers to direct reports to the extreme, Zappos, an online shoe retailer, did away with all managers in 2013. Their mantra was "no job titles, no managers, no hierarchy"—also known as holacracy. At that time, Zappos had 1,500 employees and no managers. Employees self-managed and belonged to various decision-making groups that kept the organization operating.[569] Six years later, Zappos quietly did away with holacracy as being too internally focused. Zappos wisely chose to refocus on its customers.[570]

ILLUSTRATIVE STORY

At one organization, Daniel had 25 people reporting directly to him. Unsurprisingly, he could dedicate little time to each employee and mentoring and coaching were impossible. Kayla recommended that two of his direct reports be reassigned to her. After all, these two employees had difficulty getting Daniel to review projects because his schedule was too full. Daniel agreed to reassign them. To Kayla's surprise, the two reassigned direct reports were also happy with the change.

A final thought:

- "Excellence is never an accident. It is always the result of high intention, sincere effort and intelligent execution; it represents the wise choice of many alternatives—choice, not chance, determines your destiny."[571] —Aristotle, Greek philosopher (384–322 BCE)

4.10 TECHNOLOGY

The world is currently in the fourth Industrial Revolution (IR). The first IR, from 1760 to 1840, saw the building of railroads and a shift from hand production to mechanical production using steam engines. The second IR, beginning in the late 19th century, saw mass production driven by the assembly line and the electrification of factories. The third IR, the digital or computer revolution, began in the 1960s and saw the introduction of semiconductors, mainframe computers, personal computers, and the internet. The fourth IR, beginning around 2000, merges these technologies and removes the lines between the biological, digital, and physical domains. Think of AI, big data analytics, nanotechnology, gene sequencing, robotics, etc.[572]

- Millennials and Gen Zers expect their workplaces to have the latest technology. Ask your staff to recommend new technology to help them with their jobs. Ask affected employees for feedback on these recommended tech solutions. This is another way to enable staff to help shape their workplaces and feel more in control.

- Some of the technologies with a rapid pace of implementation include AI, big data analytics, cloud computing, e-commerce, encryption, green technology, image processing (object identification), the internet of things (IoT), quantum computing, robotics, telemedicine, text mining, and voice and speech recognition.[573] These are defined below.

> **Definition of artificial intelligence (AI):** A field of computer science whose focus is to develop computer systems to mimic human intelligence to perform such tasks as recognizing speech, learning from past experiences, making decisions, and problem-solving.[574]

ILLUSTRATIVE STORY

In an October 2022 AI pilot program, ChatGPT responses to random online patient questions were compared to physician responses to the same questions. The AI responses scored much higher than physician responses in both empathy and quality of the medical response.[575]

ILLUSTRATIVE STORY

In May 2023, the IBM CEO announced that IBM would slow or stop hiring for jobs that AI will likely do soon. Their non-customer-facing staff, including HR employees, will likely be cut by 30% in the next five years.[576]

ILLUSTRATIVE STORY

In 2024, University of California engineers created an AI-assisted wearable electronic patch that allows patients with dysfunctional vocal cords to communicate verbally.[577]

Definition of adaptive AI: Software that continually revises its code without human intervention. It adapts based on assessing new experiences, which leads to quicker and better outcomes.[578] AI's adaptive analytics can help clinicians catch diseases earlier.[579]

Definition of generative AI: Algorithms that can generate new and unique content similarly to human minds.[580] For example, in life sciences, generative AI can aid in new drug discoveries; in finance, it can detect fraud; in entertainment, it can create content; in manufacturing, it can improve product design.[581]

- Building the AI foundation:

  - 59% of senior managers strongly believe that AI will improve their big data, according to a Pricewaterhouse-Coopers Global survey.[582]

  - 37% of businesses worldwide use AI, according to Gartner.[583]

□ AI will contribute \$15.7 trillion to the global economy annually by 2030, according to PricewaterhouseCoopers Global.[584] Let me put this number in context. The International Monetary Fund estimates that the global gross domestic product for 2024 will be \$109.5 trillion.[585]

Definition of big data analytics (also business analytics) (abridged): A process of collecting a high volume and variety of data and processing it at a high velocity, using advanced analytical techniques to identify hidden patterns, customer preferences, correlations, and market trends to improve customer engagement, enhance real-time business intelligence, manage risks, and make better-informed decisions.[586]

Definition of big data analytics (also business analytics) (unabridged): A process whereby big data, i.e., data sets that are immense and exceed the volume that can be processed by standard computers (high volume), is received at an unprecedented high speed (high velocity) and much of it is generated in real time. This complex and varied data is from multiple sources, i.e., devices, emails, log files, networks, sensors, texts, transactional applications, video/audio, web, and social media (high variety) and uses advanced analytical techniques to identify hidden patterns, customer preferences, correlations, and market trends to improve customer engagement, enhance real time business intelligence, manage risks, and make better-informed decisions.[587]

■ Big data analysis is used in every sector of the global economy. In manufacturing, big data can predict when equipment will fail; in retail, big data can foresee customer demand; in health care, big data can help researchers pinpoint patients' future health issues; in telecommunications, big data can enhance network performance; in financial services, big data can identify patterns that suggest fraud.[588]

ILLUSTRATIVE STORY

An article in The New York Times Magazine, *"How Companies Learn Your Secrets," illustrates the complicated issues surrounding business analytics. The story centers around a high school girl who began receiving coupons for baby clothes and baby products in the mail. Her upset father went to the store to complain, believing their advertising encourages young girls to get pregnant. Later, her father apologized to the store manager because he learned his daughter was pregnant. The store chain had determined from her online behavior that she was pregnant and then targeted her for future sales. This retailer used big data analytics, sometimes called business analytics, to identify customers and encourage them to make specific purchases.[589] Many people see this collection of information as an intrusion of privacy.*

ILLUSTRATIVE STORY

Netflix uses big data analytics to assess viewership among its 200 million viewers worldwide. The analysis allows Netflix to customize its content for different regions. This, in turn, gave Netflix a competitive edge to enter the international online streaming service successfully.[590]

Definition of cloud computing (or, simply, the cloud): Remote servers that provide on-demand computer services such as analytics, databases, intelligence, networking, servers, software, and storage via the internet. Each cloud company has many customers, which keeps costs down. Customers can scale up or down quickly.[591]

ILLUSTRATIVE STORY

Netflix migrated all of its databases to the cloud to reduce the costs of supporting and upgrading its computer system. Also, maintaining databases in-house did not allow the scalability needed to meet the rapid growth of its online streaming service.[592]

ILLUSTRATIVE STORY

Just before the Russian military invasion of Ukraine in February 2022, the Ukrainian government began migrating terabytes of crucial government data to the cloud. Ukraine's minister of digital information explained that this vital data was safe in the cloud, even from Russian missiles.[593]

ILLUSTRATIVE STORY

One organization hosted its primary and backup systems in the same computers. An experienced senior manager, not in IT, strongly suggested that the backup system be put in the cloud to improve security. The senior leadership did not understand the suggestion.

Definition of e-commerce: Online commercial transactions.

- ☐ Think Amazon, Alibaba, and MercadoLibre.

Definition of encryption: The process of scrambling readable or plain text data to an unreadable format. Once converted, the scrambled data is called cipher text. Encryption protects digital data, whether it is stored on servers or in transmission.[594] For example, websites that use credit card numbers encrypt this information to prevent identity theft.

Definition of green technology: Environmentally friendly technology.[595]

- ■ Solar and wind energy are two examples of green technology.

Definition of image processing (object identification): The process of extracting usable information from images using algorithms.

ILLUSTRATIVE STORY

The Department of Defense uses image processing to locate and identify targets.[596]

> **Definition of the internet of things (IoT):** A massive network of "things" or physical objects that contain sensors and software that allows them to exchange data via the internet.[597]

- Physical objects that contain sensors range from household objects like iPhones, cars, and security cameras to industrial tools. There will be 30 billion of these IoT devices by 2030. That is an average of three to four devices for every person on the planet.[598]

> **Definition of quantum computing:** Computing that uses special hardware and algorithms to exploit quantum mechanics to manage information. This significantly reduces the time it takes to solve complex problems.[599]

ILLUSTRATIVE STORY

Quantum computing is currently used to identify the best routes for fuel tankers worldwide in order to reduce fuel costs.[600]

ILLUSTRATIVE STORY

Assessments are underway to use quantum computing to greatly accelerate AI, model financial markets, reduce greenhouse gas emissions in the manufacturing of fertilizer, improve weather predictions, improve drug development, etc.[601]

> **Definition of robotics:** Machines that perform human actions.

ILLUSTRATIVE STORY

Ally Robotics recently developed a robot that eliminates programming. The robot learns by watching people work. Because no coding is required, it costs 70% less to produce.[602]

> **Definition of telemedicine (telehealth):** Providing medical care over the internet using computers, cameras, and other electronic devices.

- The Centers for Disease Control and Prevention reports a 154% increase in telemedicine in the last week of March 2020 over the same week in 2019 due to the COVID-19 pandemic. During the pandemic, telemedicine allowed more access to care, less facility and supplies use, and less disease exposure for patients and staff.[603]

- By December 2023, the American Medical Association reported that 74% of medical practices use telehealth.[604]

ILLUSTRATIVE STORY

In 1995, a small Air Force hospital in New Mexico volunteered to participate in the Department of Defense's telemedicine program. This hospital was too small to employ a full-time radiologist. Radiology technicians took digital X-ray images and sent them via the internet to an Army medical center in Northern California. The medical center provided quick diagnostic readings.

ILLUSTRATIVE STORY

The American College of Radiology reports that sending images via the internet to radiologists in other states and even overseas is increasing. "Teleradiology" across state and international borders raises questions about licensing and insurance reimbursements.[605]

Definition of text mining: Extracting usable information such as patterns, concepts, concealed relationships, and trends from text-based data.[606]

ILLUSTRATIVE STORY

In social media, text mining allows businesses to find thought leaders and influencers to increase brand messaging and identify new customers.[607]

Definition of voice and speech recognition (speech-to-text): Enables programs to convert human speech to a readable format.[608]

ILLUSTRATIVE STORY

At one national bank, there was high absenteeism due to illness and self-isolation at the start of the COVID-19 pandemic. At the same time, the bank had a sharp increase in phone inquiries because customers were reluctant to come to the bank in person. The bank's solution was to use speech recognition software to respond to callers. This solution was very successful, improved customer service response time, and reduced overhead costs.

Definition of wearable devices: Wearable devices are now used for assisting, monitoring, and tracking employees. They can help employees increase efficiency, improve physical well-being, and reduce injuries on the job. However, monitoring workers raises economic, legal, social, and technological concerns.[609]

ILLUSTRATIVE STORY

Some organizations offer financial incentives to employees to track their fitness and adopt healthier habits to reduce medical claims.[610] Companies have lower health care expenses, and employees are healthier—a win-win.

ILLUSTRATIVE STORY

Nontraditional data collection is on the increase. In one survey, 40% of companies said they experimented with "nontraditional" data collection methods. For example, Walmart filed for a patent on a listening device system that can record workers' activities, such as conversations at the checkout counter. This could replace customer surveys with more accurate real-time data.[611]

- Does technology create jobs? Technology has created jobs for centuries, but this trend is projected to reverse soon. Let us look at the history of technology and job creation in England and Wales to show their long-term trends. A study of census data in these two countries since 1871 shows that machines have been job creators. The study found that since 1871, the number of farmers has declined by 95%, and there has been a 20-fold increase in accountants and a 26-fold increase in nurses.[612] In 2020, the World Economic Forum projected that by 2025, 85 million jobs might be lost, but 97 million new jobs may be created as the division of labor changes between humans, machines, and algorithms.[613] In 2023, the World Economic Forum now projects that by 2027, 83 million jobs may be lost, and 69 million new jobs may be created. The report shows that machines do 34% of all business tasks, while people are doing 66% at present.[614]

- Does your staff know what is involved in replacing software?

ILLUSTRATIVE STORY

In one organization, the HR software was outdated and required time-consuming human workarounds. Jacob, a senior manager, told the HR staff that there were several steps for assessing and selecting new software.

- *The most important step is the first one: defining and prioritizing HR requirements or what you want the software to do. Jacob explained that identifying HR requirements is necessary before automating them. These requirements would also be the benchmark against which each competing software option would be measured and scored.*

- *Next, assess commercially available software and consider upgrading existing software to meet your requirements.*

- *Select the software that best meets your requirements. No software will be a perfect fit.*

- *Determine whether you want to modify the new software to add additional functionality that meets your requirements.*

- *Train the staff to operate the new software. This is especially important because all niche software, such as HR software, is never as user-friendly as Microsoft Office.*

- *Create a realistic schedule to transfer or migrate the existing HR data to the new software.*

A final thought on technology:

- "The reasonable man adapts himself to the world; the unreasonable one persists in trying to adapt the world to himself. Therefore, all progress depends on the unreasonable man."[613] —George Bernard Shaw (1856–1950), playwright

4.11 TIME MANAGEMENT

Know where you spend your time. You can and should get all your work done in less than 50 hours per week, have a good work-life balance, and have a good quality of life. It begins with knowing where you spend your time.

Do not work more than 50 hours per week. A 2013 Stanford University study concludes that 50 hours per week is the maximum that anyone can be fully productive at their jobs.[616] That certainly includes managers. To be an effective manager within these hours, you need to be extraordinarily efficient with managing your time. Your staff is always watching you. If you work beyond 50 hours per week, your staff may feel obligated to work your hours, too.

A surprising 90% of managers waste time in all kinds of unproductive activities.[617] It is less mentally taxing to do less challenging work. This is at the expense of doing higher-priority work. Some experts call this being lazy.

- Ways to improve your time management:
  - Keep a time diary. Log all your work activities in 15-minute increments for two weeks. This includes delegating, coaching, mentoring, training, planning, organizing, scheduling, budgeting, coordinating, communicating, directing, reviewing, counseling, hiring, disciplining, and firing. The results will likely surprise you. Your time diary will help you determine which work you can delegate, reduce, and eliminate.
  - Use a To-Do list. Every time you accept a task, add it to your To-Do list, electronic or on paper. At the end of each day, reprioritize the ongoing list, and you are ready for tomorrow.[618] Your To-Do list will:
    - Show you how you spend your time.
    - Ensure you never forget any tasks.
    - Enable you to prioritize tasks.
    - Be a record of tasks you gave to your employees.

- Be a record of your accomplishments and those of your employees.

ILLUSTRATIVE STORY

I have a separate section on my To-Do lists for tasks I give my employees. (Remember that even though you delegated these tasks, you have a shared responsibility to complete them.) I have found To-Do lists to be invaluable. The human mind cannot keep track of all these necessary actions. I occasionally surprise my staff by asking them about tasks they forgot about. Yes, they should use To-Do lists, too.

○ Delegate as much work as possible. You will be busy with all the work you cannot delegate, including coaching, mentoring, training, planning, organizing, scheduling, budgeting, coordinating, communicating, directing, reviewing, counseling, hiring, disciplining, and firing. Please see Section 3.5, Delegation and Empowerment, for more information.

○ Prioritize better so you always do your most important work first. Prioritize all your work, including coaching, mentoring, training, planning, organizing, scheduling, budgeting, coordinating, communicating, directing, reviewing, counseling, hiring, disciplining, firing, and completing your To-Do list items.

○ Schedule recurring work to ensure that nothing is overlooked. Include recurring work items from the list in the paragraph above.

○ Leave time for unscheduled, time-sensitive work, including communicating, directing, disciplining, firing, and other unexpected, urgent items.

○ Reduce interruptions. Employees who work in an office are often interrupted. A University of California study shows that interrupted people take between 8 to 25 minutes to recover from each interruption. The shorter recovery time is for simpler tasks, and the longer time is for more complex tasks. The interruption could be as short as two seconds. These workers make up for interruptions by working faster and experiencing more effort, frustration, stress, and time pressure.[619] To reduce interruptions: telework more, introduce quiet hours, close your door and put a DO NOT DISTURB sign on it, use white noise or sound masking, and maximize the use of noise-absorbing materials.

○ Wherever you work, you should minimize noise, maximize indoor air quality, maximize the availability of natural light, and set all thermostats at 77 degrees Fahrenheit. For more information, please see Section 4.5, Physical Work Environment.

○ Do one task at a time. Multitasking, doing two or more tasks simultaneously, does not work. Our brains do not work that way. Attempting to multitask lowers productivity, reduces quality, and causes stress and burnout.[620] "If you chase two rabbits, you will not catch either one."—Latin Proverb[621]

○ Handle each document only once, if possible.

○ Learn to say no with an explanation and a smile.

ILLUSTRATIVE STORY

Early in my career, I had a very effective and efficient boss who limited each workday to 8.5 hours with no weekend work. He arrived each morning at 6:00 a.m., took a 30-minute lunch break, and left promptly at 3:00 p.m. He told me he finished most of his work in the few hours before the others arrived. Everyone knew he left at 3:00 p.m., so there were no late afternoon meetings. Flexible work hours also improved his work-life balance and showed his staff we could finish our work in fewer than 50 hours per week. He also took all his leave each March when office activity slowed. This also taught his staff to be more independent in his absence. I should also mention that my boss managed a 300-bed medical center and was well-liked by everyone. Thanks for being a great role model, Jack!

○ I recommend that all organizations adopt one to two hours of quiet time daily; no phone calls, meetings, or drop-bys are allowed. A 2013 study published in the *European Review of Applied Psychology* shows that allowing a quiet hour is effective in improving performance.[622] Let your staff decide when to have a quiet hour or more. Please let your customers know about your quiet hours.

Final thoughts on time management:

- "Lost time is never found again."[623] —Benjamin Franklin, American statesman, writer, scientist, and inventor

- Every minute you waste is one minute less you can spend on what makes you happy.

CHAPTER 5

Partner with Your Peers

Make your work peers essential partners. You can help each other succeed by sharing ideas and frank advice, becoming mentors to each other's employees, and practicing conversations that you will have with difficult employees. Once you have established solid relationships with your peers, working together on joint projects will be easier and have better outcomes. You can even become friends with your peers outside of work.

> **Definition of peers:** People on the same organizational level.

- One study shows that managers spend more time with peers (47%) than employees (41%). More surprisingly, managers spend very little time with their bosses (12%).[624]

- An O. C. Tanner Company global study concludes that having a good friend at work improves employees' performance and productivity.[625] You should be friendly to everyone, but you can only be friends with your peers.

- Employees with a best friend at work are seven times more likely to be engaged.[626]

- How to build mutually advantageous relationships with your peers:

    ○ Meet individually with your peers during your first week on the job. Look for ways to help each other. Please see Chapter 3.1, Your First Weeks at a New Job, for more information.

    ○ Invite your peers to sit on your interview panels, especially when filling positions that work closely with their employees. Your peers will feel invested in these individuals and help ensure their success.

○ Ask your peers for their advice on your major decisions. Each of your peers has a unique background and might surprise you with their insights. They will also appreciate being asked. Of course, you should also ask your employees and customers for advice on new initiatives. Have these conversations before discussing any new initiatives with your boss.

○ Ask one of your most trusted peers to practice difficult employee conversations with you, with the peer playing the employee. Poor-performing employees sometimes try to blame you or others. Be ready and practice your responses in advance.[627] Please see Chapter 2.7, Problem Employees, for more information on counseling problem employees.

○ Ask your peers to serve as witnesses when you are counseling problem employees. You can return the favor when they are counseling their problem employees.

○ Arrange informational interviews for your employees. Ask your peers to mentor any of your staff members who plan to seek jobs in their area of expertise. No one has refused my request when I asked for their help. Agree when a peer asks you to mentor any of their staff members.

ILLUSTRATIVE STORY

On one occasion, an employee stopped by my office to ask for career advice. Matthew worked in an administrative position, but his primary career interests were accounting and finance. Since I do not have a strong background in this area, I asked our organization's senior accounting and finance officer to meet with Matthew. This senior official was a peer and friend. I asked Matthew to have a list of questions ready. Following their informational interview, I asked him to follow up with a handwritten thank-you note. Why did Matthew accept the administrative job, which is not his chosen field? A 2021 Society of Human Resource Management survey found that 96% of job candidates accept their first job offer.[628] Please see Chapter 2.2, Coaching and Mentoring, for more information on mentoring.

- Ask peers for frank advice on any services your staff provides to their staff. Constructive advice can only improve your services.

- Once you have established solid relationships with your peers, working together on joint projects will be easier and have better outcomes.

- You can never over-coordinate the review of documents that you originate. If in doubt, send documents to your peers for review. Please know that your peers will not be pleased if you under-coordinate and forget to include them when reviewing a subject that affects their areas of responsibility. Not surprisingly, I have found that peers never complain if I send them a document for review that they are not required to see but may be of interest to them.

- You should invite only your peers to lunch. If you ask one of your bosses, it will appear as if you are seeking extra face time. Also, your bosses will likely decline. If you invite one of your employees, other employees will suspect favoritism. If you ask an employee from another office, you can expect gossip.

- Please consider having a brown bag lunch with your peers at least once a month. Try to keep the number of attendees around seven. That is the optimum size for a get-together (meeting).[629] Of course, if your boss has ten direct reports, invite all ten. Please do not leave anyone out. Yes, some peers may need to dial in. The first meeting should be personal introductions, i.e., where you were born and raised, schooling, hobbies, interests, etc. Each person should add something about themselves that no one would ever guess. You might be surprised at how much you have in common. Each time you add a new member, do the introductions again. These get-togethers can start with any business subjects, and the rest can be social. You should also occasionally invite guest speakers from throughout the organization. Please let me know how it goes. I see peer relationships and cooperation as having great untapped potential. Ideally, these get-togethers will contribute to peers becoming friends. Managers need to figure out how to get the most out of peer relationships and have fun doing it. This is part of a larger effort to get the maximum benefit from our 50 hours or less per week. I want you to have a highly successful, low-stress career and a life outside of work, too. It is doable. Thanks.

ILLUSTRATIVE STORY

A peer and I became good friends when we worked in the same organization. We have a lot in common. Both of us are former military officers. We often went to lunch together and talked about things unrelated to work. Now, years later, we are both retired and stay in touch. If you check your holiday card list, the names of those you met at work will likely be peers. There will also be a few former employees on your list who want to use you as a future reference.

A final thought on peers:

- Peer relationships are very important, but I found very little research on this subject. Researchers and graduate students looking for a thesis subject should investigate the benefits of peer relations. Many of us will be interested in what you find.

CHAPTER 6

Partner with Your Bosses (Okay, You're the Junior Partner)

Employees of all ages who see their immediate boss as a partner are much happier with their lives. In terms of life satisfaction, it's worth more than doubling the income for middle-aged workers.[630] Effective managers know that working closely with their direct reports costs nothing but improves their morale, performance, and retention.

There should always be an ongoing two-way conversation with your boss. Managing upward or managing your boss is based on mutual trust, respect, and shared responsibility for common goals and objectives. Bosses ensure that adequate resources are available and set priorities. Direct reports should be loyal, trustworthy, dependable, and collaborative. They must understand their boss's priorities and key performance indicators that spell success for their boss.[631] Your most important work relationship is with your immediate boss.

- One study shows that managers spend more time with peers (47%) than employees (41%). More surprisingly, managers spend very little time with their bosses (12%).[632] In my experience, when you do not spend enough time with your boss to keep them updated on all you are doing, they assume the worst. You are wise to keep them fully informed. If you do not have a weekly coaching meeting with your boss, schedule it.

- Rules for dealing with your boss:
  - Your boss's priorities are your priorities, too.
  - Brief your boss weekly on performance measurements, recurring work and nonrecurring work, decision requests, and any

sensitive information on employees. Please see Section 2.2, Coaching and Mentoring, for details.

- For advice on your first two meetings with your new boss, see Section 3.1, Your First Weeks at a New Job.

- You are responsible for ensuring that you have adequate time scheduled to meet with your boss. Do not wait to be invited.

- Communicate with your boss in their preferred method (face-to-face, emails, texts, reports, etc.).

- Adapt to your boss.

- Present bad news as soon as possible.

- Never use your boss's name to get something done unless you get their approval first.[633]

- Bosses are responsible for clearing hurdles for you at their level. However, bosses expect you to exhaust all other options before being asked for help.

- If your boss is new to the organization, this is a timely opportunity for you to brief them on your work in detail. This is one time when more information is better. Let them know about all your responsibilities, the status of each, your office's accomplishments, and where you may need help now or in the future. Please see the form in the Appendix: Job-Related Information for Your Successor, for items to include in this update.

- Do you disagree with your boss on something important? Decide whether you think that your boss will allow respectful disagreement. If yes, please follow the steps below.

  - Do your homework. Ensure that you research your idea fully and have a plausible argument for a different solution that will work better. Discuss your idea with any affected offices to get their buy-in.

  - If you disagree with your boss's boss, work exclusively with your immediate boss. Never bypass your boss.

- Discuss your proposed solution with a trusted peer. Ask for unsparing criticism of your proposal. If it will make you feel more comfortable, ask your peer to role-play the discussion with you.

- Choose the right time to discuss your suggestion with your boss. Ensure that you will not be interrupted and that only the two of you are in the room.

- Respectfully explain that you have a different solution and ask permission to discuss it. "I would like to share with you a different way, I believe, to achieve the same outcome for less expense. Is that okay?" Focus on aligning your recommendation with the organization's interests.

- Restate your boss's decision to show that you understand it. If possible, compliment any pros of the boss's decision.

- Explain your view and speak slowly. This is calming. Choose your words carefully. If, at any point, your boss's body language tells you to wrap it up, then wrap it up.

- If your boss disagrees with your proposal, thank them for their time and let them know that you will enthusiastically support their decision.[634]

- If your boss agrees with your proposal, never take any credit at any point. "It is amazing what you can accomplish if you do not care who gets the credit."[635] —Harry S. Truman, 33rd President of the United States

A final thought on working with your bosses:

- A Society for Human Resource Management study found that 84% of workers blame badly trained managers for generating needless stress and work.[636] Please follow all the advice in this chapter to make your boss your most important partner.

CHAPTER 7

Partner with Your Unions

Cooperating with your unions will get more done than creating a hostile environment. Management and labor unions are both interested in ensuring that the organization thrives. They also have a moral obligation to create respectful and productive workplaces.[637]

- The definitions below are from the websites of the National Labor Relations Board or the Department of Labor.

  - **National Labor Relations Act** (also known as the Wagner Act): "In 1935, Congress passed the National Labor Relations Act ('NLRA'), making clear that it is the policy of the United States to encourage collective bargaining by protecting workers' full freedom of association. The NLRA protects workplace democracy by providing employees at private-sector workplaces the fundamental right to seek better working conditions and designation of representation without fear of retaliation."[638]

  - **National Labor Relations Board (NLRB):** "The NLRB is an independent federal agency enforcing the National Labor Relations Act, which guarantees the right of most private sector employees to organize, to engage in group efforts to improve their wages and working conditions, to determine whether to have unions as their bargaining representative, to engage in collective bargaining, and to refrain from any of these activities. It acts to prevent and remedy unfair labor practices committed by private sector employers and unions."[639]

  - **The Labor-Management Relations Act (also known as the Taft-Hartley Act) (1947):** "The Taft-Hartley Act made major changes to the Wagner Act. Although Section 7 was retained intact in the revised law, new language was added to provide that employees had the right to refrain from participating in union or mutual aid activities except that they could be required to become members in a union as a condition of employment.

Taft-Hartley defined six additional unfair labor practices, reflecting Congress' perception that some union conduct also needed correction. The Act was amended to protect employees' rights from these unfair practices by unions.

The amendments protected employees' Section 7 rights from restraint or coercion by unions, and said that unions could not cause an employer to discriminate against an employee for exercising Section 7 rights. They declared the closed shop illegal, but provided that employers could sign a union shop agreement under which employees could be required to join the union on or after the 30th day of employment.

The amendments also imposed on unions the same obligation to bargain in good faith that the Wagner Act placed on employers. They prohibited secondary boycotts, making it unlawful for a union that has a primary dispute with one employer to pressure a neutral employer to stop doing business with the first employer.

Unions were prohibited from charging excessive dues or initiation fees, and from "featherbedding," or causing an employer to pay for work not performed. The new law contained a "free speech clause," providing that the expression of views, arguments, or opinions shall not be evidence of an unfair labor practice absent the threat of reprisal or promise of benefit.

Several significant changes were made for representation elections. Supervisors were excluded from bargaining units, and the Board had to give special treatment to professional employees, craftsmen, and plant guards in determining bargaining units.

Congress also added four new types of elections. The first permitted employers faced with a union's demand for recognition to seek a Board-conducted election. The other three enabled employees to obtain elections to determine whether to oust incumbent unions, whether to grant to unions authority to enter into a union shop agreement, or whether to withdraw union shop authorization previously granted. (The provisions authorizing the union shop elections were repealed in 1951.)[640]

○ **Labor organization:** "'Labor organization' means a labor organization engaged in an industry affecting commerce and includes any organization of any kind, any agency, or employee representation committee, group, association, or plan so engaged in which employees participate and which exists for the purpose, in whole or in part, of dealing with employers concerning grievances, labor disputes, wages, rates of pay, hours, or other terms or conditions of employment, and any conference, general committee, joint or system board, or joint council so engaged which is subordinate to a national or international labor organization, other than a State or local central body."[641]

○ **Labor dispute:** "'Labor dispute' includes any controversy concerning terms, tenure, or conditions of employment, or concerning the association or representation of persons in negotiating, fixing, maintaining, changing, or seeking to arrange terms or conditions of employment, regardless of whether the disputants stand in the proximate relation of employer and employee."[642]

○ **Collective bargaining rights:** "The National Labor Relations Act gives you the right to bargain collectively with your employer through a representative that you and your coworkers choose." What does that mean?

"Your union and employer must bargain in good faith about wages, hours, and other terms and conditions of employment until they agree on a labor contract or reach a stand-off or 'impasse.' If negotiations reach an impasse, an employer can impose terms and conditions so long as it offered them to the union before impasse was reached. Once a contract is in place, neither party may deviate from its terms without the other party's consent, absent extraordinary circumstances. If a contract expires before the next contract is in place, almost all the terms of the expired contract continue while the parties bargain (the exceptions being union security, management rights, no-strike/no-lockout, and arbitration provisions)."[643]

- **Unfair labor practices:** Please see the National Labor Relations Act, Sec. 8. [§ 158] (a) Unfair labor practices by employer (b) Unfair labor practices by labor organization.[644]

  - **Right to Work states:** These "27 states [plus Guam] have banned union-security agreements by passing so-called 'right to work' laws. In these states, it is up to each employee at a workplace to decide whether or not to join the union and pay dues, even though all workers are protected by the collective bargaining agreement negotiated by the union."[645]

  - *These states have passed "right to work" legislation:* Alabama, Arizona, Arkansas, Florida, Georgia, Idaho, Indiana, Iowa, Kansas, Kentucky, Louisiana, Michigan, Mississippi, Nebraska, Nevada, North Carolina, North Dakota, Oklahoma, South Carolina, South Dakota, Tennessee, Texas, Utah, Virginia, West Virginia, Wisconsin, and Wyoming.[646]

- Managers and unions
  - Organizations usually only allow employee labor relations (ELR) staff members to deal directly with union representatives. Managers must defer any union questions to the ELR staff. Additionally, the ELR staff updates unions on issues affecting rank-and-file members, such as changes in HR policies and working conditions—over which the union might have a right to negotiate before implementation. If you are in the market to hire a new ELR staff member, please look for those with the best people skills.
  - Unions can be valuable partners in helping to find solutions to an organization's challenges. You can tap into their expertise and experience, turning them from adversaries into allies.[647]

ILLUSTRATIVE STORY

Labor and management relations can be significantly enhanced through open-book management organizations. These entities, by opening their financials to unions and employees, foster a culture of collaboration and innovation. This transparency encourages the workforce to seek new ideas and ways to save money, such as by improving hotel fill rates, reducing manufacturing errors, and enhancing customer service. The resulting increase in profit can then be shared with the employees, creating a win-win situation.[648]

ILLUSTRATIVE STORY

A manufacturer in Oklahoma said all his staff members were no longer employees but entrepreneurs seeking ways to increase profits.[649] *This is a great approach as long as some of the increased profits are shared with the workers.*

ILLUSTRATIVE STORY

Shortly after arriving, a new manager, Michael, became concerned that his software help desk was inefficient. He brought in an outside expert who confirmed that the organization could significantly reduce costs by outsourcing this work. However, the 56 help desk employees were represented by a strong union. First, Michael spoke to his senior managers to get approval to outsource, showing it was a good management decision to save money. The senior managers agreed. Next, Michael briefed the union on the management's decision to outsource. Since these were government employees, Michael worked with the HR staff to help staff members find new jobs. He met weekly with the senior help desk manager to track progress in finding new jobs for outgoing staff. Michael invited union representatives to attend these meetings. By the time the help desk contract was in place, about 25% of the staff had found new jobs. The remaining staff members were temporarily assigned to other positions within the agency. It took about four months to find jobs for all the staff members. The union thanked Michael for allowing them to attend his meetings. The union members saw firsthand that Michael and his staff were working to find new jobs for their members. This action reduced the agency's help desk costs by 55%, improved the quality of help desk responses, and saved American taxpayers over $2 million yearly.

- Private sector unions
  - Private sector unions primarily negotiate for pay, benefits, job security, safety and health protections, health insurance plans, retirement plans, and protections from harassment and discrimination for all workers.[650]
  - A 2022 Gallup poll finds that 71% of Americans approve of unions, the highest percentage of approval since 1965.[651] The White House Task Force on Worker Organizing and Empowerment shows that only 10.3% of U.S. workers have union representation, a significant drop from more than 30% in the 1950s. Union workers earn up to 20% more than non-union workers.[652]
  - The largest percentage of unionization rates: 31.9% of workers are in protective service occupations, and 32.7% are in education, training, and library occupations.[653]
  - 72% of Americans ages 18 to 34 approve of unions, while only 3% are union members. This group lived through the Great Recession of 2008. Their support for unions likely comes from unaffordable housing, employment insecurity, student loan debt, etc.[654]
  - The year 2023 marked a significant shift in labor relations, witnessing the highest number of work stoppages since 2000. A total of 30 major stoppages involving 464,410 workers led to 16.7 million days of work being idle.[655]

ILLUSTRATIVE STORY

Some professional athletes have unions, such as the Major League Baseball Players Association (MLBPA). These professional baseball players voted to strike in 1994 to protest the threat of a salary cap.[656] The average MLBPA player salary in 1994 was $1.17 million.[657] In 2023, the average salary was $4.52 million.[658] After adjusting for inflation, the average baseball player's salary has doubled in real dollars.

ILLUSTRATIVE STORY

In 2018, public school teachers in West Virginia successfully voted to strike for higher wages because they could not be replaced easily. Teachers' salaries in contiguous states were as much as $20,000 per year higher.[659]

ILLUSTRATIVE STORY

In November 2021, a significant union event unfolded at Columbia University as 3,000 student workers began a 10-week strike. Columbia administrators said strikers were not guaranteed jobs if they remained on strike. This action was seen as retaliation and caused outrage.[660] The strike ended in January 2022 with an agreement for a 6% raise for contract workers, hourly rates increasing from $15 to $21, and an agreement that workers could hire independent lawyers and investigators to assess their complaints.[661]

ILLUSTRATIVE STORY

Spot Coffee in Buffalo, New York, formed a union in 2019 and went on to negotiate a significant wage increase.[662] Starbucks baristas, also in Buffalo, took note of Spot Coffee's success. In December 2021, the Buffalo Starbucks staff also voted successfully to form a union.[663] Only weeks after the Starbucks employees in Buffalo voted to unionize, about 50 other Starbucks nationwide petitioned the NLRB to unionize.[664]

In retaliation, Starbucks began firing some baristas who were union leaders. A federal judge ordered the immediate reinstatement of seven Starbucks baristas in Memphis who were fired for speaking to a local TV station about their union campaign. The unionization efforts at Starbucks have contributed to a significant increase in union election filings in 2022, including first-time companies where employees voted to form unions at Amazon, Trader Joe's, Chipotle, REI, and Apple retail stores.[665]

- Government employee unions
  - Public sector unions focus on improving working conditions.
  - In 2023, there were 7.0 million U.S. public-sector workers with union membership. This is a rate of 32.5%. By comparison, also in 2023, there were 7.4 million U.S. private sector workers with union membership. This is a rate of 6.0%.[666]

Final thoughts on unions:

- Build trust with your unions, work with them cooperatively, and treat them respectfully.[667]

- Management and unions must work together to ensure that organizations thrive.

CHAPTER 8

Excite Your Customers

Customer excitement is not just a positive emotion; it is a powerful force that can significantly improve your business's success. Excited customers act as a free sales force, constantly marketing your brand through word-of-mouth.[668] Customers are also the reason we have jobs, making it even more crucial to excite them.

> **Definition of customer:** A buyer of products or services who can select from all similar competing products and services.[669]
>
> **Definition of customer excitement:** A very positive emotional response, such as joy, delight, or surprise, when your expectations are exceeded.[670]

- How to excite your customers:
  - Hire, develop, and retain great managers and employees who have exhibited high levels of engagement. Their high engagement levels will improve your customers' experience.
  - An MIT Technology Review and Genesys report shows that 91% of companies with worldwide brand recognition, i.e., Uber, Alibaba, and Zurich Insurance, use AI to improve their customer satisfaction. This compares to 42% of all companies.[671]
  - 75% of widely recognized and admired companies, i.e., BT Global Services, Nubank, Lexus, etc., embrace corporate social responsibility (CSR) compared to 21% of low-performing companies.[672] CSR describes organizations that are self-directed to act socially responsibly in areas such as their environmental impact, i.e., reducing their carbon foot-

print; philanthropy, i.e., donating money to social causes; ethical responsibility, i.e., sustainable practices, fair labor policies; and financial responsibility, i.e., investing in green energy sources.

- Benefits of CSR include improved employee engagement, productivity, retention, and more community support and customer loyalty.[673]

ILLUSTRATIVE STORY

The carbon footprint of the U.S. Air Force is the highest among American military services and is equal to that of the country of Denmark or Portugal. Plans are underway to achieve net-zero emissions by 2046.[674]

- In one study, 67% of customers said customer satisfaction was more important than price. The same study shows that 30% of companies said lowering costs was more important than customer satisfaction. Organizations must find the right balance for their customers.[675]

- Tom Peters, a highly regarded American management writer, says that the blueprint for success is to under-promise and over-deliver.[676]

ILLUSTRATIVE STORY

For many years, I had my car repairs done by the same mechanic. Every time I dropped off the car, he would give me an estimate on the price and when the car would be ready. In all cases, the car repair bill was less than the estimate, and the car was available earlier than promised. I quickly caught on, but I liked it anyway.

ILLUSTRATIVE STORY

How would you rate this customer service experience? A customer, William, bought window repair parts from a small company with new owners. The clerk said the parts would take one to two weeks to arrive. After three weeks, William called to find out if the parts were in. They were not. After four weeks, he called again, left a message, and received no response. William called the new owner, left a polite inquiry about the parts, and again received no response. After two months, he called his credit card company to request a refund. The window parts company did not respond to an inquiry from William's credit card company. He was given a full refund since he never received the parts. William got a call nearly three months after placing his order. His window parts were in. When he went to pick them up, the clerk explained that the parts were discontinued and that he needed time to search for them by contacting other window parts suppliers online. William's customer experience would have been very different if the clerk had said the following as early as possible: "Unfortunately, the parts you want are no longer made. I am checking with other window parts suppliers to see if they still have the parts you want in stock. This may take time, so I appreciate your patience. Please call me anytime if you have any questions."

ILLUSTRATIVE STORY

My wife and I bought a dishwasher from a small appliance store. We had done our research and asked for a specific model. The salesman said that the model tested by Consumer Reports was no longer made, and the replacement model substituted some metal parts with plastic. This brought the cost of the dishwasher down so they could better compete on price. The salesman said they had customer complaints about the new model and no longer carried it. He recommended another dishwasher with an excellent maintenance record. A few months after we bought the dishwasher he recommended, we received a handwritten postcard from the salesman thanking us for buying an appliance at his store. We bought the dishwasher eight years ago, and it is still working fine. I have referred a few friends and neighbors to this appliance store.

ILLUSTRATIVE STORY

The staff at a community hospital achieved an enviable 99% customer satisfaction rating. Senior hospital staff met quarterly with representatives of various community organizations to discuss changes to hospital services and why they were necessary. The hospital CEO also invited community representatives to ask questions or express concerns, which were followed up on and resolved. At each meeting, hospital senior managers reviewed the questions and answers raised since the previous meeting. For example, while reviewing urgent care clinic data, the hospital CEO noticed that new parents sometimes brought their infants to the urgent care clinic just before the 10:00 p.m. closing time. There were instances where infants had body temperatures as high as 104 degrees. The parents should have brought the infants in much earlier in the day. A body temperature that high requires immediate medical attention. Clinicians know that body temperatures often go higher as the day progresses. After consulting with the hospital staff, the CEO closed the urgent care clinic at 6:00 p.m. Another nearby hospital maintained an emergency room, so there was always an emergency option. As soon as the new hours were instituted, the urgent care clinic saw a drop in infant patients with extremely high temperatures. When the CEO explained his decision at the quarterly meeting, he emphasized that new parents do their best but do not always make the right decisions. The new hours helped remedy this situation by eliminating the option for parents to wait until later at night to bring their infants in for treatment. Everyone at the meeting agreed with the decision. Many were nodding their heads. Keeping customers updated on hospital changes and quick responses to customer questions and concerns was key to their high satisfaction rating.

A final thought on customer delight

- As Bill Gates says, you learn the most from unhappy customers.[677]

CHAPTER 9

How to Be the Best Manager Possible

In a worldwide survey of over a million employees, Gallup researchers found that highly accomplished employees need effective managers. These overachievers may join organizations for their great pay and benefits, generous telework policies, etc. However, how long they remain and how productive they are is based on their relationship with their immediate boss.[678] To be an effective manager, you must do everything possible to help your employees succeed. You can learn how to become an effective manager. This book tells you how.

9.1 WHAT IT TAKES TO BE THE BEST MANAGER POSSIBLE

Be the best manager possible. Do everything possible to make your employees successful. As an effective manager, you must hire, develop, and retain great employees; give them flexibility in their work hours and place of work; ensure they have adequate resources; hire people with dissimilar backgrounds so they challenge each other to do their best; empower them; give them motivation, mentoring, and training; grow employees through future-focused coaching that includes the creation and tracking of mutually agreed-upon performance expectations that includes goals and objectives that align with the organization's goals and objectives; establish accountability for results; treat them as partners; share responsibilities with them; always show respect; give them choices to learn and grow; and use every tool in this book. When appropriate, give them recognition and appreciation, i.e., thank you. Then please stay out of their way. Always remember that if anything goes badly, managers take all the blame. If anything goes well, employees get all the credit.

- What effective managers do:
  - Priority #1 is to achieve positive results,[679] but you must follow the guidance in the paragraph above to have the best results.
  - Provide employees with competitive pay and benefits (Chapter 1).
  - Hire, develop, and retain great employees (Chapter 2).
  - Be an effective manager at work (Chapter 3).
  - Use all these managers' tools (Chapter 4).
  - Partner with your peers (Chapter 5).
  - Partner with your bosses (Chapter 6).
  - Partner with your unions (Chapter 7).
  - Excite your customers (Chapter 8).
  - Be the best manager possible (Chapter 9).
  - Create the best organization possible (Chapter 10).
  - Grow your direct reports through performance development, an approach based on future-focused coaching that allows the creation and tracking of mutually agreed-upon performance expectations to include goals and objectives that align with the organization's goals and objectives, establishes employee accountability for results, and gives employees autonomy.[680] Please see Section 2.4, Performance Development, for more information. An essential part of your help to your direct reports takes place in your weekly coaching meetings. Please see Section 2.2, Coaching and Mentoring, for more information on the importance of coaching.
  - Do not merely react—plan. Effective managers create plans and revise them along the way. These plans include goals and objectives for themselves and their direct reports. The plans should be linked to your organization's strategic plan and discussed at coaching meetings. Without plans, you are directionless.

- Give your employees appropriate compensation, benefits, and perks. For more information, please see Section 1.2, What Employees Want.

- Involve your staff in decision-making.

ILLUSTRATIVE STORY

Jeanne, the CEO of a community hospital, arrived the week after a scheduled inspection by The Joint Commission (TJC). TJC is the accrediting organization for all U.S. hospitals and clinics. The departing CEO and two department heads had recently been fired, and the hospital was in complete chaos. Staff morale was as low as it could be. TJC completed its inspection as scheduled, only a few days before Jeanne's arrival. The result was 18 Type-1 write-ups. One Type-1 write-up is damaging, but 18 threatened to shut down the hospital. This would have been disastrous for the community that relied on this hospital. Jeanne immediately created 18 committees—one to address each Type-1 write-up. Each staff member was on at least one committee, with some on several. Some Type-1 write-ups overlapped, and committees could work on them together. Jeanne attended numerous committee meetings to show support but sat in the back of the room and never spoke. She wanted staff to find their own solutions. The TJC team returned after eight months to examine progress. During the TJC in-briefing, each committee chair provided input on the hospital's progress. At the end of the in-depth three-hour briefing, the senior TJC inspector rose from her chair and said, "This is the most remarkable turnaround of a hospital I have seen in 15 years. Your hospital accreditation is extended for the full three years." The re-inspection was scheduled to take two days, but the satisfied inspection team left immediately after the in-brief. Jeanne gave all the credit to the staff for this success.

- Nurture the great potential in every employee because they all have it. Harvard psychologist Robert Rosenthal and an elementary school principal, Lenore Jacobson, *randomly* identified some elementary school students as having the greatest academic potential. Their teachers were told that these students were exceptional and gave the selected students more attention. Four years later, the selected students' test results continued to show higher scores than their classmates, reflecting their teachers' extra attention rather than their innate abilities. The teacher's belief in the student's ability became self-fulfilling.[681]

- Every one of your employees has the potential to be great, and you have the potential to be a great manager. As Mark Twain said, "Keep away from people who try to belittle your ambitions. Small people always do that, but the really great make you feel you, too, can be great."[682]

○ Always let your staff make as many decisions about their work and environment as possible. If you want someone to implement a new program enthusiastically, let them do it their way and credit them for every idea and achievement. People are slow to implement the ideas of others.

○ Nothing beats timely and heartfelt words of praise. They are free and priceless.[683]

○ Set high standards for quality and live by them. If you do not set high standards for the quality of your employees' work, who will?

○ Motivate, recognize, and show appreciation to your staff. Thank you. For more information, please see Section 3.8, Motivation, Recognition, and Appreciation.

○ Know your employees' strengths. Gallup research shows that employees who use their strengths daily are six times more likely to be engaged at work and three times more likely to say they have an excellent quality of life.[684] For more information on employee engagement, please see Section 3.6, Employee Engagement.

○ Encourage your staff to look for ways to improve their performance.

- Suggest to your direct hires to check out best practices in your industry and attend conferences to find new ideas.

- Effective managers also work with each direct report in coaching meetings to help them raise their performance bar. You can ask coaching questions like, "Do you see any way to reduce costs?" For more information, please see Section 2.2, Coaching and Mentoring.

- Finally, you can arrange for your staff to participate in electronic brainstorming meetings. Electronic brainstorming meetings of four or fewer members have no performance advantages over face-to-face meetings, but electronic brainstorming meetings with six or more participants have proven successful. As the size of these groups increases, the productivity of electronic brainstorming meetings improves.[685] For more information on electronic brainstorming meetings, please see Section 4.3, Meetings.

○ Delegate as much work to your staff as possible. For more information, please see Section 3.5, Delegation and Empowerment, and Section 4.11, Time Management.

○ Know where you spend your time. For more information, please see Section 4.11, Time Management. Ninety percent of managers waste time in unproductive activities.[686]

○ Address poor performance as soon as possible. A KEYGroup Consulting survey found that employees rated a mere 31% of managers as confronting poor performance.[687] That means that 69% of managers are not addressing poor performance and should not be managers. For more information, please see Section 2.7, Problem Employees.

○ Limit your work week to no more than 50 hours and ensure that none of your employees works more than 50 hours per week. A 2013 Stanford University study shows that 50 hours per week is the maximum number of hours in which you can be fully productive.[688] If you work late, some employees will feel they must stay at the office, too. For more information on getting the most from your working hours, please see Section 4.11, Time Management.

- Give your employees praise and recognition. A Gallup survey of 4 million employees worldwide across more than 30 industries shows that *praise* and *recognition* increase employee engagement, productivity, and retention.[689] For more information, please see Section 3.8, Motivation, Recognition, and Appreciation, and Section 3.6, Employee Engagement.

- Prioritize your work and do your must-do items first.

  - Excite your customers and seek feedback to improve. Please see Chapter 8, Excite Your Customers, for more information.

  - Engage in big-picture thinking: Work with your direct reports to create goals, objectives, and milestones that align with the corporate strategy. Please see Section 3.11, Strategic Planning, for more information.

- Focus on staff:

  - Hire and retain great people by following the guidance in Section 2.1, Hire and Retain Great Employees. Be sure to always perform background and reference checks.

  - Coach and mentor your direct reports by following the guidance in Section 2.2, Coaching and Mentoring.

- Provide regularly scheduled feedback to your boss(es) using the performance measurements from your staff. Your boss(es) will not need the same level of detail as you, nor will they need updates on all the subjects you receive. Please see Section 2.4, Performance Development, and Chapter 6, Partner with Your Bosses (Okay, You're the Junior Partner), for more information.

- For all other work, ask yourself: Is it necessary?

> **ILLUSTRATIVE STORY**
> *At one organization, an eager new employee completed a report
> and gave it to her boss. The boss did nothing with the report for
> a few weeks. The employee asked her boss if he had forwarded it
> to the corporate office. The experienced boss smiled and said the
> report was no longer necessary. Since the corporate-level office
> had not asked for it well past the due date, it was all the proof the
> boss needed to stop turning in these reports.*

- Always do your best. Soon, it will become a habit. "I do the very best I know how—the very best I can; and I mean to keep doing so until the end."[690] —Abraham Lincoln, 16th President of the United States

  - How long does it take to develop a stable, long-term habit? According to a study published in the *European Journal of Social Psychology*, the average is 66 days. The range is between 18 and 254 days and depends on the person, the circumstances, and the behavior.[691]

- Ensure that your employees take all their vacation days every year—no exceptions. In Section 1.2, What Employees Want, we learned that over half of U.S. employees do not take all their vacation days each year for fear of being let go. You want your employees to take their vacation days, so they return to work with renewed energy. Encouraging employees to take all their vacation days will also dramatically improve their productivity, morale, and retention at no cost.

- Always reserve your opinion until you have heard all sides of an issue. You do not want to be biased or even appear to be biased.

- Always provide your staff with *good top cover*. Managers provide good top cover when they ensure that no one outside their immediate organization interferes with their employees or their work.

- Never accept perks that are not offered to everyone. Here are a few examples.

ILLUSTRATIVE STORY

At one organization, the CEO had a "reserved" parking space. This was no ordinary parking space. This CEO parked in an accessible space. Everyone knew it was his personal parking space. The CEO was not a person with a disability and did not qualify for an accessible space. This space, like most accessible parking spaces, was the parking space closest to the rear entrance to the building. Why did the CEO park in an accessible parking space? If a company offers a designated parking space, the user of that space must pay taxes on the value of that space. To avoid paying taxes, the CEO parked in an accessible space. In this scenario, there were four accessible parking spaces next to each other. No one ever parked in the other accessible parking spaces, even if they had a disability parking pass, for fear of offending the CEO. One of the employees, a military veteran with severe disabilities, had major surgery for a service-related injury. This surgery required the veteran to use crutches for six months. He chose to park in one of the vacant accessible spaces because his surgeon had given him a disability parking pass, allowing him to do this. When the CEO saw the veteran in the accessible parking space, he berated him for parking there. Several times, he shouted, "You have no right to park there." Ironically, the military veteran with severe disabilities had a right to park in an accessible parking space, but the CEO did not.

ILLUSTRATIVE STORY

Use whatever office supplies are available to everyone else in the organization. Never order any expensive office supplies for yourself. Over the years, I have had bosses who ordered expensive office supplies, often pens, which cost much more than those offered to the rest of the staff. In every case, the rest of the staff learned about these purchases within days and rolled their eyes.

ILLUSTRATIVE STORY

Under no circumstances should you ask any of your employees to run an errand for you or any other personal request. This is often a violation of company rules. If not, it should state in your employee handbook that providing personal assistance to managers is prohibited.

○ Collaborate and negotiate. Do not try to dominate those around you. The notion that strong, domineering managers are more effective has been discredited. Effective managers collaborate, negotiate, and understand that no one has all the answers.[692]

○ Do not tolerate your direct report supervisors who are responsive and even solicitous to you but treat their employees badly. This *kiss-up, kick-down management style* is very destructive.[693] How do you find out about this type of behavior? As an effective and trusted manager, people will tell you all about it because they know you will discreetly fix the problem without using their names.

○ Learn and maintain technical competence. As a manager, you will gain an understanding of your employees' jobs over time. Asking your employees questions will enhance your expertise and let them know you are interested in their work. Please ask politely and thank them for their advice.

> ***ILLUSTRATIVE STORY***
>
> *In one software development organization, an inquisitive manager, Sarah, met individually with senior code writers to get to know them and their products better. In these discussions, she learned that all of the code writers were convinced that their largest software product would continue to fail often. They explained that there was no solution except to start over. Sarah asked why they continued to work there if the flagship product would continue to fail. Each of them said that the pay and benefits were very good, so they chose to stay. Several of them also commented that they were surprised that no one had ever asked them about the long-term viability of their largest product. Since the top leadership was not interested in what the code writers had to say, Sarah quit. A few years later, she was not surprised to learn that the corporate board decided to start over with the largest product.*

○ In the United States Marine Corps, *officers eat last.* They put the needs of their enlisted men and women above their own at all times.[694] Effective managers should follow their example by doing everything they can to ensure their employees succeed. If your employees are successful, you will be successful.

- Follow the Golden Rule: "Do unto others as you would have them do unto you." All major religions and cultures, from ancient times to today, embrace this rule.

- Outstanding personal qualities that help managers succeed:

  - Be a giver (up to a point). In his bestseller, *Give and Take: Why Helping Others Drives Our Success* (Penguin, 2013), Dr. Adam Grant identifies three types of people in the workplace: givers, takers, and matchers. These three groups differ in how they deal with others. Takers like to take more than they give. The largest group, matchers, will help others but expect help in return. Givers, the smallest group by far, help others without expecting return favors. Surprisingly, givers end up on both ends of the success continuum. Givers help by mentoring others, are quick to share credit, and are happy to make connections for others. They also selflessly help others while building trust and goodwill. Givers at the bottom of the success continuum are far too generous at the expense of their own productivity.[695]

    - Dr. Grant's bestseller is a remarkable book that gives you practical advice on how to work effectively with others and reach the top of your organization. You will also understand why Dr. Grant is an award-winning researcher, author of six *New York Times* #1 bestsellers, and Wharton's highest-rated professor.

  - Have high emotional intelligence.

> **Definition of emotional intelligence:** Emotional intelligence is the capacity to recognize and manage your emotions and those of others.[696] You can learn to improve your emotional intelligence, and it is an important factor in determining success in life.

- Learn to recognize the emotions you are feeling. When you can name them, you better understand what you are feeling. You can then regulate your emotions by thinking before acting. The book *Emotional Intelligence 2.0* (TalentSmart, 2009) teaches you strategies to increase your emotional intelligence. You begin by taking the Emotional Intelligence Appraisal online to create a baseline. You can then review the 66 strategies in the book to improve your score over time. Please note that each *Emotional Intelligence 2.0* book contains one password that is only good for one use. If you are not the first owner of this book, the password will likely have already been used.[697]

- Be ethical.

> **Definition of ethics:** Moral principles that govern our behavior and say what is and is not acceptable.

ILLUSTRATIVE STORY
Air Force officers and enlisted men and women are taught that just following laws and regulations is not enough. They are taught that they must avoid even the appearance of impropriety.

- "Wrong is wrong, even if everyone is doing it. Right is right, even if no one is doing it."[698] —William Penn, founder of Pennsylvania as a place where people could enjoy religious freedom. His colony became a sanctuary for minority religious sects from Germany, Great Britain, Holland, and Scandinavia.

- Be reserved, even shy.[699] Let the spotlight always be on your employees.

- Be forgiving. None of us is perfect. Also, take the blame if anything fails. The great French philosopher Voltaire said, "Common sense is not so common."[700]

- Be humble. "Let nothing be done through strife or vainglory; but in lowliness of mind let each esteem others better than themselves." —King James Bible, Philippians 2:3

o Be humble. "The servants of the Most Merciful are those who walk upon the earth in humility, and when the ignorant address them, they say words of peace." —Verse 25:63 of the Quran, also known as Surah Al-Furqan

o Acknowledge mistakes and accept criticism graciously.[701]

o Be self-effacing (do not draw attention to yourself).[702] Always credit your employees for all successes, even if you made a major contribution to them. Never take credit for anything unless something goes badly. Think of this as part of your job description.

o Have stamina. Stamina is grit, passion, perseverance, effort, and determination. Make a decision and never stop until it is completed successfully. As Mark Twain said, "The secret of getting ahead is getting started. The secret of getting started is breaking your complex overwhelming tasks into small manageable tasks and starting on the first one."[703]

o Put effort into your work. Without effort, you achieve nothing, even if you have education, talent, and potential. As Alexander Hamilton said, "People sometimes attribute my success to my genius; all the genius I know anything about is hard work."[704]

o Have empathy (understanding others' feelings and thoughts). Empathy improves human connections and is learnable. Appreciate others' views and backgrounds. Listen carefully to your employees. Example: "You sound worried. How can I help you?"[705] Then, do everything you can to help.

o Give your employees updates on their questions and concerns so they do not think you have forgotten them. If you enjoy helping others, you are in the right job. The Confucian term, *ren*, which translates today as empathy, is to feel the needs of others and to act accordingly. Empathy is the founding pillar of Confucian ethics.[706]

- Be optimistic. Optimism is contagious. As Winston Churchill says, "a pessimist sees the difficulty in every opportunity; the optimist sees the opportunity in every difficulty."[707]

- Do not micromanage your staff. One very irritating way that managers micromanage is by having too many meetings. Even with all the stresses of the American Civil War, President Lincoln was an excellent example of a manager leaving his generals and cabinet secretaries alone to do their jobs.[708]

- Lead by example.

ILLUSTRATIVE STORY

If anything fails, take all the blame. General Dwight Eisenhower, Supreme Commander of the Allied Expeditionary Force, understood that he must take the blame if anything went wrong and give all the credit to his troops when things went well. During World War II, just before the D-Day invasion, General Eisenhower wrote a message to broadcast should the invasion fail. It reads, "Our landings in the Cherbourg-Havre area have failed to gain a satisfactory foothold, and I have withdrawn the troops. My decision to attack at this time and place was based on the best information available. The troops, the air, and the navy did all that bravery and devotion to duty could do. If any blame or fault attaches to the attempt, it is mine alone."[709] The mission was successful, but this handwritten note shows that Eisenhower was ready to take all the blame if the D-Day invasion failed.

ILLUSTRATIVE STORY

Jack stopped by Stephanie's office for advice. He was recently hired to be a manager. Jack would now manage his former peers, so he was anxious to ensure they would accept him as their new boss. Stephanie agreed that managing former peers can be challenging. She suggested that Jack meet one-on-one with other applicants for his new job, ask about any changes they had planned to make if they had been chosen, and offer to try to implement their ideas and give them credit. After speaking with each new employee, Jack returned to Stephanie's office with a big smile. His former peers appreciated him reaching out to them. About a month later, Jack came to Stephanie's office with another problem. Before being chosen for the new position, he and his peers occasionally met for drinks after work. Now that he was in charge, he felt he could no longer join them. Stephanie said that if Jack did not attend, his staff might believe he now thinks he is too good to be around them in a social setting. She recommended that Jack show up on time, greet each person as they arrive, buy them a drink, and make small talk about anything but work. Stephanie also said he should leave after an hour. Jack agreed to go but could not understand why he should leave after an hour. Stephanie said that as a junior military officer, she was instructed to attend all non-commissioned officer functions to which she was invited and always depart after one hour. After more than an hour and a few drinks, your enlisted personnel may say things you do not want to hear. Following the event, Jack returned to Stephanie's office to update her on how things went. He said he showed up on time, greeted each person as they arrived, bought each a drink, and asked about their families or hobbies. After an hour, he stood up and said, "I need to leave now so you can talk about me." Stephanie laughed and said that his parting remark was not in her script.

○ Be cheerful and smile often. The act of smiling creates a positive feeling. Even though the smile is not genuine, your brain does not know that, and you feel good anyway. You can teach yourself to be cheerful and smile. It will have a positive effect on you and those around you.[710] Begin smiling as you enter your office and greet each employee by name the first time you see them. Say goodnight to each employee by name. In no time, this will become natural to you. Smiling can elevate your mood, is contagious, and helps you stay positive.[711] As Mark Twain said, "The best way to cheer yourself up is to cheer someone else up."[712]

○ Be friendly, but not friends, with your staff. For example, do not single out any employees for lunches or coffee breaks. If you want to go to lunch with someone, ask one of your peers. Please see Chapter 5, Partner with Your Peers, for more information.

ILLUSTRATIVE STORY

The director of finance became too friendly with his deputy. Both were avid sports fans of the same teams. They often met at each other's houses to watch sports. The senior of the two noted that the deputy's performance was dropping. As a result, he did not plan to give him a bonus. The finance director's boss, Lauren, replied that their friendship outside the workplace could have contributed to the deputy's performance drop. She advised the senior of the two to keep a professional distance between himself and his employee. As stated above, you should be friendly, but not friends, with your employees. Lauren overruled the director of finance and gave his deputy a bonus.

○ "The single most important ingredient in the formula for success is knowing how to get along with people."[713] —Theodore Roosevelt, 20th President of the United States

○ Model good behavior. Never gossip. You can always find something kind to say about each person or say nothing. Your staff sees you and hears everything you say. You are always on stage performing. Make sure to give them a good show. "All the world's a stage, and all the men and women merely players . . . " —William Shakespeare, from *As You Like It*, Act 2, Scene 7, spoken by Jacques[714]

- ○ Listen more than you speak. "Wisdom is the reward you get for a lifetime of listening when you'd rather have been talking."[715] —Aristotle, Greek philosopher (384–322 BCE)

- ○ Communicate clearly. Tell your staff the good and bad news clearly and with compassion.

- ○ Be consistent and treat everyone the same.

A final thought on what it takes to be the best manager possible:

- As Sam Walton, founder of Walmart and Sam's Club, says, employees treat their customers exactly how their bosses treat them.[716]

9.2 HAPPINESS AND PRODUCTIVITY

"Happiness depends more upon the internal frame of a person's own mind than on the externals in the world."[717] —George Washington, 1st President of the United States

Oxford University research shows that happy employees are 13% more productive than unhappy ones.[718]

Recent research in positive psychology and neuroscience confirms that developing positive brains increases our creativity, efficiency, motivation, and resilience, which improves our productivity.[719]

- Each of us can create our own happiness. Sonja Lyubomirsky, a professor in the Department of Psychology at the University of California, Riverside, and a leading researcher in the scientific study of well-being, prefers the term *creating happiness* rather than *chasing happiness* because research shows that we create happiness from within.[720]

  - Monks spend years meditating and expanding their left prefrontal cortex, which is the area of the brain primarily responsible for happiness. Anyone can achieve the same results. Close your eyes and sense your breath go in and out for five minutes daily. Your entire focus should be on breathing, while you tune out everything else. Remain silent and patient. If you're a beginner, you may find your mind wandering. If so, gently refocus on your breathing. Meditation is a powerful way to create happiness and lower stress. Other ways to create happiness include looking forward to something, performing acts of kindness, filling your surroundings with positivity, exercising, spending money on experiences (not stuff), and doing something you do well (like being a very effective manager).[721]

  - Numerous studies find a strong link between being outdoors and mental health.[722] Not all of us can work outdoors, but office designs can increase natural light, add plants, add bird chirping sounds, and much more. Please see Section 4.5, Physical Work Environment, for more information on bringing nature into your offices.

- The Sydney-based Happiness Institute suggests that happiness requires practicing a few simple but powerful disciplines daily:

  - Think optimistically. You can train yourself to find and question unhelpful thoughts and replace them with more optimistic ones.

  - Improve relationships. Happy people have better-quality relationships. You can practice this by learning to help others.

  - Clarify your goals and execute them, and using your strengths will give you a sense of achievement and happiness.[723]

- Enjoy the present moment. You can only experience happiness in the present moment or the "now." Unhappiness comes from too much time thinking about the past and the future.[724] "Do not dwell in the past; do not dream of the future, concentrate the mind on the present moment."[725] —The Buddha, founder of Buddhism, 6th or 5th century BCE

ILLUSTRATIVE STORY

I spent a week at a monastery nearly 50 years ago. The monks gathered several times each day for meditation and prayers. One of the monks' jobs was to clean the guest rooms. His schedule was the same every day. While working, he had no reason to dwell on the past or the future. He was living in the now. After almost 50 years, I still remember his big smile as he cleaned the guest rooms.

- The world's longest study on happiness, ongoing at 80 years, concludes that the happiest, healthiest, and longest-lived are those with the strongest relationships.[726] Since we spend many waking hours at work, having your peers as friends is a win-win.

- Managing by chocolate.

  - A University of Warwick, UK, study shows a link between happiness and productivity. In one experiment, workers who were given chocolate, fruit, and drinks were happier, and the increase in happiness made them more productive.[727]

  - Keep a bowl of assorted wrapped chocolates on your desk and encourage staff to help themselves even if you are not there. Even extreme introverts will stop by for a piece of their favorite chocolate.

    - Your office will be less threatening, and people will feel more comfortable talking with you.

    - Chocolate is a great conversation starter because almost everyone has a favorite type of chocolate.

      ILLUSTRATIVE STORY

      At one organization, Nicholas, a well-liked and very efficient administrative officer, teleworked four days per week. He only liked one type of chocolate, and his boss was sometimes out of it. The creative senior manager took a nondescript empty binder, attached a plastic document protector, and labeled it, "Misc. Budget Documents, 2018." This would ensure that no one would ever pull it off the shelf. Then, the senior official filled it with Nicholas's favorite chocolate and told him where to find it. It put a smile on Nicholas's face. About a year later, when the senior manager retired, she presented Nicholas with a binder full of his favorite chocolate.

ILLUSTRATIVE STORY

One senior manager, Elizabeth, kept a bowl of individually wrapped chocolates in the corner of her desk near the door. If anyone wanted chocolate, they could grab some without disturbing her. She refilled the bowl often and gave out more than 250 pounds of chocolate each year. Often, people from outside her office stopped by for chocolate. In time, they trusted Elizabeth for advice and sometimes would vent about their offices. She never repeated anything she was told. Chocolate never fails to put a smile on people's faces. Everyone seems to have a favorite type. Elizabeth's office was consistently recognized as the best in the organization.

ILLUSTRATIVE STORY

Christine Lagarde, president of the European Central Bank, understands the value of chocolate in tense negotiations. People often call her Madame M&Ms. When she was the French finance minister, Ms. Lagarde sometimes had to negotiate late into the evening or overnight. In the small hours of the morning, everyone was starving. At that point, Ms. Lagarde passed around large bags of M&Ms, making negotiations easier.[728]

Final thoughts on happiness:

- "Those are happiest who do the most for others."[729] —Booker T. Washington, American author, orator, and educator

- "Happiness is not a goal; it is a by-product. Paradoxically, the one sure way not to be happy is deliberately to map out a way of life in which one would please oneself completely and exclusively."[730] —Eleanor Roosevelt, an American political crusader, activist, and diplomat

- You are in the right job if helping your employees succeed makes you happy.

9.3 **CREATING A POSITIVE WORK ENVIRONMENT**

Effective managers must advocate for their employees' interests to ensure they can do their jobs without interference (provide *good top cover*), that their workplaces are comfortable, and that they are able to realize their ambitions.[731]

- Managers are the primary players in creating a positive work environment. They drive 70% of a team's engagement.[732]
  - What percentage of employers think their employees leave for more money? Answer: 89%. What percent of employees leave for more money? Answer: 12%.[733]
  - In 1998, almost 50% of those surveyed said they were treated discourteously at least once a month. This percentage increased to 55% in 2011 and to 62% by 2016. There is more than one reason for this increase. The primary attribute that earned engagement and commitment from employees was *respect* from managers.[734]
    - In a 2025 Gallup poll, only 37% of responders said they are treated with respect at work.[735]

    ILLUSTRATIVE STORY
    During my more than 50 working years, I had 25 to 30 bosses. About two in three were effective, and the rest were less so. If you've been in the workforce long enough, your experience may be similar. A remarkable 84% of workers blame badly trained managers for generating needless stress and work.[736] These managers are not bad people; they just don't know what they're doing, but many think they're doing great. That is the reason I wrote this book. It is based on a large body of current behavioral research and my 45 years as a successful manager. This book tells you what to do and how to do it. It shows you how to be an effective manager and create a positive work environment.

Final thoughts on creating a positive work environment:

- "We can complain because rose bushes have thorns, or rejoice because thorn bushes have roses."[737] —Abraham Lincoln, 16th President of the United States

- "The positive thinker sees the invisible, feels the intangible, and achieves the impossible."[738] —Winston Churchill, British statesman, writer, and soldier

CHAPTER 10

How to Build the Best Organization Possible

This chapter offers effective options for improving recruiting, morale, retention, and productivity. The best organizations offer these to their employees, most of which are free or low-cost.

- Please look at the chapter titles below and see if any involve significant expenses. The answer is "no," except for offering competitive pay and the "big three" benefits described in Section 1.2, What Employees Want. You must offer competitive pay and benefits or lose employees to organizations that do. Now, does any other subject below have a hefty price tag? The answer is no. Throwing money at a problem rarely works.
  - Provide employees with competitive pay and benefits (Chapter 1).
  - Hire, develop, and retain great employees (Chapter 2).
  - Be an effective manager at work (Chapter 3).
  - Use all these managers' tools (Chapter 4).
  - Partner with your peers (Chapter 5).
  - Partner with your bosses (Chapter 6).
  - Partner with your unions (Chapter 7).
  - Excite your customers (Chapter 8).
  - Be the best manager possible (Chapter 9).
  - Create the best organization possible (Chapter 10).
- Effective organizations are safe, fair, and tolerant workplaces. These attributes cost nothing and improve recruiting, morale, retention, and productivity.

○ Do not tolerate harassment.

> **Definition of harassment:** According to the U.S. Equal Employment Opportunity Commission, "Harassment is unwelcome conduct that is based on race, color, religion, sex (including sexual orientation, gender identity, or pregnancy), national origin, older age (beginning at age 40), disability, or genetic information (including family medical history)."
>
> Furthermore, "Harassment becomes unlawful where 1) enduring the offensive conduct becomes a condition of continued employment, or 2) the conduct is severe or pervasive enough to create a work environment that a reasonable person would consider intimidating, hostile, or abusive. Anti-discrimination laws also prohibit harassment against individuals in retaliation for filing a discrimination charge, testifying, or participating in any way in an investigation, proceeding, or lawsuit under these laws; or opposing employment practices that they reasonably believe discriminate against individuals, in violation of these laws."
>
> "Petty slights, annoyances, and isolated incidents (unless extremely serious) will not rise to the level of illegality. To be unlawful, the conduct must create a work environment that would be intimidating, hostile, or offensive to reasonable people."
>
> "Offensive conduct may include, but is not limited to, offensive jokes, slurs, epithets or name calling, physical assaults or threats, intimidation, ridicule or mockery, insults or put-downs, offensive objects or pictures, and interference with work performance. Harassment can occur in a variety of circumstances, including, but not limited to, the following:
>
> - The harasser can be the victim's supervisor, a supervisor in another area, an agent of the employer, a co-worker, or a non-employee.
> - The victim does not have to be the person harassed, but can be anyone affected by the offensive conduct.
> - Unlawful harassment may occur without economic injury to, or discharge of, the victim."
>
> "Prevention is the best tool to eliminate harassment in the workplace. Employers are encouraged to take appropriate steps to prevent and correct unlawful harassment. They should clearly communicate to employees that unwelcome harassing conduct will not be tolerated. They can do this by establishing an effective complaint or grievance process, providing

anti-harassment training to their managers and employees, and taking immediate and appropriate action when an employee complains. Employers should strive to create an environment in which employees feel free to raise concerns and are confident that those concerns will be addressed."

"Employees are encouraged to inform the harasser directly that the conduct is unwelcome and must stop. Employees should also report harassment to management at an early stage to prevent its escalation."[739] See more information on harassment at https://www.eeoc.gov/harassment.

- "Harassment is a form of employment discrimination that violates Title VII of the Civil Rights Act of 1964, the Age Discrimination in Employment Act of 1967, (ADEA), and the Americans with Disabilities Act of 1990, (ADA)."[740]

- Significant hostile work environment harassment court case. "Notice Concerning the Supreme Court's Decision in Vance v. Ball State University, 133 S. Ct. 2434 (2013). The standard for employer liability for hostile work environment harassment depends typically on whether or not the harasser is the victim's supervisor. An employer is vicariously liable for a hostile work environment created by a supervisor. In Vance v. Ball State University, 133 S. Ct. 2434 (2013), the Supreme Court rejected in part the EEOC's definition of "supervisor." The Court held that an employee is a 'supervisor' if the employer has empowered that employee to take tangible employment actions against the victim, i.e., to effect a significant change in employment status, such as hiring, firing, failing to promote, reassignment with significantly different responsibilities, or a decision causing a significant change in benefits." The Court stated that an employer is liable for hostile work environment harassment by employees who are not supervisors if the employer was 'negligent in failing to prevent harassment from taking place.' In assessing such negligence, the Court explained, 'the nature and degree of authority wielded by the harasser is an important factor to be considered in determining whether the employer was negligent.' Also relevant is '[e]vidence that an employer did not monitor the workplace, failed to respond to complaints, failed to provide a system for registering complaints, or effectively discouraged complaints from being filed.' "[741]

- Significant sexual harassment court cases. Two sexual harassment cases are *Faragher v. City of Boca Raton* (1998) and *Burlington Industries v. Ellerth* (1998). These cases established a standard of liability, the U.S. Supreme Court asserting that "an employer is responsible for the acts of its supervisors," and "employers should be encouraged to prevent harassment . . . "[742]

- Forms of harassment. According to a 2022 Gallup survey of 74,000 people worldwide, 23% of employees have experienced harassment or violence at work in their lives. These include psychological violence and harassment, i.e., bullying, insults, intimidation, and threats; physical violence and harassment, i.e., hitting, spitting, or restraining; and sexual violence and harassment, i.e., unwanted comments, emails, pictures, requests, or sexual touching. 55% of the workplace assault and harassment victims never told anyone about what happened to them. They felt it would be pointless.[743]

- What needs to change? In one survey, HR professionals said the two top factors that can stop sexual harassment are changes in workplace culture (75% of respondents checked this category) (see Section 3.10, Organizational Culture) and senior management commitment (69% of respondents checked this category).[744]

- Are harassment complaints being handled satisfactorily? In a SourceMedia survey, less than half of respondents think harassment is handled satisfactorily. Women who experienced the most grievous forms of unwelcome sexual harassment and violence are the least confident that organizations in their industry will take appropriate action.[745]

- U.S. women's experience with harassment. A *Wall Street Journal/NBC News* poll showed that 48% of working women in the U.S. said they had experienced verbal or physical harassment or unwelcome sexual advances at work.[746]

- Types of workplace sexual misconduct. An Employment Law Alliance study showed that 43% of survey respondents scored "language, jokes, and teasing" an 8 or 9 on a scale of 0 to 10 (with 10 being high) as the most widespread workplace sexual misconduct. This was followed by "comments about looks, dress, or physical appearance" and then "flirting and sexual advances." The same survey found that 81% of respondents said their in-house HR staff was only "somewhat competent" enough to conduct internal investigations about misconduct complaints.[747]

- Sexual relationships between managers and their employees. Legal claims may result from consensual sexual relationships between managers and their employees. The employee may assert that they agreed to the sexual behavior due to threats of negative repercussions for refusing, another person may claim that the sexual relationship resulted in favorable treatment by the manager, and if this sexual relationship deteriorates, the employee may assert that the resulting unfavorable treatment by the manager is retaliatory. For consensual relationships, the organization's management should redistribute job duties to avoid real or perceived advantages or disadvantages to the employee.[748] Organizational management should strongly consider adding a statement to their employee handbooks requiring managers to disclose or prohibit their romantic or sexual relationships with their employees. Please see Section 4.1, Employee Handbook, for more information.

- An increase in non-fraternization policies. In the #MeToo era, more companies are adding non-fraternization policies prohibiting intimate relationships or workplace romances among employees with different power, status, or influence levels. Debra Katz, a lawyer representing employees in workplace harassment cases, said she has been involved in many cases of sexual harassment that began as consensual.[749]

○ Do not tolerate sex discrimination.

> **Definition of sex discrimination:** According to the U.S. Equal Employment Opportunity Commission: "Sex discrimination involves treating someone (an applicant or employee) unfavorably because of that person's sex, including the person's sexual orientation, gender identity, or pregnancy."
>
> "Discrimination against an individual because of gender identity, including transgender status, or because of sexual orientation is discrimination because of sex in violation of Title VII."[750] See more information on sex-based discrimination at https://www.eeoc.gov/sex-based-discrimination.

- Statistics on sex discrimination. In 1997, 24,728 sex discrimination cases were filed, according to the EEOC. This was 30.7% of all discrimination cases filed in 1997. By fiscal year 2023, the number of sex discrimination cases was 25,473, representing 31.4% of all discrimination cases filed that year. These numbers, of course, only reflect formally filed cases.[751]

- Significant sex discrimination court case. A sex discrimination case is Bostock v. Clayton County (2020). The United States Supreme Court held that "An employer who fires an individual merely for being gay or transgender violates Title VII" of the Civil Rights Act of 1964.[752]

○ Do not tolerate race/color discrimination.

> **Definition of race/color discrimination:** According to the U.S. Equal Employment Opportunity Commission: "Race discrimination involves treating someone (an applicant or employee) unfavorably because he/she is of a certain race or because of personal characteristics associated with race (such as hair texture, skin color, or certain facial features)."
>
> "Color discrimination involves treating someone unfavorably because of skin color complexion. Race/color discrimination can also involve treating someone unfavorably because the person is married to (or associated with) a person of a certain race or color. Discrimination can occur when the victim and the person who inflicted the discrimination are of the same race or color."[753]

- □ The following table from the U.S. Bureau of Labor Statistics shows the March 2025 unemployment rate for various races.

U.S. Unemployment Rate for March 2025[754]

Overall	4.2%
Black	6.2%
Hispanic	5.1%
White	3.7%
Asian	3.5%

- Statistics on race discrimination. In 1997, 29,199 race discrimination cases were filed, according to the EEOC. This is 36.2% of all discrimination cases filed in 1997. By fiscal year 2023, the number of race discrimination cases dropped to 27,505, representing 33.9% of all discrimination cases filed that year. These numbers, of course, only reflect formally filed cases.[755]

- A significant example of a race discrimination lawsuit was *EEOC v. Gonnella Baking Co.* (2017). The EEOC successfully proved that Gonnella Baking Co. violated the Civil Rights Act when it did not adequately respond to an African American employee's racial harassment complaints and that he suffered an egregious pattern of denigrating racial comments made by coworkers.[756]

- "Color discrimination" is often and incorrectly seen as another way of saying "race discrimination."[757] Color discrimination is a distinct type of prejudice, as illustrated by *EEOC v. Hooters of America*, LLC, Civil Action No.: 1:23-cv-00722. The EEOC proved that the retail chain violated Title VII when a Hooters Greensboro, NC, location failed to recall Black and dark-skinned "Hooters Girls" after the 2020 pandemic layoffs. The workforce shifted from 51% Black/dark-skinned to 8% post-recall.[758]

- Statistics for color discrimination. In 1997, 762 color discrimination cases were filed, according to the EEOC. This is 0.9% of all discrimination cases filed in 1997. By fiscal year 2023, the number of color discrimination cases jumped to 5,819, representing 7.2% of all discrimination cases filed that year. These numbers, of course, only reflect formally filed cases.[759]

○ Do not tolerate religious discrimination.

> **Definition of religious discrimination:** According to the U.S. Equal Employment Opportunity Commission: "Religious discrimination involves treating a person (an applicant or employee) unfavorably because of his or her religious beliefs. The law protects not only people who belong to traditional, organized religions, such as Buddhism, Christianity, Hinduism, Islam, and Judaism, but also others who have sincerely held religious, ethical, or moral beliefs. Religious discrimination can also involve treating someone differently because that person is married to (or associated with) an individual of a particular religion."[760]

- "Title VII of the Civil Rights Act of 1964 prohibits employers with at least 15 employees, as well as employment agencies and unions, from discriminating in employment based on race, color, religion, sex, and national origin. It also prohibits retaliation against persons who complain of discrimination or participate in an EEO investigation. With respect to religion, Title VII prohibits:

  1. Treating applicants or employees differently based on their religious beliefs or practices—or lack thereof—in any aspect of employment, including recruitment, hiring, assignments, discipline, promotion, and benefits (disparate treatment);

  2. Subjecting employees to harassment because of their religious beliefs or practices—or lack thereof—or because of the religious practices or beliefs of people with whom they associate (e.g., relatives, friends, etc.);

3. Denying a requested reasonable accommodation of an applicant's or employee's sincerely held religious beliefs or practices—or lack thereof—if an accommodation will not impose more than a de minimis cost or burden on business operations; and,

4. Retaliating against an applicant or employee who has engaged in protected activity, including participation (e.g., filing an EEO charge or testifying as a witness in someone else's EEO matter) or opposition to religious discrimination (e.g., complaining to the human resources department about alleged religious discrimination)."[761]

- Four tendencies add to religious discrimination in the workplace. They are:

  □ Legal confusion.

  □ Religious diversity in the U.S. workforce continues to expand.

  □ Increasing assertion of religious beliefs.

  □ The special or unique nature of religion.[762]

- Statistics on religious discrimination. In 1997, 1,709 religious discrimination cases were filed, according to the EEOC. This is 2.1% of all discrimination cases filed in 1997. By fiscal year 2023, the number of religious discrimination cases was 4,341, representing 5.4% of all discrimination cases filed that year. These numbers, of course, only reflect formally filed cases.[763]

- Significant religious discrimination case. The *EEOC v. Abercrombie & Fitch Stores, Inc.* (2015) is a religious discrimination case in which the clothing retailer fired a Muslim employee for refusing to remove her hijab. A hijab is a headscarf some Muslim women wear and is governed by a Muslim religious code. Abercrombie & Fitch argued that this violated their company-wide dress code. The retailer lost the case and was found liable for religious discrimination.[764]

- Do not tolerate national origin discrimination.

> **Definition of national origin discrimination:** According to the U.S. Equal Employment Opportunity Commission: "National origin discrimination involves treating people (applicants or employees) unfavorably because they are from a particular country or part of the world, because of ethnicity or accent, or because they appear to be of a certain ethnic background (even if they are not)."
>
> "National origin discrimination also can involve treating people unfavorably because they are married to (or associated with) a person of a certain national origin. Discrimination can occur when the victim and the person who inflicted the discrimination are the same national origin."[765]

- Statistics on national origin discrimination. In 1997, 6,712 national origin discrimination cases were filed, according to the EEOC. This is 8.3% of all discrimination cases filed in 1997. By FY2023, the number of national origin discrimination cases was 6,963, representing 8.6% of all discrimination cases filed that year. These numbers, of course, only reflect formally filed cases.[766]

- Significant national origin discrimination case. The *EEOC v. Chas. S. Winner, Inc.* (2017) is an example of a national origin discrimination lawsuit. The EEOC proved in court that the Winner car dealership violated Title VII of the CRA by paying Chinese technicians less than non-Chinese technicians. Further, when a Chinese technician complained about the wage disparity, the company reprimanded him, telling him he would be fired if he complained or sought a legal remedy.[767]

- Do not tolerate age discrimination.

> **Definition of age discrimination:** According to the U.S. Equal Employment Opportunity Commission: "Age discrimination involves treating an applicant or employee less favorably because of his or her age."

> "The Age Discrimination in Employment Act (ADEA) forbids age discrimination against people who are age 40 or older. It does not protect workers under the age of 40, although some states have laws that protect younger workers from age discrimination. It is not illegal for an employer or other covered entity to favor an older worker over a younger one, even if both workers are age 40 or older. Discrimination can occur when the victim and the person who inflicted the discrimination are both over 40."[768]

- Approximately 3% of victims of age discrimination complained to their employers or a government agency. Studies show that more than 75% of workers surveyed report that their age is a barrier to getting a job. Even with low unemployment and a strong economy, older workers struggle to get jobs.[769]

- A 2018 Urban Institute study on aging in America found that employment is increasingly uncertain as workers age. Just over half of full-time, full-year workers, ages 51 to 54, with long-term experience are still involuntarily laid off after age 50. This results in a lengthy period of unemployment or less pay of over 50% for at least two years. These involuntarily laid-off workers include those in all U.S. geographic areas, demographic groups, and industries.[770] Older workers are not involuntarily laid off because they are less productive. Following a review of 74 peer-reviewed studies, researchers concluded that the productivity of older and younger workers is the same. Older workers perform work better but are absent from work more.[771] Older workers often have multiple skills and experience and remain longer in jobs.[772]

- Statistics on age discrimination. In 1997, 15,785 age discrimination cases were filed, according to the EEOC. This is 19.6% of all discrimination cases filed in 1997. By FY2023, age discrimination cases were 14,144, representing 15.6% of all discrimination cases filed that year. These numbers, of course, only reflect formally filed cases.[773]

- Significant age discrimination court case. The *EEOC v. Texas Roadhouse, Inc.* (2017) is an example of an age discrimination lawsuit. The EEOC proved in court that the nationwide restaurant chain violated applicants' rights under the Age Discrimination in Employment Act. Texas Roadhouse refused to hire individuals aged 40 or older for visible, front-of-house positions, such as bartenders and servers, because of their age.[774]

- Do not tolerate disability discrimination.

  - "The Americans with Disabilities Act (ADA) prohibits discrimination against people with disabilities in several areas, including employment, transportation, public accommodations, communications, and access to state and local government programs and services."[775]

> **Definition of a person with a disability:** "The ADA directs that the definition of disability is construed broadly, in favor of extensive coverage, to the maximum extent allowed by the law. Nonetheless, not everyone with a medical condition is protected from disability discrimination. Under the law, a person has a disability if the person:
>
> - Has a physical or mental condition that substantially limits a major life activity (such as walking, talking, seeing, hearing, or learning, or operation of a major bodily function, such as brain, musculoskeletal, respiratory, circulatory, or endocrine function).
>
> - Has a history of disability.
>
> - Is subject to an adverse employment action because of a physical or mental impairment the individual has or is perceived to have, except if it is transitory (lasting or expected to last six months or less) and minor. A medical condition does not need to be long-term, permanent, or severe to be substantially limiting. Also, if symptoms come and go, what matters is how limiting the symptoms are when they are active."[776]

- "Disability discrimination occurs when an employer or other entity covered by Title I of the Americans with Disabilities Act (ADA) (which protects private and state and local employees) or the Rehabilitation Act (which protects federal employees) treats a qualified employee or applicant unfavorably because of disability. The disability laws forbid discrimination when it comes to any aspect of employment, including hiring, firing, pay, job assignments, promotions, layoff, training, fringe benefits, and any other term or condition of employment."[777]

Definition of a reasonable accommodation: A "reasonable accommodation is any change or adjustment to a job or work environment that permits a qualified applicant or employee with a disability to participate in the job application process, to perform the essential functions of a job, or to enjoy benefits and privileges of employment equal to those enjoyed by employees without disabilities."

"For example, reasonable accommodation may include:

- Providing or modifying equipment or devices

- Job restructuring

- Part-time or modified work schedules

- Reassignment to a vacant position

- Adjusting or modifying examinations, training materials, or policies

- Providing readers and interpreters

- Making the workplace readily accessible to and usable by people with disabilities."

- An employer is required to provide a reasonable accommodation to a qualified applicant or employee with a disability unless the employer can show that the accommodation would be an undue hardship—that is, that it would require significant difficulty or expense.[778]

- Statistics on disability discrimination. In 1997, 18,101 disability discrimination cases were filed, according to the EEOC. This is 22.4% of all discrimination cases filed in 1997. By 2023, the number of disability discrimination cases was 29,106, representing 36% of all discrimination cases filed that year. These numbers, of course, only reflect formally filed cases. As the U.S. workforce ages, more become workers with disabilities.[779]

- According to the U.S. Bureau of Labor Statistics (BLS), in 2023, only 22.5% of people with disabilities were working. The BLS report also states that the unemployment rate for people with a disability was 7.2%. The BLS defines those who are counted in the unemployment rate as those who are jobless, actively looked for work in the prior four weeks, and are available for work.[780]

- Significant disability discrimination court case. The *EEOC v. Starbucks Corporation* (2007) is an example of a disability discrimination lawsuit. The EEOC proved in court that Starbucks violated an employee's rights under the ADA. A barista with bipolar, major depression, and attention-deficit disorders performed satisfactorily when given extra training and support. However, a new manager stopped providing this accommodation, which caused the employee's performance to suffer. As a result, the manager cut her hours and discharged her.[781]

ILLUSTRATIVE STORY

At one organization, the senior managers chose to go beyond providing ADA-required accommodations and offered customized office equipment to anyone who asked. The most requested accommodation was larger computer screens for aging staff with impaired eyesight. The organization chose to offer bigger screens to everyone. Another common accommodation was customized computer mice for those with carpal tunnel syndrome. The organization believed providing customized computer mice to everyone who asked might prevent some cases of carpal tunnel. This organization also offered sit-stand desks to any employee who asked. Sit-stand desks sound good until you have been standing on a concrete floor for hours. In addition to the desks, the employees were given thick rubber pads called anti-fatigue mats to stand on. The organization offered footrests for shorter employees whose feet did not touch the floor when seated to avoid restricting circulation. Some employees complained that the fluorescent lights gave them headaches. The remedy was to replace fluorescent lighting with desk lamps. A few employees wore golf hats, keeping the fluorescent lights' overhead glare out of their eyes. Soon, it was common to see employees in meetings wearing golf hats. Whatever it took, the organization responded. The total cost of all these accommodations was minimal. The happy employee response was priceless.

○ Support equal pay for equal work.

Definition of equal pay/compensation discrimination: According to the U.S. Equal Employment Opportunity Commission: "The Equal Pay Act (EPA) requires that men and women in the same workplace be given equal pay for equal work."

"The jobs need not be identical, but they must be substantially equal. Job content (not job titles) determines whether jobs are substantially equal. All forms of pay are covered by this law, including salary, overtime pay, bonuses, stock options, profit sharing and bonus plans, life insurance, vacation and holiday pay, cleaning or gasoline allowances, hotel accommodations, reimbursement for travel expenses, and benefits. If there is an inequality in wages between men and women, employers may not reduce the wages of either sex to equalize their pay. An individual alleging a violation of the EPA may go directly to court and is not required to file an EEOC charge beforehand. The time limit for filing an EPA charge with the EEOC and the time limit for going to court are the same: within two years of the alleged unlawful compensation practice or, in the case of a willful violation, within three years. The filing of an EEOC charge under the EPA does not extend the time frame for going to court."[782] More information on equal pay/compensation discrimination is found at https://www.eeoc.gov/equal-paycompensation-discrimination.

- A Glassdoor survey shows that 93% of employed Americans believe that men and women should be compensated equally for equal work.[783]

- Statistics on Equal Pay Act discrimination case. In 1997, 1,134 Equal Pay Act (EPA) discrimination cases were filed, according to the EEOC. This is 1.4% of all discrimination cases filed in 1997. In FY2023, the number of EPA cases was 1,012, representing 1.2% of all discrimination cases filed that year. These numbers, of course, only reflect formally filed cases.[784]

- Significant equal pay and sex discrimination court case. In a 2021 EPA case, *EEOC v. Dell*, Dell Inc. agreed to pay $75,000 to resolve an equal pay and sex discrimination lawsuit filed by the EEOC. According to the lawsuit, Kea Golden and three male workers were hired as information technology analysts for Dell, Inc. beginning in September 2017. While working at Dell, Golden did the same work as one of her male coworkers. Nonetheless, Dell paid Golden $17,510 less yearly than her male coworker.[785]

- A Pew Research Center analysis of U.S. Census Bureau data shows that full-time, year-round working women under the age of 30, on average, have salaries equal to or greater than men in Washington, D.C., Los Angeles, New York, and 19 other major metropolitan areas. Nationally, women 30 and younger are paid 93% of what men make. All women who work full-time nationally are paid only 82% of what men make.[786]

- Effective organizations provide these low or no-cost initiatives that directly influence recruitment and retention.

  - Work-life balance.

> **Definition of work-life balance:** Employees spend sufficient amounts of time at work, not more than 50 hours per week, while giving them enough time for their pursuits of happiness, such as spending time with family and friends, worship, hobbies, and reading this book.[787]

ILLUSTRATIVE STORY

A savvy manager improves an employee's work-life balance at no cost. Brandon, a skilled technician, told Emily he would retire a year earlier than planned. After saying she would hate to lose him, Emily asked Brandon why he decided to retire early. Emily needed far more than the customary two weeks' notice to find and train Brandon's replacement. Was there any way to delay his retirement? Brandon said the traffic was getting worse, and it sometimes took him two hours to commute home on his work-at-the-office days. Emily immediately suggested that he try leaving two hours earlier than normal each day to telework the last two hours at home. At first, Brandon thought Emily was joking. When he was assured that she was serious, Brandon said he wanted to try it, starting the next day. His new schedule worked perfectly for him and those with whom he worked. Brandon worked for two more years, and Emily had more than sufficient time to hire and train his successor.

- According to a 2022 Morning Consult survey on behalf of Prudential, 22% of employees changed jobs during the pandemic, and of those, one in three took a new job with less pay so they could have a better work-life balance.[788]

ILLUSTRATIVE STORY

Deloitte created a family leave program that allow up to 16 weeks of paid family leave per year, which covered the birth or adoption of children, caring for an ill family member, or caring for elderly parents. This program offered coverage for all age groups rather than just new parents. For example, Deloitte allowed a middle-aged, single man to take several months off to care for a sick parent. There is something for everyone.[789]

ILLUSTRATIVE STORY

In 1998, the beloved animated movie, Toy Story 2, was accidentally deleted during production. Worse yet, the studio's onsite backup failed. These were the days before cloud backup. Galyn Susman, Pixar's technical director, came to the rescue. Although on maternity leave, Susman was working on the film on her laptop at home.[790] Let us never underestimate the abilities of employees on extended leave to continue making significant contributions to their organizations. Managers should look for ways to allow them to continue contributing while on extended leave.

ILLUSTRATIVE STORY

Organizations should invite valuable former employees to quarterly meetings where senior managers provide high-level organizational updates and arrange one-on-one discussions with their former bosses. The information at these meetings should flow both ways. Managers should ask these former employees for their thoughts on organizational strategy and challenges. Their fresh and well-thought-out insights will be invaluable. They have more time to think strategically and consider solutions to the organization's challenges. Another way organizations can benefit from this talent is through electronic brainstorming sessions. As we learned in Section 4.3, Meetings, electronic brainstorming works wonderfully; the more participants, the better. Electronic brainstorming is ideally suited to include these former employees. These quarterly meetings incentivize former employees to keep up with their industry and organization. In return for employees' participation in these activities, organizations should pay their salaries for these meetings at an hourly rate adjusted for inflation, maintain former employees' health benefits, and maintain their professional credentials and professional publications. These employees who leave organizations to care for children, ill family members, or elderly parents may also have time to work part-time or periodically when workloads peak or their expertise is needed. When these valuable employees return to work full-time, every effort should be made to return them to positions of responsibility higher than those they left. This recommendation goes beyond the traditional unpaid leave of absence. The Family and Medical Leave Act of 1993 defines instances under which approval of a leave of absence is required.

○ Offer a financial wellness program.

> **Definition of financial wellness:** Successfully managing your finances. This includes creating and sticking to a budget, paying your bills on time, minimizing debt, being financially prepared for emergencies, and planning for long-term financial objectives like retirement or college costs for your children.[791]

- A 2021 Bank of America survey showed that 84% of employers agree that financial wellness programs increase retention.[792]

- Your employees need the best financial wellness training available. They need to know how to get the most benefit from each dollar. A staggering 66.2% of Americans report struggling between paychecks, according to a 2024 MarketWatch Guides survey.[793]

- Employees' stress costs organizations through increasing medical expenses, lower productivity and morale, and increased time off due to injuries and illnesses. To be effective for every employee, organizations should ensure that their financial wellness programs meet the needs of all generations in their workforce. Many financial wellness programs are designed for baby boomers and focus on retirement savings and planning. Millennials and Gen Zers want financial wellness programs that teach them financial basics such as developing a budget, paying back student loans, and saving for retirement. If your organization offers a financial wellness program and you have checked that box, look at your program carefully. Are you meeting the financial planning needs of all generations in your organization? If you're unsure, you can survey your employees or look at the participation rate by generation to see who is using it. Offering a financial wellness program that meets everyone's needs is not a significant expense; it improves retention and lowers stress.

  ○ Offer a health wellness program.

> **Definition of a health wellness program:** An organization-sponsored program that offers employees and their family members a variety of ways to improve their health, which increases employee retention and reduces health care costs.

- In a Society for Human Resource Management survey, 62% of respondents said an organization's wellness program was "extremely or very important."[794]

- In 2018, 51.8% of civilian U.S. adults, 129 million, had at least one chronic condition (arthritis, cancer, asthma, chronic obstructive pulmonary disease, coronary heart disease, diabetes, hepatitis, hypertension, stroke, weak or failing kidneys) and 27.2%, or 68 million people, have more than one chronic condition.[795]

  - Employees with fair or poor mental health miss four times more work than other workers.

  - 23% of women are likelier to report poor or fair mental health than men (15%).

  - 36% of women under 30 report poor or fair mental health.

  - 40% of U.S. workers say their job has an extremely negative (7%) or somewhat negative (33%) effect on their mental health.

  - Among workers who report that their workplace adversely affects their mental health, 57% are unaware of mental health services in their workplace.[796] Effective managers frequently make all employees aware of available mental health services and work with their direct reports to reduce stress. For more information on reducing stress, please see Section 2.1, Hire and Retain Great Employees.

- Understand the effects of the COVID-19 pandemic on the U.S. workforce. The following table shows the change in self-reported anxiety and depression symptoms from 2019 to 2024.

U.S. Change in Self-Reported Anxiety and Depression Symptoms, January 2019–July 2024

	Percent of responders who self-identified as having anxiety symptoms	Percent of responders who self-identified as having depression symptoms	Percent of responders who self-identified as having both anxiety and depression symptoms
2019 average[797]	8.1%	6.5%	10.8%
2024 (Jan–June) average[798]	17.4%	13.6%	21%
% of increase from 2019 to 2024	114%	109%	94%

> **Definition of long COVID:** COVID-19 symptoms that last at least three months after first contracting the virus.[799] There is no cure for long-term COVID-19, so healthcare providers treat the symptoms, i.e., fatigue, fever, headaches, etc.[800]

- The Centers for Disease Control and Prevention advise that over 40% of American adults say they have had COVID-19, and 19% currently have symptomatic long COVID.[801]

- The #1 priority of businesses is not profit; it is survival. Effective managers and engaged employees will help you survive and thrive.

A final thought on creating a positive work environment:

- Managers have a moral obligation to ensure that each of their employees looks forward to coming to work every day.[802]

"Job-Related Information for Your Successor" Form

TO: (Your replacement's name and job title here) _______________

OBJECTIVE: We want everyone leaving our organization to complete this form so their successor can smoothly transition into their new job.

This information is also helpful for anyone filling in for you temporarily before your successor arrives.

Your name: ____

Your future contact information for questions: _______________

Your successor's name (if known): _______________________

Name of interim replacement (if applicable): _______________

YOUR JOB INFORMATION

- Your job title:

- Please attach your job description. If the job description needs any revisions, please show the revisions with Track Changes so that your successor can discuss them with your boss:

- Your boss's name and job title:

- Whom do you manage by name and job title?

- Please attach an organization chart with all your employees' names and duty titles. The organization chart should also show your organization's relationship with all others within the enterprise.

- Do you currently have any job vacancies? What is the status of hiring replacements? Some departing managers prefer to delay hiring new employees so their replacements can choose them.

- Key people inside the organization that you deal with regularly and the nature of your business with them (names, job titles, phone numbers, and email addresses):

- Key people outside the organization that you deal with regularly and the nature of your business with them (names, job titles, phone numbers, and email addresses):

- Help your successor and transition your work.
  - List projects with which you are currently involved and your role. Give details on any goals, objectives, milestones, and challenges.

  - Contracts/delivery orders for which you are a task manager:

  - Reports for which you are responsible (name of each report, date dues, your employees that are responsible for preparing each report, contact information where the reports are submitted):

  - Regular meetings that you attend and your role (chair, committee chair, secretary, voting member, non-voting member):

- What should your replacement look for during the following periods?
  - Week 1 (May 1–7):
  - Week 2 (May 8–14):
  - Week 3 (May 15–21):
  - Week 4 (May 22–30):
  - Second Month (June):
  - Third month (July):

- Did you put "Out of Office" messages in your email and voice-mail stating the contact information of the person filling in/taking over for you?

- Any additional suggestions and advice for your successor?

- Date this form was last revised:

ENDNOTES

1. Joanne Sujansky, "The Poor Performer Confrontation Handbook: Eight Rules for Dealing with Employees Who Are Bringing Your Company Down," *Cost Engineering Volume 49,* Issue 8 (August 2007): pp. 14–15

2. Effective People Managers: The Linchpin of Organizational Success," *Society for Human Resource Management,* June 12, 2024, p. 3.

3. "Survey: 84 Percent of U.S. Workers Blame Bad Managers for Creating Unnecessary Stress," *Society for Human Resource Management,* August 12, 2020, https://www .shrm.org/about/press-room/survey-84-percent-u-s-workers-blame-bad -managers-creating-unnecessary-stress.

4. John Pencavel, "The Productivity of Working Hours," discussion paper, Stanford Institute for Economic Policy Research, Stanford, October 2013, p. 21, https:// siepr.stanford.edu/sites/default/files/publications/FatiguepaperSIEPRcover _0.pdf.

5. Paul O'Keefe et al., "Implicit Theories of Interest: Finding Your Passion or Developing It?" *Psychol Sci.* 2018 Oct;29(10):1653-1664. doi: 10.1177 /0956797618780643. Epub 2018 Sep 6. PMID: 30188804; PMCID: PMC6180666.

6. Lao Tzu quoted in Mark Robert Polelle, *Leadership: Fifty Great Leaders and the Worlds They Made* (Westport, Connecticut: Greenwood Press, 2008), p. xiv.

7. Pauline Graham, *Mary Parker Follett: Prophet of Management* (Cambridge: Harvard Business School Press, 1995), p. 178.

8. Sir Isaac Newton quoted in Andrew May, *Isaac Newton: Scientist* (New York: Cavendish Square Publishing, 2016), p. 15.

9. Tom Northup, *Five Hidden Mistakes CEOs Make: How to Unlock the Secrets that Drive Growth and Profitability* (Newport Beach: Solutions Press, 2008), p. 68.

10. Ibid., Mary Parker Follett quoted in *Mary Parker Follett: Prophet of Management* and in Shivanand Bhanje, *Principles of Management,* (Raleigh, SC: Lulu Publications, 2023), p. 3.

11. Henri Fayol, *Administration industrielle et générale —prévoyance organization—commandment, coordination—contrôle,* (Paris: H. Dunod et E. Pinat, 1917).

12. Gary L. Neilson et al., "The Secrets to Successful Strategy Execution," *Harvard Business Review Magazine,* June 1, 2008, https://hbr.org/2008/06/the -secrets-to-successful-strategy-execution.

13. W. Edwards Deming, *Out of the Crisis* (Cambridge, MA: The MIT Press, 2000), p. xi.

14. Joshua Rothman, "Shut Up and Sit Down: Why the Leadership Industry Rules," *The New Yorker Magazine,* February 29, 2016, p. 66.

15. Barbara Kellerman, *The End of Leadership* (New York: HarperCollins, 2012), p. xxi.

16. Peter F. Drucker, *The Essential Drucker: The Best of Sixty Years of Peter Drucker's Essential Writings on Management* (New York: Harper, 2001), p. 268–71.

17. Kellerman, *The End of Leadership*, p. xiv.

18. Ben Wigert, "The Top 6 Things Employees Want in Their Next Job," *Gallup Workplace*, February 21, 2022, https://www.gallup.com/workplace/389807/top-things-employees-next-job.aspx.

19. Marcus Buckingham and Curt Coffman, *First, Break All the Rules: What the World's Greatest Managers Do Differently* (New York: Gallup Press, 1999), pp. 7–8.

20. Leigh Branham, *The 7 Hidden Reasons Employees Leave,* (New York: American Management Association, 2005), p. 3.

21. "The Frontline Leader Project: Exploring the Most Critical Segment of Leaders," *Development Dimensions International,* 2019, p. 59.

22. David P. Costanza et al., "Generational Differences in Work-Related Attitudes: A Meta-analysis," *Journal of Business and Psychology,* Vol. 27, Iss. 4 (December 2012): pp. 375–394.

23. Brent W. Roberts et al., "It Is Developmental Me, Not Generation Me: Developmental Changes Are More Important Than Generational Changes in Narcissism-Commentary on Trzesniewski & Donnellan (2010)," *Perspectives on Psychological Science: A Journal of the Association for Psychological Science* vol. 5, 1 (2010): pp. 97–102. doi:10.1177/1745691609357019.

24. Robert Half, "12 Employee Benefits and Perks for Your Hiring and Retention Plan," *Robert Half,* October 11, 2023.

25. Adam Grundy et al., "Medical Expenditure Panel Survey—Insurance Component Shows 86% of Private-Sector Employees Worked for Establishments that Offered Health Insurance," U.S. Census Bureau, February 29, 2024.

26. "Questions and Answers on Employer Shared Responsibility Provisions Under the Affordable Care Act," *Internal Revenue Service,* https://www.irs.gov/affordable-care-act/employers/questions-and-answers-on-employer-shared-responsibility-provisions-under-the-affordable-care-act.

27. Lindsey Dawson et al., "Access to Employer-Sponsored Health Coverage for Same-Sex Spouses: 2020 Update," *KFF,* November 30, 2021, https://www.kff.org/private-insurance/issue-brief/access-to-employer-sponsored-health-coverage-for-same-sex-spouses-2020-update/.

28. "TED: The Economic Daily," *U.S. Bureau of Labor Statistics,* April 9, 2019.

29. Amy Heine, "Paid Time Off: Definition and Comparison to Vacation Time," *Indeed Career Guide,* July 7, 2023.

30. Quentin Fottrell, "The sad reason half of Americans don't take all their paid vacation," *Market Watch,* May 28, 2017, https://www.marketwatch.com/story/55-of-american-workers-dont-take-all-their-paid-vacation-2016-06-15.

31. Jena McGregor, "What's the One Benefit Employees Want Most? More Time Off, Study Shows," *The Washington Post,* March 28, 2019.

32. Sarah Green Carmichael, "Goldman Sacks Now Has Wall Street's Best Vacation Policy," *Bloomberg*, May 19, 2022.

33. Ashley V. Whillans, "Time for Happiness: Why the pursuit of money isn't bringing you joy—and what will," *Harvard Business Review*, January 24, 2019, https://hbr.org/2019/01/time-for-happiness.

34. John F. Helliwell et al., "Happiness at Different Ages: The Social Context Matters," *National Bureau of Economic Research*, October 2018, doi: 10.3386/w25121.

35. "Retirement plans for workers in private industry and state and local government in 2022," *TED: The Economic Daily*, U.S. Bureau of Labor Statistics, February 1, 2023.

36. Katherine T. Smith, "Work-Life Balance Perspectives of Future Marketing Professionals," *Services Marketing Quarterly* 31, no. 4 (2010): p. 434.

37. Kim Parker et al., "COVID-19 Pandemic Continues to Reshape Work in America," *Pew Research Center*, February 16, 2022, https://www.pewresearch.org/social-trends/2022/02/16/covid-19-pandemic-continues-to-reshape-work-in-america/.

38. Melanie S. Brucks and Jonathan Levav, "Virtual Communication Curbs Creative Idea Generation," *Nature* 605, pp. 108–112 (2022). https://doi.org/10.1038/s41586-022-04643-y.

39. Sean Nehlsen, "Boomers need benefits, too: What you need to consider," *Benefits Pro*, February 5, 2020.

40. "What Benefits Appeal Most to Gen X Employees?" *BenefitEd*, March 4, 2024.

41. What Benefits Appeal Most to Millennial Employees?" BenefitsEd, February 12, 2024.

42. "Millennials at Work: Reshaping the Workplace," *Price, Waterhouse & Cooper*, pp. 18–19, https://www.pwc.com/co/es/publicaciones/assets/millennials-at-work.pdf.

43. "Benefits and Perks That Attract Gen Z Employees," Monster, https://hiring.monster.com/resources/recruiting-strategies/emerging-workforce/attract-gen-z-employees/

44. Aaron Terrazas, "Glasdoor's 2024 Workplace Trends," *Glassdoor*, November 15, 2023.

45. Kevin S. Dubina et al., "Projections overview and highlights, 2030," Monthly Labor Review, U.S. Bureau of Labor Statistics, October 2021, https://doi.org/10.21916/mlr.2021.20.

46. "Research: Here's What Generation Z Candidates Want at Work," *Yello*.

47. Socrates quoted in Patrick Kelly, "Why Socrates Hates Millennials," *The Junto Club*, January 4, 2016.

48. Jeanne Batalova, "Frequently Requested Statistics on Immigrants and Immigration in the United States," *Migration Policy Institute*, March 14, 2024, https://www.migrationpolicy.org/sites/default/files/publications/frs-print-2023.pdf.

49. Jonathan Vespa et al., "Demographic Turning Points for the United States: Population Projections for 2020 to 2060," *U.S. Census Bureau*, revised February 2020, p. 3.

50. Sarah Jane Glynn, "Breadwinning Mothers Are Critical to Families' Economic Security," *The Center for American Progress*, March 29, 2021, https://www.americanprogress.org/article/breadwinning-mothers-critical-familys-economic-security/

51. Kim Parker and Ruth Igielnik, "On the Cusp of Adulthood and Facing an Uncertain Future: What We Know About Gen Z So Far," *Pew Research Center*, May 14, 2020, https://www.pewresearch.org/social-trends/2020/05/14/on-the-cusp-of-adulthood-and-facing-an-uncertain-future-what-we-know-about-gen-z-so-far-2/.

52. "U.S. Census Bureau Projections Show a Slower Growing, Older, More Diverse Nation a Half Century from Now," *U.S. Census Bureau*, December 12, 2012.

53. Vespa, et al., "Demographic Turning Points for the United States: Population Projections for 2020 to 2060."

54. "The Demographic Outlook: 2022 to 2052," *Congressional Budget Office*, July 27, 2022.

55. Batalova, "Frequently Requested Statistics on Immigrants and Immigration in the United States."

56. Bradford D. Smart, *Topgrading: How Leading Companies Win by Hiring, Coaching, and Keeping the Best People* (New York: Penguin Group, 2005), p. 36.

57. Stephanie Neal et al., "CEO Leadership Report 2023," *Development Dimensions International*, 2023, p. 11.

58. Jesse Schell quoted in Reginald Wilkinson, *Leadership and Management: Connecting the Dots* (Bloomington, IN: Xlibris, 2018), p. 167.

59. "Your slow recruiting process costs your organization more than lost revenue," *Field of Talent, 2023*, https://fieldoftalent.com/slow-recruiting-process-costs-more-than-lost-revenue/.

60. Kelli Delfosse, "8 Things You Need To Know About Applicant Tracking Systems," *McKelvey School of Engineering*, Washington University in St. Louis, February 4, 2022.

61. Ava Abbott, "Top 10 Gartner Competitors and Alternatives," *Business Strategy Hub*, March 8, 2024.

62. "Job Seekers Are Now in the Driver's Seat and Expect Next-Gen Recruiting and New Hire Experiences, Survey Finds," *CareerBuilder*, October 30, 2018, https://press.careerbuilder.com/2018-10-30-Job-Seekers-Are-Now-in-the-Drivers-Seat-and-Expect-Next-Gen-Recruiting-and-New-Hire-Experiences-Survey-Finds.

63. "What is Job Analysis?" *Indeed*, https://www.indeed.com/hire/c/info/what-is-job-analysis

64. Iryna Veter, "Mastering Workload Analysis: 5 Tips to Get Started," Runn, May 28, 2024.

65. "The Americans with Disabilities Act (ADA) protects people with disabilities from discrimination," ADA.gov, *U.S. Department of Justice, Civil Rights Division*, updated May 22, 2024.

66. "SFA Knowledge, Skills, & Abilities (KSA) Bank: Frequently Asked Questions," Stephen F. Austin State University.

67. David Kirkpatrick, "Google: 53% of mobile users abandon sites that take over 3 seconds to load," *Marketing Dive*, September 12, 2016.

68. Roy Maurer, "Employee Referrals Remain Top Source for Hires," *Society for Human Resource Management,* June 23, 2017, https://www.shrm.org/topics-tools/news/talent-acquisition/employee-referrals-remain-top-source-hires.

69. Indeed Editorial Team, "Q&A: How Long Do Job Postings Stay Up?" *Indeed,* July 2, 2024.

70. Charlotte A. Burrows (Chair), "Meeting of January 31, 2023—Navigating Employment Discrimination in AI and Automated Systems: A New Civil Rights Frontier—Transcript," Tuesday, *U. S. Equal Employment Opportunity Commission,* January 31, 2023.

71. Paul Lyons and Randall Bandura, "An Expanded Value of College GPA in Recruitment? As Related to U.S. Organizations," *Development and Learning in Organizations* 31, no. 2 (2017): pp. 13–15. DOI:10.1108/DLO-08-2016-0072

72. "Employment Tenure in 2022," Economic News Release, *U.S. Bureau of Labor Statistics,* U. S. Department of Labor, September 22, 2022.

73. "Over Half of Employees Report Lying on Resumes," *HRO Today,* https://www.hrotoday.com/news/over-half-of-employees-report-lying-on-resumes.

74. Chad Brooks, "Even Small Resume Lies Raise Red Flags," Fox Business, August 11, 2014, https://www.foxbusiness.com/features/even-small-resume-lies-raise-red-flags.

75. Chris Platts, "Predictive Hiring Analytics: How to Use Them," *ThriveMap,* September 4, 2020, https://thrivemap.io/predictive-hiring-analytics/

76. Glen Rifkin, "Big Data, Predictive Analytics, and Hiring," *Briefings Magazine,* Korn Ferry, https://www.kornferry.com/insights/briefings-magazine/issue-19/big-data-predictive-analytics-and-hiring.

77. "Best of Bamboo HR," *Bamboo HR,* chrome extension://efaidnbmnnnibpca jpcglclefindmkaj/https://www.bamboohr.com/resources/assets/ebooks/top-onboarding-advice.pdf

78. Alison Doyle, "Interview Questions About Skills and Experience," *the balance,* October 18, 2021.

79. William Way in an email response recommending interview questions, March 17, 2023.

80. Joseph T. Straub, *The Rookie Manager: A Guide to Surviving Your First Year in Management* (New York: American Management Association, 2000), p. 94.

81. "Leading America's Workforce, Policy, Data, Oversight," Senior Executive Service, Office of Personnel Management.

82. Ibid.

83. Ibid.

84. Ibid.

85. Ibid.

86. Suzy Welch, "The Single Best Question to Ask in an Interview," *NBC,* last modified May 23, 2017.

87. Marci Martin, "Illegal Job Interview Questions to Avoid," *Business News Daily,* updated October 23, 2023.

88. "7 in 10 Companies Will Use AI in the Hiring Process in 2025, Despite Most Saying It's Biased," *Resume Builder,* last updated October 22, 2024.

89. Rob Porter, "AI in Job Interviews: Pros and Cons," *Vault,* December 1, 2023.

90. Greg J. Sears et al., "A Comparative Assessment of Videoconference and Face-to-Face Employment Interviews," *Management Decision* 51, no. 8 (2013): pp. 1733–1752.

91. Jay J. Van Bavel and Tessa V. West, "Seven Steps to Reduce Bias in Hiring: The Key is to Take Bias Out of the Hiring Process Instead of Trying to Take It Out of the People Doing the Hiring," *The Wall Street Journal,* February 21, 2017, https://www.wsj.com/articles/seven-steps-to-reduce-bias-in-hiring-1487646840.

92. "The ADA: Your Employment Rights as an Individual With a Disability," *U.S. Equal Employment Opportunity Commission.*

93. "Employers and the ADA: Myths and Facts," *Office of Disability Employment Policy,* U.S. Department of Labor, https://www.dol.gov/agencies/odep/publications/fact-sheets/americans-with-disabilities-act.

94. Straub, *The Rookie Manager: A Guide to Surviving Your First Year in Management,* p. 41.

95. Susan Cain, *Quiet: The Power of Introverts in a World That Can't Stop Talking* (New York: Broadway Paperbacks, 2012), p. 3.

96. Santhosh Damera, "The Ideal Number of Interviews: Striking the Right Balance for Candidate Experience," *LinkedIn,* September 4, 2023.

97. Rifkin, "Big Data, Predictive Analytics, and Hiring."

98. Mitchell Hoffman et al., "Discretion in Hiring," *National Bureau of Economic Research,* NBER Working Paper Series, Working Paper 21709, last revised October 27, 2022, https://www.nber.org/system/files/working_papers/w21709/w21709.pdf.

99. "Background Evaluation/Investigation," *U.S. Office of Personnel Management.*

100. Jund-Ming Wang and Brain H. Kleiner, "Effective Employment Screening Practices," *Management Research News* 27, no. 4/5 (2004): pp. 97–107.

101. Ibid.

102. Aaron Hotfelder, "What to Do If Your Former Employer Badmouths You," NOLO, 2024.

103. "Guide to Reference Checks" (University of Wisconsin-Madison Human Resources), accessed April 10, 2025, https://hr.wisc.edu/docs/recruitment/guide-to-reference-checks.pdf.

104. Ibid.

105. Ibid.

106. "8 Useful Questions to Ask When Conducting a Reference Check," *Indeed for Employers.*

107. Ibid.

108. Ibid.

109. Christine Porath, *Mastering Civility: A Manifesto for the Workplace* (New York: Grand Central Publishing, 2016), p. 127.

110. Tanyu Zhang et al., *"Do Follower Characteristics Moderate Leadership and Employee Engagement?"* Journal of Global Responsibility, Volume 5, Issue 2 (2014): pp. 269–288.

111. Sara Sameen and Samia Cornelius, "Social Networking Sites and Hiring: How Social Media Profiles Influence Hiring Decisions," *Journal of Business Studies Quarterly,* Volume 7, no. 1 (2013): pp. 27–35, www.joycerain.com/uploads/2/3/2/0/23207256/social_networking_sites_and_employers.pdf.

112. Margaret Vroman et al., "Employer Liability for Using Social Media in Hiring Decisions," *Journal of Social Media for Organizations* 3, no. 1 (2016): p. 5, https://www2.mitre.org/public/jsmo/pdfs/03–01-employer-liability.pdf.

113. Lisa Wirthman, "How to (Legally) Use Social Media to Recruit," *Forbes,* October 24, 2016, https://www.forbes.com/sites/adp/2016/10/24/how-to-legally-use-social-media-to-recruit/?sh=78d317a029f4.

114. Kimberly Fitch and Sangeeta Agrawal, "Why Women Are Better Managers Than Men: U.S. employees with female bosses are more engaged than employees with male bosses," *Gallup Business Journal,* October 16, 2014, pp. 26–28, https://news.gallup.com/businessjournal/178541/why-women-better-managers-men.aspx.

115. Ibid.

116. "State of the Global Workforce 2024 Report: The Voice of the World's Employees," *Gallup,* p. 35, file:///C:/Users/Owner/Downloads/state-of-the-global-workplace-2024-download%20(15).pdf

117. "Large-cap companies with at least one woman on the board have outperformed their peer group with no women on the board by 26% over the last six years, according to a report by Credit Suisse Research Institute," *Press Release,* July 31, 2012.

118. Olivia Konotey-Ahuhu, "Female Managers Make Fairer Pay Decisions Than Male Counterparts," *Bloomberg,* September 1, 2022, https://www.bloomberg.com/news/articles/2022-09-01/female-managers-make-fairer-pay-decisions-than-male-counterparts?embedded-checkout=true.

119. Chris Gilligan, "States With the Highest percentage of Female Top Executives," *U.S. News and World Report,* March 6, 2023, https://www.usnews.com/news/best-states/articles/2023-03-06/states-with-the-highest-percentage-of-women-in-business-leadership-roles.

120. Cain, *Quiet: The Power of Introverts in a World That Can't Stop Talking,* p. 265.

121. Menelaos L. Batrinos, "Testosterone and Aggressive Behavior in Man," *International Journal of Endocrinology and Metabolism.* 2012 Summer; 10(3): 563–568. Published online 2012 Jun 30. doi: 10.5812/ijem.3661.

122. "Probationary Periods for New Employees," *Indeed for Employers.*

123. Vanessa Fuhrmans and Lindsay Ellis, "Half of College Grads Are Working Jobs That Don't Use Their Degrees: Choice of Major, Internships and Getting the Right First Job After Graduation Are Critical to Career Paths, New Study Shows," *The Wall Street Journal,* February 22, 2024, https://www.wsj.com/lifestyle/careers/college-degree-jobs-unused-440b2abd.

124. Matthew J. Bidwell, "Paying More to Get Less: The Effects of External Hiring versus Internal Mobility," *Administrative Science Quarterly* Volume 56, Issue 3 (2011): pp. 369–407.

125. Roy Maurer, "Survey Finds Half of Candidates Have Accepted a Job Offer Before Reneging," *Society of Human Resource Management,* September 27, 2023, https://www.shrm.org/topics-tools/news/talent-acquisition/survey-finds-half-candidates-accepted-job-offer-reneging.

126. "Your slow recruiting process costs your organization more than lost revenue."

127. *Mark Twain, Mark Twain in Eruption: Hitherto Unpublished Pages About Men and Events,* (New York: Grosset & Dunlap, Publishers, 1922)

128. Mary Buffett and David Clark, *The Tao of Warren Buffett* (New York: Scribner, 2006), p. 58.

129. Sarah Jane Thomas, "How Long Should You Give a Candidate to Mull Over a Job Offer," *LinkedIn,* January 21, 2016.

130. Jan B. Schmutz et al., "How effective is teamwork really? The relationship between teamwork and performance in healthcare teams: a systematic review and meta-analysis," *BMJ Open,* September 12, 2019, doi: 10.1136/bmjopen-2018-028280.

131. "New Employee Onboarding Checklist," *Department of the Interior, Office of the Chief Information Officer,* https://www.doi.gov/sites/doi.gov/files/uploads/OCIO-Employee-Checklist.pdf.

132. "Why the Onboarding Experience is Key for Retention," *Gallup Workplace,* https://www.gallup.com/workplace/235121/why-onboarding-experience-key-retention.aspx#:~:text=Gallup%20finds%20that%20only%2012,can%20make%20or%20break%20retention

133. Orianna Rosa Royle, "80% of new hires who receive poor onboarding plan to quit- especially if they are remote workers," *Fortune,* March 15, 2023, https://fortune.com/2023/03/15/new-hires-plan-quit-poor-onboarding-experience-remote-workers-paychex/.

134. Tess Taylor, "Why Do 28% of Employees Quit in Their First 90 Days? Poor Onboarding Practices," *HR Dive,* April 25, 2017.

135. Rachel Saltsgaver, "Employee onboarding software: 15 employee engagement stats," *Seismic,* December 21, 2020.

136. John F. Truitt, *Executive's Manual of Professional Recruiting* (New York: Facts on File Publishing, 1985), p. 135.

137. Eleanor Roosevelt quoted in H. James Harrington and Frank Voehl, *Knowledge Management Excellence: The Art of Excelling in Knowledge Management,* (Chico, CA: Paton Press LLC, 2007) p. 62.

138. "2012 Allied Workforce Mobility Survey: Onboarding and Retention," *Allied HR,* May 2012, p. 4, https://www.allied.com/docs/default-source/pdf/alliedworkforcemobilitysurvey.pdf.

139. Andrew Chamberlain, "How Long Does It Take to Hire? Interview Duration in 25 Countries," *Glassdoor Economic Research,* August 9, 2017, https://www.glassdoor.com/research/time-to-hire-in-25-countries.

140. Katherine Reynolds Lewis, "Diverse Interview Panels May Be a Key to Workplace Diversity," *The Verna Myers Company,* June 16, 2017, https://www.vernamyers.com/2017/06/16/diverse-interview-panels-may-be-a-key-to-workplace-diversity/.

141. Richard Alaniz, "How to Conduct an Effective Job Interview," *CPA Practice Advisor 28,* no. 7 (2018): p. 33, https://www.cpapracticeadvisor.com/contributor/richard-alaniz/.

142. Ibid.

143. Felix Richter, "The Great Resignation Is Over: Quits Return to Pre-Covid Level," *Statistica, January 8, 2024.*

144. Kim Parker and Juliana Menasce Horowitz, "Majority of workers who quit in 2021 cite low pay, no opportunities for advancement, feeling disrespected," *Pew Research Center,* March 9, 2022, https://www.pewresearch.org/short reads/2022/03/09/majority-of-workers-who-quit-a-job-in-2021-cite-low-pay-no-opportunities-for-advancement-feeling-disrespected/.

145. Samantha Delouya, "The job market enters a new phase as the Great Resignation ends," *CNN* Business, updated June 13, 2023.

146. Shane McFeely and Ben Wigert, "This Fixable Problem Costs U.S. Businesses $1 Trillion," *Gallup,* March 13, 2019, https://www.gallup.com/workplace/247391/fixable-problem-costs-businesses-trillion.aspx.

147. Matthew O'Connell and Mei-Chuan Kung, "The Cost of Employee Turnover," *Industrial Management* 49, no. 1 (2007): pp. 14–19.

148. John F. Helliwell et al., "Happiness at Different Ages: The Social Context Matters," *National Bureau of Economic Research,* October 2018, doi: 10.3386/w25121.

149. Kathleen Doheny, "Respect: How Managers Can Deliver What Workers Want," *Society for Human Resource Management,* April 13, 2022, https://www.shrm.org/topics-tools/news/managing-smart/respect-how-managers-can-deliver-workers-want.

150. Stephanie Neal et al., Development Dimension International: Global Leadership Forecast 2023, *Development Dimension International,* https://www.ddiworld.com/global-leadership-forecast-2023#.

151. Ibid., "Pencavel, "The Productivity of Working Hours" p. 11.

152. Camilla Frumar et al., "How to Make Hybrid Work for Women," *Gallup,* March 8, 2023, https://www.gallup.com/workplace/471239/hybrid-work-women.aspx.

153. Carol Hymowitz, "Though Now Routine, Bosses Still Stumble During Layoff Process," *The Wall Street Journal,* June 25, 2007.

154. Ben Horowitz, *The Hard Thing About Hard Things: Building a Business When There Are No Easy Answers* (New York: HarperCollins Publishers, 2014), pp. 70–72.

155. Pranshu Verma, "AI is starting to pick up who gets laid off: As layoffs ravage the tech industry, algorithms once used to help hire could now be deciding who gets cut," *The Washington Post,* February 20, 2023, https://www.washingtonpost.com/technology/2023/02/20/layoff-algorithms/.

156. Theodore Roosevelt quoted in Colin Combe, *Introduction to Management* (Oxford: Oxford University Press, 2014), p. 27.

157. "Approaches to Coaching and Mentoring," *Vitae: Realizing the Potential of Researchers, 2024,* https://www.vitae.ac.uk/doing-research/leadership-development-for-principal-investigators-pis/developing-individual-researchers/mentoring-and-coaching-researchers/approaches-to-coaching-and-mentoring.

158. Gotakh Bobde, *The Banyan Tree: Compilation of Great Thoughts,* 2019, p. 55.

159. John H. Eggers and Doug Clark, "Executive Coaching That Wins," *The Ivey Business Journal,* Sep-Oct 2000, p. 67.

160. "2024 Employee Engagement Strategies Checklist," *Gallup,* https://www.gallup.com/workplace/388685/2024-guide-employee-engagement.aspx.

161. "The Best One-on-One Meeting Frequency According to Research," *Quantum Workplace,* March 29, 2022.

162. John Whitmore, *Coaching for Performance: GROWing Human Potential and Purpose—The Principles and Practice of Coaching and Leadership,* 4th edition, People Skills for Professionals (Boston: Nicholas Brealey Publishing, 2009), ISBN 9781857885354. OCLC 314840903.

163. George T. Doran, "There is a S.M.A.R.T. Way to Write Management's Goals and Objectives," *Management Review (AMA Forum)* 70, no. 11 (1981): 35–36, http:// community.mis.temple.edu/mis0855002fall2015/files/2015/10/S.M.A.R.T-Way -Management-Review.pdf.

164. Whitmore, *Coaching for Performance.*

165. "From Benjamin Franklin to Joseph Priestley, 19 September 1772," Founders Online, *National Archives,* https://founders.archives.gov/documents/Franklin /01-19-02-0200.

166. Whitmore, *Coaching for Performance.*

167. Doran, "There is a S.M.A.R.T. Way to Write Management's Goals and Objectives," pp. 35–36.

168. Ibid.

169. Ibid.

170. Ibid.

171. F. John Reh, "A Guide to Understanding the Role of a Mentor," *The Balance Careers,* August 14, 2019.

172. Gracey Cantalupo, "Does Mentoring Still Matter For Fortune 500 Companies?" *Forbes,* May 19, 2022.

173. "Time to talk: What has to change for women at work," *PricewaterhouseCoopers,* 2018, p.4, https://www.pwc.com/gx/en/about/diversity/iwd/international- womens-day-pwc-time-to-talk-report.pdf.

174. "Women in the Workplace study: The State of Women in Corporate America," 2023, *LeanIn*.Org & McKinsey & Company, p. 8, https://www.mckinsey. com/~/media/mckinsey/featured%20insights/diversity%20and%20inclusion /women%20in%20the%20workplace%202022/women-in-the-workplace-2022 .pdf.

175. Fitch and Agrawal, "Why Women Are Better Managers Than Men."

176. Andy Grove, *High Output Management* (New York: Random House, 1983), p. xxvi.

177. Ei Mon Mon and Lee Lu, "An Action Research Study on the Impact of Human Resource Practices Towards the Employee Job Satisfaction: A Case Study of Private Hospital in Myanmar," *International Journal of Economics and Business Administration,* Volume X, Issue 3, 2022, p. 119. Also found in C. Fey and I. Borkman, "The Effect of Human Resource Management Practices on MNC Subsidiary Performance in Russia," 2001.

178. Fuhrmans and Ellis, "Half of College Grads Are Working Jobs That Don't Use Their Degrees."

179. Saadia Zahidi et al., "The Future of Jobs Report 2023," *World Economic Forum,* May 2023, p. 7, https://www3.weforum.org/docs/WEF_Future_of_Jobs_2023. pdf.

180. Jonathan Rothwell, "The American Upskilling Study shows workers want skills training," *Gallup and Amazon*, September 9, 2021, pp. 12 & 14, https://www.aboutamazon.com/news/workplace/the-american-upskilling-study-shows-workers-want-skills-training.

181. Lauraine Genota, "Generation Z Prefers Learning From YouTube, Not Books," *Education Week*, August 24, 2018, https://www.edweek.org/technology/generation-z-prefers-learning-from-youtube-not-books/2018/08

182. Bill Gates and Collins Hemingway, *Business @ the Speed of Thought* (New York: Warner Books, 1999), p. 248.

183. Ben Wigert et al., "Re-Engineering Performance Management," *Gallup*, 2017, p. 15, https://www.gallup.com/workplace/238064/re-engineering-performance-management.aspx.

184. Mary Walton, *The Deming Management Method* (New York: Penguin Books, 1986), p. 36.

185. Robby Brumberg, "The demise of the annual performance review has been greatly exaggerated," *PR Daily*, August 31, 2021, https://www.prdaily.com/the-demise-of-the-annual-performance-review-has-been-greatly-exaggerated/.

186. Marcus Buckingham, "Annual Reviews are a Terrible Way to Evaluate Employees," *The Wall Street Journal*, April 30, 2022, https://www.wsj.com/articles/annual-reviews-are-a-terrible-way-to-evaluate-employees-11651291254.

187. Wigert et al., "Re-Engineering Performance Management," p. 15.

188. "2024 Employee Engagement Strategies Checklist."

189. Mark Benjamin, "Strategies and Tips for Dealing with Difficult Employees," *Employee Benefits Plan Review*, Volume 62, Issue 12, (June 2008): pp. 11–12, https://www.autodealertodaymagazine.com/308726/strategies-and-tips-for-dealing-with-difficult-employees.

190. "13 Justifications for Termination," Indeed for Employers, accessed April 10, 2025, https://www.indeed.com/hire/c/info/reasons-for-termination.

191. Joseph R. Biden, Jr., "Executive Order on Diversity, Equity, Inclusion, and Accessibility in the Federal Workforce," The White House, June 25, 2021.

192. Ibid.

193. Ibid.

194. Ibid.

195. "Best Practice" Definition, *National Institute of Standards and Technology*, Information Technology Laboratory, Computer Security Resource Center.

196. "What is Inclusion?" *Inclusive Employers*.

197. Rachel Minkin, "Diversity, Equality and Inclusion in the Workplace," *Pew Research Center Report, May 17, 2023*, https://www.pewresearch.org/social-trends/2023/05/17/diversity-equity-and-inclusion-in-the-workplace/.

198. Kellie Wong, "Diversity and Inclusion in the Workplace: Benefits and Challenges," *Achievers*, updated on March 25, 2024, https://www.achievers.com/blog/diversity-and-inclusion/.

199. Katherine W. Phillips, "How Diversity Makes Us Smarter: Being around people who are different from us makes us more creative, diligent, and hard-working," *Scientific American*, October 1, 2014.

200. Vivian Hunt et al., "Diversity matters even more: The case for holistic impact," *McKinsey & Company*, December 5, 2023, https://www.mckinsey.com/featured-insights/diversity-and-inclusion/diversity-matters-even-more-the-case-for-holistic-impact.

201. Christine Smith and Stephanie Turner, "The Radical Transformation of Diversity and Inclusion: The Millennial Influence," *The Leadership Center for Inclusion*, Deloitte University, 2015, p. 5, https://www2.deloitte.com/content/dam/Deloitte/us/Documents/about-deloitte/us-inclus-millennial-influence-120215.pdf.

202. Emaline Soken-Huberty, "Examples pf Equality and Equity in the Workplace," *Human Rights Careers*.

203. Biden, Jr., "Executive Order on Diversity, Equity, Inclusion, and Accessibility in the Federal Workforce."

204. Johanna Maleh and Tiffany Bosley, "Disability and Death Probability Tables for Insured Workers Who Attain Age 20 In 2022," Actuarial Note, Number 2022.6, *Social Security Administration*, December 2022.

205. "Why Hire Persons With Disabilities," Fact Sheet 3, United Nations Enable, United Nations.

206. Nicole Maestas and Kathleen J. Mullen, "Unmet Need for Workplace Accommodation," *Journal of Policy Analysis and Management*, May 16, 2019, Volume 38, Issue 4, pp. 1004–1017.

207. "Employers and the ADA: Myths and Facts."

208. "Resources for Finding Candidates with Disabilities: Explore resources your organization can use to source candidates with disabilities," *Employer Assistance and Resource Network for Disability Inclusion*, https://askearn.org/page/finding-candidates-with-disabilities-2.

209. Ray Kurzweil, *The Age of Spiritual Machines: When Computers Exceed Human Intelligence*, (New York: Penguin Group, 1999), p. 268.

210. Kristine Larsen, *Stephen Hawking: A Biography* (Amherst, New York: Prometheus Books, 2007).

211. "Diversity Primer," *Diversity Best Practices, Chapter 6: Diversity and Inclusion Officers*, September 23, 2009, p. 97.

212. Ibid.

213. Anke Mogannam, "Leveraging Differences to Drive Success: 5 Best Practices for Building a Diverse Workforce and an Inclusive Workplace," *Oracle Fusion Cloud Human Capital Management Blog*, March 10, 2014.

214. "Want to improve productivity? Make friends at workplace," *The Economic Times*, last updated July 3, 2017, https://economictimes.indiatimes.com/jobs/want-to-improve-productivity-make-friends-at-workplace/articleshow/59428190.cms?from=mdr.

215. Laura Colby, *Road to Power: How GM's Mary Barra Shattered the Glass Ceiling* (Hoboken, NJ: John Wiley & Sons, Inc.; 2015), p. 58.

216. "Diversity Primer," p. 97.

217. Adedayo Akala, "Cost of Racism: U.S. Economy Lost $16 Trillion Because Of Discrimination, Bank Says", *National Public Radio*, September 23, 2020.

218. Ryan Pendell, "Avoid Virtue Signaling; Embrace Culture-Changing DEI Initiatives," *Gallup,* August 16, 2022, https://www.gallup.com/workplace/396593 /avoid-virtue-signaling-embrace-culture-changing-dei-initiatives.aspx.

219. "The Importance of Inclusion in the Workplace," *Korn Ferry, 2024.*

220. John Stuart Mill quoted in J.W. Parker, *Principles of Political Economy with Some of the Applications to Social Philosophy,* 1848 and in Ellen Ernst Kossek and Kyung-Hee Lee, Creating Gender-Inclusive Organizations: Lessons from Research and Practice (Toronto: University of Toronto Press, 2020).

221. Peter J. Klein and Angelia Berrie, *A Passion for Giving: Tools and Inspiration for Creating a Charitable Foundation,* (Hoboken, NJ: John Wiley & Sons, Inc.; 2012), p. 67.

222. Sara Rowe, "How to Succeed as an Introvert in an Extroverted World," *Vibrant Life* 31, no. 5 (Sept/Oct 2015): pp. 38–41.

223. Henry Ford Health Staff, "Introvert Or Extrovert? How Your Personality Type Can Impact Your Brain," *Henry Ford Health,* September 8, 2022.

224. Marti Olsen Laney, *The Introvert Advantage: How to Thrive in an Extrovert World* (New York: Workman Publishing, 2002), p. 43.

225. Jennifer B. Kahnweiler, *The Introverted Leader: Building on Your Quiet Strength,* (San Francisco: Berrett-Koehler Publishers, Inc., 2013), pp. 2–3.

226. Dan Buettner, "Are Extroverts Happier Than Introverts? Extroverts and Introverts Interact with the World in Different Ways," *Psychology Today,* May 14, 2012, https:// www.psychologytoday.com/us/blog/thrive/201205/are-extroverts-happier -introverts.

227. Cain, *Quiet: The Power of Introverts in a World That Can't Stop Talking,* p. 265.

228. Cain, *Quiet: The Power of Introverts in a World That Can't Stop Talking,* p. 168.

229. Cain, *Quiet: The Power of Introverts in a World That Can't Stop Talking,* p. 11.

230. "Extroversion," *Psychology Today,* https://www.psychologytoday.com/us/basics /extroversion#:~:text=People%20who%20identify%20as%20extroverts,spend %20too%20much%20time%20alone.

231. Cain, *Quiet: The Power of Introverts in a World That Can't Stop Talking,* p. 167.

232. Cain, *Quiet: The Power of Introverts in a World That Can't Stop Talking,* p. 168.

233. David Kalt, "How I Empower the Introverts on My Staff," *The Wall Street Journal,* April 30, 2018.

234. Ibid.

235. Annette Clancy, "Help Introverts Excel," *Accountancy Ireland* 49, no. 5 (Oct 2017): p. 19.

236. Christine Thompson, "Introverts and Employee Engagement: A Manager's Guide," *Quantum Workplace,* August 30, 2018.

237. Ron Edmondson, "7 Ways to Help Introverts on Your Team Better Engage in Meetings," August 21, 2019.

238. Donna M. Owens, "Quiet Time," *HR Magazine* Vol. 58, no. 12 (Dec 2013): pp. 26–27.

239. Leslie Gordon, "Introverts in an Extroverts' World," *ABA Journal* 102, no. 1 (January 2016): pp. 36–41.

240. Rowe, "How to Succeed as an Introvert in an Extroverted World," pp. 38–41.

241. Cain, *Quiet: The Power of Introverts in a World That Can't Stop Talking,* p. 350.

242. Adam M. Grant et al., "Reversing the extraverted leadership advantage: The role of employee proactivity," *Academy of Management Journal,* 54(3), pp. 528–550. https://doi.org/10.5465/AMJ.2011.61968043

243. "Employee Engagement Indicators," *Gallup,* 2024, https://www.gallup.com/394373/indicator-employee-engagement.aspx#:~:text=In%20the%20latest%20reading%2C%20from,than%202020's%20high%20of%2036%25.

244. Pete Ross, "If You're an Introvert, You're Probably Getting Screwed at Work," *Observer,* January 30, 2017, https://observer.com/2017/01/introverts-underrepresented-managerial-positions/.

245. Elena Lytkina Botelho et al., "What Sets Successful CEOs Apart," *Harvard Business Review,* May-June 2017, https://hbr.org/2017/05/what-sets-successful-ceos-apart.

246. Fitch and Agrawal, "Why Women Are Better Managers Than Men."

247. Joanne Sujansky, "The Poor Performer Confrontation Handbook: Eight Rules for Dealing with Employees Who Are Bringing Your Company Down," *Cost Engineering Volume 49,* Issue 8 (August 2007): pp. 14–15.

248. John Shetcliffe, "Managing Difficult Employees," *Insurance Brokers Monthly,* Lye, Vol. 55, Iss. 6 (June 2005): pp. 21–23.

249. Benjamin, "Strategies and Tips for Dealing with Difficult Employees," pp. 11–12.

250. "Progressive Discipline," *Indiana University Human Resources,* updated 2021.

251. Ibid.

252. "Employee Assistance Programs," U.S. Office of Personnel Management, accessed April 10, 2025, https://www.opm.gov/policy-data-oversight/worklife/employee-wellness-programs/employee-assistance-programs/.

253. John Foltz and Joan Fulton, "Dealing with Problem Employees," Feed and Grain 44, no. 4 (Jun/Jul 2005): pp. 38–41.

254. Gary Hobson, "Dealing with Employee Problems," *SuperVision* Volume 50, Issue 9 (September 1989): pp. 9–11.

255. Benjamin, "Strategies and Tips for Dealing with Difficult Employees," pp. 11–12.

256. Ibid., "How to Create a Performance Improvement Plan."

257. "What Is a Performance Improvement Plan (PIP)?," Indeed for Employers, accessed April 10, 2025, https://www.indeed.com/hire/c/info/pip-meaning.

258. Dan Hoppen, "10 Examples of Effective and Ineffective Employee Feedback," Quantum Workplace, November 28, 2018.

259. Jim Olsztynski, "Dealing with Difficult Employees," National Driller 29, no. 9 (September 2008): 14, pp. 16–17.

260. Ibid.

261. Ibid.

262. Ibid.

263. Ibid.

264. Christine Organ, "How to Create a Performance Improvement Plan," Forbes Advisor, June 3, 2024.

265. Ibid.

266. Ibid.

267. "Cognitive Bias 101: What It Is and How To Overcome It," *Cleveland Clinic*, May 2, 2023.

268. "13 Justifications for Termination," Indeed for Employers.

269. "What is a Termination Letter," *Bamboo HR, 2024.*

270. "Termination Guidance for Employers," USAGov, accessed April 10, 2025, https://www.usa.gov/termination-for-employers.

271. Elisabeth Kübler-Ross, *On Death and Dying*, (New York: Macmillan Publishing Company, 2014).

272. Ibid.

273. Everett Spain and Boris Groysberg, "Making Exit Interviews Count: This underused practice can be a powerful tool for retention," *Harvard Business Review*, April 2016, https://hbr.org/2016/04/making-exit-interviews-count.

274. Branham, *The 7 Hidden Reasons Employees Leave*, p. 212.

275. "The Frontline Leader Project: Exploring the Most Critical Segment of Leaders," *Development Dimensions International*, 2019, p. 59.

276. Eli Amdur, "Costs of the 'Great Resignation' Starting to Add Up," *Forbes,* January 19, 2023, https://www.forbes.com/sites/eliamdur/2023/01/19/costs-of-the-great-resignation-starting-to-add-up/?sh=3a1df60359eb.

277. Martha Frase-Blunt, 'Making Exit Interviews Work,' *Society for Human Resource Management*, August 1, 2004, https://www.shrm.org/topics-tools/news/hr-magazine/making-exit-interviews-work.

278. "What Are the Benefits and Drawbacks of Using Online Exit Surveys vs. Face-to-Face Interviews?," *Linkedin*, accessed April 10, 2025, https://www.linkedin.com/advice/1/what-benefits-drawbacks-using-online-exit-surveys.

279. Frase-Blunt, "Making Exit Interviews Work."

280. Frase-Blunt, "Making Exit Interviews Work."

281. Christina Pavlou, "How to Conduct an Effective Exit Interview," *Workable Resources for Employers,* September 2023.

282. Frase-Blunt, "Making Exit Interviews Work."

283. Patrick Ball, "11 Exit Interview Questions You Should Always Ask," Care.Com (blog), September 3, 2021, https://www.care.com/c/11-exit-interview-questions-you-should-always/.

284. Ibid.

285. Ibid.

286. "13 Must-Ask Exit Interview Questions," *Glassdoor,* February 3, 2021.

287. Ibid.

288. Ibid.

289. "18 Standard Exit Interview Questions," bestjobinterview.com.

290. Ibid.

291. Ibid.

292. Richard Titmuss, *The Gift Relationship: From Human Blood to Social Policy,* edited by Ann Oakley and John Ashton, expanded and updated edition (New York: New York Press, 1977). Also found in Daniel H. Pink, Drive: The Surprising Truth About What Motivates Us, (New York: Riverhead Books, 2009), p. 45.

293. Daniel Ariely et al., Doing Good or Doing Well? Image Motivation and Monetary Incentives in Behaving Prosocially," *Federal Reserve Bank of Boston Working Paper No. 07-9*, August 2007. Also found in Pink, Drive, pp. 46–47.

294. Spain and Groysberg, "Making Exit Interviews Count."

295. Beth N. Carvin, "How to Improve Exit Interview Response Rates, *Nobscot Corporation*, February 5, 2020.

296. The Buddha quoted in Maya Annika Dayal, *Off the Beaten Path: My Roundabout Journey to Humanitarianism*, (Morrisville, NC: Lulu Press, 2016) p. 34.

297. Michael Watkins et al., "Hit the Ground Running: Transitioning to New Leadership Roles," *International Institute for Management Development* 33 (2014), p. 1.

298. Mark Twain quoted in Thorsten Fögen and Mireille M. Lee, *Bodies and Boundaries in Graeco-Roman Antiquity*, (Berlin: Walter de Gruyter, 2009), p. 181.

299. Sandi Mann, *Managing Your Boss* (London: Hodder Education, 2012), p. 34.

300. Thomas Edison quoted in Barbara Bonner, *Inspiring Courage*, (Somerville, MA: Wisdom Publications, 2017)

301. Louis Pasteur quoted in Robert I. Fitzhenry, editor, *The Harper Book of Quotations*, Third Edition, (New York: Quill/HarperResource, 1993) p 5.

302. "Getting More by Working Together—Opportunities for Linking Planning and Operations," U.S Department of Transportation, Federal Highway Administration, https://ops.fhwa.dot.gov/publications/lpo_ref_guide/prim0406 .htm#:~:text=Performance%20measurement%20is%20a%20process,which%20 clients%20are%20satisfied)%20and.

303. "Measure performance and set targets," *The Chamber of Commerce of Metropolitan Montreal*.

304. Claire C. Caruso et al., "Overtime and Extended Work Shifts: Recent Findings on Illnesses, Injuries, and Health Behaviors," *U.S. Department of Health and Human Services, Centers for Disease Control and Prevention*, 2004, p. 27.

305. Amy Witkoski Stimpfel, Douglas M. Sloane, and Linda H. Aiken, "The Longer the Shifts for Hospital Nurses, the Higher the Levels of Burnout and Patient Dissatisfaction," *Health Affairs (Project Hope)* 31, no. 11 (November 2012): 2501–9, https://doi.org/10.1377/hlthaff.2011.1377.

306. Lydia Saad, "The '40-Hour' Workweek Is Actually Longer by Seven Hours," *Gallup*, August 29, 2014, https://news.gallup.com/poll/175286/hour-workweek -actually-longer-seven-hours.aspx

307. Pencavel, "The Productivity of Working Hours," p. 21.

308. Noor Nanji, "Elon Musk tells Twitter staff to work long hours or leave," BBC, November 16, 2022.

309. Kinsey Crowley and Max Hauptman, "Down 80%: Fidelity says X has plummeted in value since Elon Musk's takeover," *USA Today*, October 2, 2024.

310. "GDP per capita (current US$) – Germany," World Bank Group, https://data .worldbank.org/indicator/NY.GDP.PCAP.CD?locations=DE.

311. Jeffrey A Hall et al., "Which mediated social interactions satisfy the need to belong?" *Journal of Computer-Mediated Communication*, Volume 28, Issue 1, January 2023, zmac026, https://doi.org/10.1093/jcmc/zmac026

312. Lisa Evans, "Why You Need to Actually Talk to Your Coworkers Face-to-Face," *The Future of Work*, October 13, 2014.

313. Susan Pinker, *The Village Effect: How Face-to-Face Contact Can Make Us Healthier, Happier and Smarter* (New York: Spiegel & Rau, 2014), p. 262.

314. "Millennials as Bosses—Forget Face-to-Face, Online Messaging New Norm for Communicating with Direct Reports, According to Korn Ferry," *Korn Ferry*, March 12, 2018, https://ir.kornferry.com/news-events/press-releases/detail/227 /millennials-as-bosses-forget-face-to-face-online-messaging-new-norm-for -communicating-with-direct-reports-according-to-korn-ferry-survey.

315. Vicky Hallett, "Should I be insulted if my name is listed last on a group email? *The Washington Post*, May 9, 2017, https://www.washingtonpost.com/national /health-science/should-i-be-insulted-if-my-name-is-listed-last-on-an-group -email/2017/05/05/35c9a344-2f3d-11e7-9534-00e4656c22aa_story.html.

316. Deborah Tannen, "The (Sometimes Unintentional) Subtext of Digital Conversations," *The Atlantic*, April 27, 2017, https://www.theatlantic.com/technology /archive/2017/04/the-sometimes-unintentional-subtext-of-digital-conversations /524106/.

317. Blaise Pascal quoted in *Lettres Provinciales Ou Les Lettres Escrites Par Louis De Montalte*, VN Provincial De Ses Amis & Aux RR. Pp. Jesuites (Cologne: Pierre de la Valle, M. DC. VII. (1657))

318. Evan DeFilippis et al., "Collaborating During Coronavirus: The Impact of Covid-19 on the Nature of Work," *National Bureau of Economic Research*, July 2020.

319. Vanessa K. Bohns, "A Face-to-Face Request is 34 Times More Successful Than An Email," *Harvard Business Review*, April 11, 2017, https://hbr.org/2017/04 /a-face-to-face-request-is-34-times-more-successful-than-an-email.

320. Pinker, *The Village Effect*, p. 262.

321. Carl Sagan, *Broca's Brain, Reflections on the Romance of Science*, (New York: The Random House Publishing Group, 1974), p. 35.

322. Iskandar Aminov, "Decision making in the age of urgency," *McKinsey & Company*, April 30, 2019, https://www.mckinsey.com/capabilities/people-and -organizational-performance/our-insights/decision-making-in-the-age-of -urgency.

323. Marcia W. Blenko et al., *Decide & Deliver: 5 Steps to Breakthrough Performance in Your Organization* (Boston: Harvard Business Review Press, 2010), p. 88.

324. Ibid.

325. William James quoted in Mary Elizabeth Croft, *How I Clobbered Every Cash-Confiscatory Agency Known to Man: A Spiritual Economics Book on $$$ and Remembering Who You Are* (Create Space Independent Publishing Platform, 2017), p. 32.

326. Auguste Rodin quoted in Gene C. Hayden, *The Follow-Through Factor: Getting from Doubt to Done* (Toronto: McClelland & Stewart, 2009), p. 224.

327. Michael Johnson quoted in "50 Leaders' Inspirational Quotes on Employee Engagement and Workplace Culture," *Quantum Workplace*.

328. "You Want It When?" Time Management Practitioner Consensus Survey, *Institute for Corporate Productivity*, June 27, 2007, https://www.i4cp.com /news/2007/06/26/you-want-it-when.

329. Reginald Bell and Nancy Dusty Bodie, "Delegation, Authority, and Responsibility: Removing the Rhetorical Obstructions in the Way of an Old Paradigm," *Journal of Leadership,* Accountability and Ethics 9, no. 2, (May 2012): pp. 94–108.

330. Lynne Joy McFarland, "Leading the Way," *Entrepreneur,* Vol. 22, January 1994, p. 224.

331. Jack Welch, "Three Ways to Take Your Company's Pulse," *Small Business Journal,* February 16, 2016.

332. "State of the Global Workplace 2024 Report: The Voice of the World's Employees," *Gallup Workplace,* p. 3, https://www.gallup.com/workplace/349484/state -of-the-global-workplace.aspx?thank-you-report-form=1.

333. Ibid., "Employee Engagement Indicators."

334. Ibid.

335. "State of the Global Workplace 2024 Report," p. 4.

336. Ibid., "Employee Engagement Indicators."

337. Ibid.

338. "State of the Global Workplace 2024 Report:," p. 4.

339. Ibid., "Employee Engagement Indicators."

340. Ibid.

341. "State of the Global Workplace 2024 Report," p. 2.

342. Schmutz et al., "How effective is teamwork really?"

343. "2024 Employee Engagement Strategies Checklist."

344. Tom Rath and Donald O. Clifton, "The Power of Praise and Recognition: Research shows they are crucial for increasing employee productivity and engagement," *Gallup Business Journal,* July 8, 2004, https://news.gallup.com /businessjournal/12157/power-praise-recognition.aspx.

345. Wigert et al., "Re-Engineering Performance Management," p. 15,.

346. Abagail Johnson Hess, "LinkedIn: 94% of employees say they would stay at a company longer for this reason—and it's not a raise," *LinkedIn,* February 27, 2019, https://www.linkedin.com/posts/linkedinlearning_94-of-employees-say -that-they-would-stay-activity-6372632932300963840-k9hI/.

347. Brent Gleeson, "5 Powerful Steps to Improve Employee Engagement," *Forbes,* October 15, 2017, https://www.forbes.com/sites/brentgleeson/2017/10/15/5 -powerful-steps-to-improve-employee-engagement/?sh=7cd7cbaf341d.

348. Helliwell et al., "Happiness at Different Ages."

349. Tom Rath, *StrengthsFinder 2.0,* (New York: Gallup Press, 2007), p. iii.

350. "Live Your Best Life Using Your Strengths," *Gallup, 2024.*

351. Brian Brim and Jim Asplund, "Driving Engagement by Focusing on Strengths," *Gallup,* November 12, 2009.

352. Jackie Wiles, "Is it Time to Toss Out Your Old Employee Engagement Survey?" *Gartner,* November 26, 2018, https://www.gartner.com/smarterwithgartner /is-it-time-to-toss-out-your-old-employee-engagement-survey.

353. Aaron De Smet et al., "Three types of modern flexibility today's workers demand," McKinsey & Company, April 25, 2022, https://www.mckinsey .com/capabilities/people-and-organizational-performance/our-insights/the -organization-blog/three-types-of-modern-flexibility-todays-workers-demand.

354. Beth M. McFarland, "Leveraging Workplace Flexibility for Engagement and Productivity," *SHRM Foundation Effective Practice Guidelines Series,* 2014, p. viii.
355. Ibid., p. 9.
356. Brucks and Levav, "Virtual Communication Curbs Creative Idea Generation."
357. Ibid.
358. Jack Kelly, "Belgium Is The Latest Country to Join the Four-Day Workweek," *Forbes,* April 14, 2022.
359. Stefano de Luca Tamajo, "The right to disconnect around the world," *Ius Laboris: Global HR Lawyers,* January 3, 2024.
360. Tatiana Pignon et al., "Making It Stick: The UK Four Day Week Pilot One Year On," *Autonomy Research Ltd,* February 2024, https://autonomy.work/portfolio/making-it-stick/.
361. Emerson M. Wickwire et al., "Shift Work and Shift Work Sleep Disorder," Chest. 2017 May; 151(5): 1156–1172. Published online 2016 Dec 21. doi: 10.1016/j.chest.2016.12.007.
362. Stimpfel, Sloane, and Aiken, "The Longer the Shifts for Hospital Nurses, The Higher the Levels of Burnout and Patient Dissatisfaction," pp. 2501–2509.
363. McFarland, "Leveraging Workplace Flexibility for Engagement and Productivity."
364. Ibid.
365. Ibid.
366. Ibid.
367. "Telework Basics," *U.S. Office of Personnel Management.*
368. Kate Lister, "The State of Remote Work 2022," *Owl Labs Global Workplace Analytics.*
369. Brucks and Levav, "Virtual Communication Curbs Creative Idea Generation."
370. Mayo Clinic Staff, "Caregiver stress: Tips for taking care of yourself," Mayo Clinic, August 9, 2023.
371. "Get paid as a caregiver for a family member," *USA.gov,* updated July 22, 2024.
372. Gloria Mark, Daniela Gudith, and Ulrich Klocke, "The Cost of Interrupted Work: More Speed and Stress," in *Proceedings of the SIGCHI Conference on Human Factors in Computing Systems,* CHI '08 (CHI '08: CHI Conference on Human Factors in Computing Systems, Florence, Italy: Association for Computing Machinery, 2008), 107–10, https://doi.org/10.1145/1357054.1357072.
373. Frumar et al., "How to Make Hybrid Work for Women."
374. Brucks and Levav, "Virtual Communication Curbs Creative Idea Generation."
375. "65% of remote workers do not want to return to the office—here's why," *World Economic Forum,* April 27, 2021, https://www.weforum.org/agenda/2021/04/survey-65-of-remote-workers-do-not-want-to-return-to-the-office/.
376. John M. Bremen, "Where Will Return-To-Office Mandates Land In 2025? *Forbes,* February 18, 2025.
377. Kevin J. Delaney, "The sweet spot for hybrid," Charter Works, Inc., *McKinsey,* July 30, 2023, https://www.charterworks.com/hybrid-work-mckinsey-katy-george/.

378. Rachel Lerman et al., "Elon Musk tells Tesla, Space X workers to go back to the office or go away," *The Washington Post,* June 1, 2022, https://www.washingtonpost.com/technology/2022/06/01/elon-musk-tesla-office/.

379. C. Mandler, "Elon Musk's X worth 71.5% less than it was when he bought the platform in 2022, Fidelity says," *CBS News,* January 22, 2024.

380. Chantal DaSilva, "Apple workers launch petition over company's reported return-to-office plan," *NBC News,* August 22, 2022.

381. Sam Tabahriti, "Apple is threatening to take action against staff who aren't coming into the office 3 days a week, report says," *Business Insider,* March 24, 2023.

382. Taylor Telford, "Ordered back to the office, top tech talent left instead, study finds," *The Washington Post,* updated May 13, 2024.

383. Benjamin Pimentel, "Microsoft exec weights in on Silicon Valley remote work trash talk." *San Francisco Examiner,* updated June 9, 2023.

384. Yuye Ding and Mark (Shuai) Ma, Return-to-Office Mandates (December 25, 2023). Available at SSRN: https://ssrn.com/abstract=4675401 or http://dx.doi.org/10.2139/ssrn.4675401

385. "Labor Shortages are Here to Stay," International Strategy Analysis, April 29, 2024.

386. Pinker, *The Village Effect, p. 268.*

387. Aleks Krotoski, "Robin Dunbar: We can only ever have 150 friends at most...," *The Guardian,* March 13, 2010, https://www.theguardian.com/technology/2010/mar/14/my-bright-idea-robin-dunbar.

388. Pinker, *The Village Effect,* p. 268.

389. Nicholas Bloom et al., "How Hybrid Working From Home Works Out," National Bureau of Economic Research, NBER Working Paper Series, Working Paper 30292, revised January 2023.

390. Jack Kelly, "'Quiet Vacationing' Raises Ethical Questions This Summer," *Forbes,* May 29, 2024.

391. Ibid.

392. Aimee Groth, "Richard Branson Says That Marissa Meyer Got It Wrong About Remote Employees," Business Insider, February 25, 2013.

393. Pink, *Drive,* p. 9.

394. Ibid., p. 36.

395. Ibid., p. 10.

396. Alfie Kohn, "Why Incentive Plans Cannot Work," *Harvard Business Review,* September–October 1993.

397. Wigert et al., "Re-Engineering Performance Management," p. 15.

398. Becki Hall, "Recognizing employees isn't enough – and here's why," *Interact,* February 25, 2019, https://www.interactsoftware.com/blog/recognizing-employees-isnt-enough-and-heres-why/.

399. Ibid.

400. Ibid.

401. Mike Robbins quoted in "The Power of Appreciation," *TED Talk,* https://www.ted.com/talks/mike_robbins_the_power_of_appreciation.

402. Rainer Strack, "Decoding Global Talent: 200,000 Survey Responses on Global Mobility and Employment Preferences," The Boston Consulting Group, October 2014, p. 16.

403. "4 Surprising Benefits of Peer-to-Peer Recognition Programs," O.C. Tanner, accessed April 16, 2025, https://www.octanner.com/articles/4-surprising-benefits-of-peer-to-peer-recognition-programs.

404. "How peer-to-peer recognition boosts employee engagement," People Matters Global.

405. "The Importance of Employee Recognition: Low Cost, High Impact," Gallup Workplace, updated January 12, 2024.

406. "4 Surprising Benefits of Peer-to-Peer Recognition Programs."

407. Marcus Tullius Cicero quoted in Amy Newmark, *Chicken Soup for the Soul: Attitude of Gratitude: 101 Stories About Counting Your Blessings & the Power of Thankfulness,* (Cos Cob Connecticut: Chicken Soup for the Soul Publishing, LLC, 2022), p. Introduction.

408. Schmutz et al., "How effective is teamwork really?"

409. Bradley Kirkman et al., "Teamwork Works Best When Top Performers Are Rewarded," *Harvard Business Review,* March 14, 2016.

410. Ray Fisman, "Forget About That Cash Bonus, Harvard Business Review," March 4, 2013.

411. Amit Kumar and Nicholas Epley, "Undervaluing Gratitude: Expressers Misunderstand the Consequences of Showing Appreciation," *Psychological Science* 29, no. 9 (September 2018): pp. 1423–35, doi.org/10.1177/0956797618772506.

412. "2024 Employee Engagement Strategies Checklist."

413. Ibid.

414. Jeff Hyman et al., "Take 5: How to Keep Your High Performers Happy: Plus, Ways to Prevent Toxic Workers from Corrupting Your Team," Kellogg School of Management at Northwestern University, May 2, 2018, https://insight.kellogg.northwestern.edu/article/take-5-how-to-keep-your-high-performers-happy.

415. George Washington quoted in John Walcott, "17 Rules of Presidential Behavior from George Washington," *The Atlantic,* December 16, 2018.

416. William James quoted in Dale Carnegie, *How to Win Friends and Influence People* (New York: Gallery Books, 1936), p. 18.

417. W. Somerset Maugham, *Of Human Bondage* (Garden City, N.Y: The Sun Dial Press, 1915), p. 267.

418. Caitlin Szikora, "Fostering Employee Engagement Through Work Social Events," *Mentor Works,* September 11, 2019.

419. Adam Grant, "The One Question You Should Ask About Every New Job," *The New York Times,* December 19, 2015, https://www.nytimes.com/2015/12/20/opinion/sunday/the-one-question-you-should-ask-about-every-new-job.html.

420. Shivaram Rajgopal, "CEOs and CFOs Share How Corporate Culture Matters," *Columbia Business School Newsroom,* November 19, 2015, https://business.columbia.edu/newsroom.

421. Christina Lee, "2016 Employee Job Satisfaction and Engagement: Revitalizing a Changing Workforce," *Society for Human Resource Management,* 2016.

422. Evgueni Ivantsov, "Strategic risk failure is what unites Credit Suisse and SVB," *Financial Times*, May 15, 2023.

423. K. R. Goswami, *Master Your Managerial Behavior: 21 Secrets to Scale Up Excellence in an Organization,* (Gurgaon, India: Zorba Books, 2021), p. 90.

424. Sun Tzu quoted in Lieutenant General David W. Barno, "Fighting 'The Other War:' Counterinsurgency Strategy in Afghanistan, 2003–2005," *Military Review,* The Professional Journal of the U.S. Army, January-February 2008, p. 87.

425. Indeed Editorial Team, "10 Business Strategy Examples (And Why It Helps To Have One)," *Indeed Career Guide,* updated May 26, 2023, https://www.indeed.com/career-advice/career-development/business-strategy-examples.

426. Ibid.

427. Ricardo Viana Vargas, "Closing the Gap: Designing and Delivering a Strategy that Works," *The Economist, Intelligence Unit,* 2017.

428. Robert S. Kaplan and David P. Norton, "The Office of Strategic Management," *Harvard Business Review,* October 2005, https://hbr.org/2005/10/the-office-of-strategy-management.

429. Gary L. Neilson et al., "The Secrets to Successful Strategy Execution," *Harvard Business Review Magazine,* June 1, 2008, https://hbr.org/2008/06/the-secrets-to-successful-strategy-execution.

430. Robert S. Kaplan and David P. Norton, *The Balanced Scorecard: Translating Strategy into Action,* (Boston, MA: Harvard Business School Press, 1996), pp. 7-15.

431. Robert S. Kaplan and David P. Norton, *The Balanced Scorecard: Translating Strategy into Action* (Boston, MA: Harvard Business Review Press, 1996), pp. 7–15.

432. W. Chan Kim and Renee Mauborgne, *Blue Ocean Strategy: How to Create Uncontested Market Space and Make the Competition Irrelevant,* (Boston: Harvard Business Review Press, 2015), https://hbr.org/2004/10/blue-ocean-strategy.

433. Ted Jackson, "The Blue Ocean Strategy: What It Is & How to Use It [+4 Examples]," *ClearPoint Strategy,* May 29, 2024.

434. J. Michael Scott et al., "Gap Analysis: a Geographic Approach to Protection of Biological Diversity," Wildlife Monographs, *The Wildlife Society,* No. 123, 1993.

435. Francis J. Aguilar, *Scanning the Business Environment,* (New York: McMillan Publishers, 1967).

436. Biplab Paul, "Background and development of the PESTEL analysis," LinkedIn, November 7, 2023.

437. Albert S. Humphrey, "SWOT Analysis for Management Consulting," *SRI International Alumni Association,* December 2005 Newsletter, December 2005, https://alumni.sri.com/newsletters/2005/AlumNews-Dec-2005.pdf.

438. Richard W. Puyt et al., "The Origins of SWOT Analysis," article in *Long Range Planning,* February 2023, DOI: 10.1016/j.lrp.2023.102304.

439. Michael E. Porter, "How Competitive Forces Shape Strategy," *Harvard Business Review,* May 1979 (Vol. 57, No. 2), pp. 137–145, https://hbr.org/1979/03/how-competitive-forces-shape-strategy.

440. Ibid.

441. Ibid.

442. Sun Tzu quoted in Barno, "Fighting 'The Other War'," p. 87.

443. John Kelly, "Key Performance Indicators," *Score, April 25, 2014.*

444. Heyden Enochson, "KPI Meaning + 27 Examples of Key Performance Indicators," *OnStrategy* (blog), accessed April 16, 2025, https://onstrategyhq.com /resources/27-examples-of-key-performance-Indicatoro/.

445. "2.8 million workplace injuries and illnesses in private industry in 2022, up 7.5% from 2021," TED: The Economics Daily, *U.S. Bureau of Labor Statistics,* December 14, 2023.

446. Geetha M. Waehrer and Ted R. Miller, "Does Safety Training Reduce Work Injury in the United States?" The Ergonomics Open Journal 2(1):26–39, December 20092(1):26–39, DOI:10.2174/1875934300902010026.

447. Enochson, "KPI Meaning + 27 Examples of Key Performance Indicators."

448. Mark Twain quoted in Randy Bartlett, *A Practitioner's Guide to Business Analytics,* (New York: McGraw-Hill, 2013), p. 8.

449. Albert Einstein quoted in Marelize Gergens and Jody Zall Kusek, *Making Monitoring Systems and Evaluation Systems Work: A Capacity Development Toolkit,* (Washington D.C.: The World Bank, 2009), p. 249.

450. Leo Tolstoy quoted in Paul E. Heacock, *Basic Relationship and Leadership Strategies,* (Bloomington, IN: Trafford Publishing, 2014) p. 2.

451. "What Are Workers' Rights? *Bureau of International Labor Affairs,* U.S. Department of Labor.

452. Morgan Rush, "Why Is it Important for an Employee Handbook to Include a Letter from the Chief?" *Bizfluent,* September 26, 2017.

453. "Employee Handbooks," Society for Human Resource Management, https:// www.shrm.org/business-solutions/partner-products/employee-handbooks.

454. "Employee Handbook (With Downloadable Templates)," *Indeed for Employers,* updated January 21, 2025)

455. "Make A Free Employee Handbook," Form Swift.

456. "Make Your Free Employee Handbook," Rocket Lawyer.

457. *Valve Handbook for New Employees: A fearless adventure in knowing what to do when no one's there telling you what to do,* Valve Press, 2012.

458. John Girard and JoAnn Girard, "Defining Knowledge Management: Toward an Applied Compendium," *Online Journal of Applied Knowledge Management* 3, no. 1 (2015): 1–20.

459. Ibid., pp. 1–20.

460. Ibid., pp. 1–20.

461. Kevin Desouza, and Yukika Awazu, "Knowledge Management," *Society of Human Resource Management HR Magazine,* November 1, 2003.

462. Mike Burk, "Knowledge Management: Everyone Benefits By Sharing Information," U.S. Department of Transportation, Federal Highway Administration, *Public Roads,* Nov/Dec 1999, Volume 63, Number 3.

463. "Knowledge Management," *Deloitte Services.*

464. Melany Gallant, "Why Knowledge Management Matters," *Saba,* August 24, 2015.

465. Simon Winchester, *Knowing What We Know: The Transmission of Knowledge From Ancient Wisdom to Modern Magic,* (New York: HarperCollins, 2023), pp. 20–24.

466. Plato, *Theaetetus,* Translated by Benjamin Jewett. Also found in Winchester, Knowing What We Know, pp. 340, 380.

467. Girard and Girard, "Defining Knowledge Management."

468. Benjamin Laker et al., "Dear Manager, You're Holding Too Many Meetings," *Harvard Business Review,* March 9, 2022, https://hbr.org/2022/03/dear-manager -youre-holding-too-many-meetings.

469. "Survey: 84 Percent of U.S. Workers Blame Bad Managers for Creating Unnecessary Stress," SHRM, August 12, 2020, https://www.shrm.org/about/press-room /survey-84-percent-u-s-workers-blame-bad-managers-creating-unnecessary -stress.

470. Janice M. Francisco, "How to Create and Facilitate Meetings that Matter," *Information Management Journal 41,* no. 6 (Nov/Dec 2007): pp. 54–56, 58.

471. Ibid.

472. Ibid.

473. Ibid.

474. Blenko et al., *Decide & Deliver,* p. 88.

475. Katherine A. Karl et al., "Virtual Work Meetings During the COVID-19 Pandemic: The Good, Bad, and Ugly," Small Group Research Journal. 2022 Jun; 53(3): 343–365. doi: 10.1177/10464964211015286.

476. Vasu Unnava et al., "Coffee with Co-Workers: Role of Caffeine on Evaluations of the Self and Others in Group Settings," *Journal of Psychopharmacology,* Vol. 32, April 5, 2018, https://doi.org./10.1177/0269881118760665.

477. Oliver Staley, "One of the world's biggest companies found the secret to better meetings: a wooden box," *Quartz,* March 30, 2018, https://qz.com/work/1241058/ one-of-the-worlds-biggest-companies-found-the-secret-to-better-meetings-a -wooden-box.

478. Henry M. Robert III et al., *Robert's Rules of Order, Newly Revised,* 12th Edition (New York: Hachette Book Group, 2020).

479. Robert Townsend, *Up the Organization: How to Stop the Corporation from Stifling People and Strangling Profits,* commemorative ed. (Hoboken: John Wiley & Sons, Inc., 2007), p. 130.

480. Allen C. Bluedorn et al., "The Effects of Stand-Up and Sit-Down Meeting Formats on Meeting Outcomes," *Journal of Applied Psychology* 84, no. 2 (1999): p. 284.

481. Donald Rumsfeld, "Donald Rumsfeld's Rules for Successful Meetings," *The Wall Street Journal,* May 10, 2013, https://www.wsj.com/articles/SB100014241278873 24326504578467211739938822.

482. Alex F. Osborne, *Applied Imagination: Principles and Procedures of Creative Problem Solving* (New York: Charles Scribner's Sons, 1953), p. 156.

483. Brian Mullen et al., "Productivity Loss in Brainstorming Groups: A Meta-Analytica Integration," *Basic and Applied Social Psychology* 12, no. 1 (1991): pp. 3–23, doi.org/10.1207/s15324834basp1201_1.

484. R. Brent Gallupe et al., "Electronic Brainstorming and Group Size," *Academy of Management Journal* 35, no. 2 (2017): pp. 352, doi.org/10.5465/256377.

485. Alan R. Dennis and Joseph S. Valacich, "Computer Brainstorming: More Heads Are Better Than One," *Journal of Applied Psychology* 78, no. 4 (1993): pp. 531–537.

486. Cain, *Quiet: The Power of Introverts in a World That Can't Stop Talking*, 265.

487. Marc T. Hamilton, Deborah G. Hamilton, and Theodore W. Zderic, "A Potent Physiological Method to Magnify and Sustain Soleus Oxidative Metabolism Improves Glucose and Lipid Regulation," *iScience* 25, no. 9 (September 16, 2022), https://doi.org/10.1016/j.isci.2022.104869.

488. "Warby Parker: Impact Report," Warby Parker, 2022.

489. Ibid.

490. Ibid.

491. Mark Zuckerberg, "Bringing the World Closer Together," Facebook, last edited March 15, 2021.

492. "15 Examples Mission Statements, Visions, and Values," Deliberate Directions, https://www.deliberatedirections.com/inspiring-missions/

493. Ibid.

494. "Purpose, Vision, and The Southwest Way," *Southwest.*

495. Ibid.

496. Ibid.

497. Ibid.

498. Andrew Van Dam, "The happiest, least stressful, most meaningful jobs in America," *The Washington Post,* January 6, 2023.

499. N. Kamarulzaman et al., "An Overview of the Influence of Physical Office Environments towards Employee," *Procedia Engineering* 20 (2011): pp. 262–268, doi.org/10.1016/j.proeng.2011.11.164.

500. Susan S. Lang, "Study Links Warm Offices to Fewer Typing Errors and Higher Productivity," *Cornell Chronicle*, October 19, 2004, https://news.cornell.edu/stories/2004/10/warm-offices-linked-fewer-typing-errors-higher-productivity.

501. R. Ferraro et al., "Lower sedentary metabolic rate in women compared with men," *J Clin Invest,* 1992 Sep; 90(3): pp. 780–4. doi: 10.1172/JCI115951. PMID: 1522233; PMCID: PMC329930.

502. M. Y. Beshir and J. D. Ramsey, "Comparison between male and female subjective estimates of thermal effects and sensations," *Appl Ergon,* 1981 Mar; 12(1): pp. 29–33. doi: 10.1016/0003–6870(81)90091–0. PMID: 15676395.

503. Christopher Ingraham, "Why Crowded Conference Rooms and Meetings Make You So, So, Tired," *The Washington Post*, June 16, 2019, https://www.washingtonpost.com/business/2019/06/06/why-crowded-meetings-conference-rooms-make-you-so-so-tired/.

504. "Why plants in the office make us more productive," *University of Exeter*, September 1, 2014.

505. Virginia I. Lohr, "What Are the Benefits of Plants Indoors and Why Do We Respond Positively to Them? *Washington State University,* 2010.

506. Kristi Kellogg, "21 Air-Purifying Plants to Cleanse Your Space," *Architectural Digest,* March 23, 2021, https://www.architecturaldigest.com/gallery /best-air-purifying-plants.

507. David Trilling, "Daylight, windows and workers' well-being: Research review," *The Journalist's Resource,* Harvard Kennedy School /Shorenstein Center on Media, Politics and Public Policy, September 15, 2017.

508. Mohamed Boubekri et al., "Impact of Windows and Daylight Exposure on Overall Health and Sleep Quality of Office Workers: A Case-Control Pilot Study," *Journal of Clinical Sleep Medicine* 10, no. 6 (2014): pp. 603–611, doi: 10.5664/jcsm.3780. PMID: 24932139; PMCID: PMC4031400.

509. Alan Hedge, "Study: Natural Light Is the Best Medicine for the Office," *Cornell University,* Department of Design and Environmental Analysis, January 31, 2018, https://www.prnewswire.com/news-releases/study-natural-light-is-the-best-medicine-for-the-office-300590905.html#:~:text=31%2C%202018%20%2FPRNewswire%2F%20%2D%2D,which%20can%20detract%20from%20productivity.

510. Thomas Schielke, "Light Matters: Whiteness in Nordic Countries," *Arch Daily,* August 29, 2014.

511. Nick Perham et al., "Mental Arithmetic and Non-Speech Office Noise: An Exploration of Interference-by-Content," *Noise Health* 15, no. 62 (Jan-Feb 2013): pp. 73–8, doi: 10.4103/1463–1741.107160.

512. Eric Sundstrom et al., "Office Noise, Satisfaction, and Performance," *Environment and Behaviour* 26, no. 2 (1994): pp. 195–222, doi: 10.1177/0013916594026 00204.

513. "Occupational Noise Exposure," *Occupational Safety and Health Administration,* U.S. Department of Labor.

514. Sarah Kessler, "Thanks to Open Offices, There's a Booming Market for Fancy Noise-Absorbing Objects," *Quartz,* May 11, 2017.

515. Christopher Calisi and Justin Stout, "Stop Noise from Ruining Your Open Office," *Harvard Business Review,* March 16, 2015, https://hbr.org/2015/03/stop -noise-from-ruining-your-open-office.

516. "Sound Masking Versus White Noise," Steelcase QTPro.

517. Cornelius J. König, M. Kleinmann, and W. Höhmann, "A Field Test of the Quiet Hour as a Time Management Technique," *European Review of Applied Psychology* 63, no. 3 (May 1, 2013): 137–45, https://doi.org/10.1016/j.erap.2012.12.003.

518. "Constitution of the United States—A History," America's Founding Documents, *National Archives.*

519. Erin Largo-Wight, "Cultivating healthy places and communities: evidenced-based nature contact recommendations," *Int J Environ Health Res,* 2011 Feb; 21(1): pp. 41–61. doi: 10.1080/09603123.2010.499452. PMID: 21246432.

520. "What Is Biophilia? A Quick Overview..." *Plant Plan,* December 9, 2019. Also found in Nicole Ridder, "Cultivating the City: Establishing the Presence of Nature in Urban Architecture," *University of Cincinnati,* March 2018, https:// etd.ohiolink.edu/acprod/odb_etd/etd/r/1501/10?clear=10&p10_accession _num=ucin1522342247782963

521. Jena McGregor, "Amazon opens a different kind of office," *The Washington Post,* January 30, 2018.

522. Brucks and Levav, "Virtual Communication Curbs Creative Idea Generation."

523. J. Pejtersen et al., "Indoor Climate, Psychosocial Work Environment and Symptoms in Open-Plan Offices," *Indoor Air 16,* no. 5 (October 2006): 392–401, https://doi.org/10.1111/j.1600-0668.2006.00444.x.

524. Ethan S. Bernstein and Stephen Turban, "The Impact of the 'Open' Workspace on Human Collaboration," *Philosophical Transactions of the Royal Society B: Biological Sciences* 373, no. 1753 (July 2, 2018), https://doi.org/10.1098/rstb.2017.0239.

525. John Triano, "Office Chair: How to Reduce Back Pain?" *SPINE-health,* last updated December 2, 2010.

526. Sal Vaglica, "Are Standing Desks Actually Better for Your Aching Backs?" *The Wall Street Journal,* February 9, 2022, https://www.wsj.com/articles/standing-desks-better-for-your-back-11644438302.

527. WebMD Editorial Contributors," Can I Prevent Prostatitis? *WebMD Men's Health Guide,* May 23, 2023.

528. Matthew Lieberman, *Social: Why Our Brains Are Wired to Connect* (New York: Crown Publishers, 2013), pp. 4–5.

529. Chip Heath and Dan Heath, *Switch: How to Change Things When Change Is Hard* (New York: Crown Business, 2010), p. 221.

530. Stuart Bloom and Evan Dold, "A Guide to Developing a Policies and Procedures Manual," *Management World* 10, no. 6 (June 1981): 27–31, 44.

531. Ibid.

532. Ibid.

533. Ibid.

534. Ibid.

535. Ibid.

536. Ibid.

537. "How to Enter a Cleanroom," *wikiHow,* last updated May 4, 2023, https://www.wikihow.life/Enter-a-Cleanroom. The steps cited here are a condensed version of those on the website.

538. Susan A. Randolph, "Developing Policies and Procedures," *American Association of Occupational Health Nurses Journal,* Vol. 54, no. 11 (November 2006): pp. 501–504.

539. Rachel Nizinski, "What is a Continuous Improvement Process? Tips for IT Leaders," *Appian,* March 24, 2024.

540. Mark Gershon, "Choosing Which Process Improvement Methodology to Implement," *The Journal of Applied Business and Economics 10,* no. 5 (March 2010): pp. 62 and 64.

541. Michael E. Porter, *Competitive Advantage: Creating and Sustaining Superior Performance* (New York: The Free Press, 1985), pp. 36–59.

542. Ibid., pp. 36–59.

543. Ibid., pp. 36–59.

544. Ibid., p. 37.

545. Ibid., pp. 39–40.

546. Ibid., pp. 40–43.

547. Ibid., pp. 40–43.

548. Ibid.

549. Confucius quoted in V. K. Bali, *Military Wisdom (Military Quotes on War, Peace and Valor)* (Delhi, India: Ocean Books, 2013) p.142.

550. "Risk Management Fundamentals," *Homeland Security,* April 2011, p. 23.

551. "Risk Management for a Small Business," U.S. *Small Business Administration.*

552. Roger Goodman, "The ascent of risk: risk and the Guide to the project management body of knowledge (PMBOK guide), 1987-1996-2000-2004." Paper presented at PMI® Global Congress 2005—Asia Pacific, Singapore. Newtown Square, PA: Project Management Institute.

553. "Risk Management Fundamentals," p. 23.

554. "Travel Advisories," *U.S. Department of State,* https://travel.state.gov/content/travel/en/traveladvisories/traveladvisories.html/.

555. "What is Risk Reduction?" *Founder Shield,* accessed April 17, 2025, https://foundershield.com/insurance-terms/definition/risk-reduction/#:~:text=Risk%20reduction%20refers%20to%20identifying,the%20impact%20of%20unexpected%20events.

556. Joanne Sammer, "Is Self-Insurance for You?" *Society of Human Resource Management,* May 1, 2011, https://www.shrm.org/topics-tools/news/hr-magazine/self-insurance.

557. "Contracts: Transferring and Financing Risk," *Department of Enterprise Services,* State of Washington, May 1999.

558. Knut Alicke, Ed Barriball, and Vera Trautwein, "How COVID-19 is reshaping supply chains," *McKinsey & Company,* November 23, 2021, https://www.mckinsey.com/capabilities/operations/our-insights/how-covid-19-is-reshaping-supply-chains.

559. Victoria Walker, *Subsidizing the Microchip Race: The Expanding Use of National Security Arguments in International Trade,* 57 U. MICH. J. L. REFORM 661 (2024), https://repository.law.umich.edu/mjlr/vol57/iss3/4.

560. Peter Schroeder, "FDIC says it should have supervised First Republic more closely," *Reuters,* September 8, 2023.

561. "Span of Control vs. Span of Support," *The Journal of Quality and Participation 23,* no. 4 (Fall 2000): p. 15.

562. "Span of Control vs. Span of Support," p. 15.

563. Tiffany McDowell, Trevor Page, and Don Miller, "Organizational Design: The Rise of Teams," Deloitte Insights, March 1, 2016, https://www2.deloitte.com/content/www/us/en/insights/focus/human-capital-trends/2016/organizational-models-network-of-teams.html.

564. Ashin Gupta, "Organization's Size and Span of Control," *Practical Management,* January 10, 2010.

565. Chip Heath and Dan Heath, *Switch: How to Change Things When Change Is Hard* (New York: Crown Business, 2010), p. 221.

566. Wigert et al., "Re-Engineering Performance Management," p. 15.

567. König, Kleinmann, and Höhmann, "A Field Test of the Quiet Hour as a Time Management Technique."

568. Pencavel, "The Productivity of Working Hours," p. 21.

569. Aimee Groth, "Zappos is going holacratic: no job titles, no managers, no hierarchy," *Quartz*, December 30, 2013.

570. Aimee Groth, "Zappos has quietly backed away from holacracy," *Quartz*, January 29, 2020.

571. Aristotle quoted in Robert Shimonski, *AI in Healthcare: How Artificial Intelligence Is Changing IT Operations and Infrastructure Services,* (Indianapolis, IN: John Wiley & Sons, Inc., 2021), p. 93.

572. Klaus Schwab, *The Fourth Industrial Revolution* (New York: Penguin Random House LLC, 2016), pp. 6–8.

573. Zahidi et al., "The Future of Jobs Report 2023," p. 24.

574. Cole Stryker and Eda Kavlakoglu, "What Is Artificial Intelligence (AI)?," IBM, August 9, 2024, https://www.ibm.com/think/topics/artificial-intelligence.

575. John W. Ayers et al., "Comparing Physician and Artificial Intelligence Chatbot Responses to Patient Questions Posted to a Public Social Media Forum," *JAMA Intern Med.* Published online April 28, 2023. doi:10.1001/jamainternmed.2023.1838.

576. Brody Ford, "IBM to Pause Hiring Jobs That AI Could Do," *Bloomberg*, May 1, 2023.

577. Christine Wei-Li Lee, "Speaking without vocal cords, thanks to a new AI-assisted wearable device," *UCLA Newsroom*, March 14, 2024.

578. Notomoro, "Adaptive AI: Explore the Use Cases, Examples, and Others," *Webisoft,* February 11, 2024, https://webisoft.com/articles/adaptive-ai/.

579. Karen L. Howard et al., "Artificial Intelligence in Health Care Benefits and Challenges of Machine Learning Technologies for Medical Diagnostics," *United States Government Accountability Office and the National Academy of Medicine,* GAO-22–104629, September 2022.

580. "What is the future of AI?" *McKinsey & Company, April 30, 2024,* https://www.mckinsey.com/featured-insights/mckinsey-explainers/whats-the-future-of-ai.

581. Sushill Kumar Behera, "Generative AI in Practice" Real-World Applications and Impact," LinkedIn, September 30, 2023, https://www.linkedin.com/pulse/generative-ai-practice-real-world-applications-impact-behera/.

582. Giselle Abramovich, "PwC: Artificial Intelligence Will Be The Business Advantage of The Future," *Adobe Blog* (blog), April 14, 2017, https://blog.adobe.com/en/publish/2017/04/14/pwc-artificial-intelligence-will-be-the-business-advantage-of-the-future-tlp.

583. Katie Costello, "Gartner Survey Shows 37% of Organizations Have Implemented AI in Some Form," Gartner, Press Release, January 21, 2019.

584. Dr. Anand S. Rao and Gerard Verveij, "Sizing the Prize: What's the real value of AI for your business and how can you capitalize?" *Pricewaterhouse Coopers,* 2017.

585. "Real GDP Growth," *International Monetary Fund.*

586. Alexander S. Gillis, Scott Robinson, and Wesley Chai, "What Is Big Data Analytics?" TechTarget Business Analytics, accessed April 17, 2025, https://www.techtarget.com/searchbusinessanalytics/definition/big-data-analytics.

587. Ibid.

588. "Top big data analytics use cases," *Oracle,* 2020, https://www.oracle.com/dz/a/ocom/docs/top-22-use-cases-for-big-data.pdf.

589. Charles Duhigg, "How Companies Learn Your Secrets," *The New York Times Magazine*, February 16, 2012, "https://www.nytimes.com/2012/02/19/magazine/shopping-habits.html.

590. VivekR, "How Did Netflix Use Big Data to Transform Their Company and Dominate the Streaming Industry?" Medium, June 18, 2023.

591. "What is Cloud Computing? A Beginner's Guide," *Microsoft.*

592. Chaadrack Boudzoumou, "A Case Study of Netflix's Migration to the Cloud," LinkedIn, January 6, 2023.

593. Frank Konkel, "Ukraine Tech Chief: Cloud Migration 'Saved Ukrainian Government and Economy,'" *NEXTGOV*, December 1, 2022.

594. Alison Grace Johansen, "What is encryption, and how does it protect your data?" Norton.

595. Muhammad Zaid Qamar et al., "Green Technology and its Implications Worldwide," The Inquisitive Meridian Multidisciplinary Journal, Volume 3, Issue 1, March 30, 2021.

596. The role of image and video processing," *Military + Aerospace Electronics,* March 2, 2023

597. What is IoT?" *Oracle.*

598. Fabio Duarte, "Number of IoT Devices (2024)," *Exploding Targets,* February 19, 2024.

599. "What is quantum computing?" *IBM.*

600. Charlie Campbell, "Quantum Computers Could Solve Countless Problems—And Create a Lot of New Ones," *Time Magazine,* January 26, 2023.

601. Stephen Gossett, "10 Quantum Computing Applications and Examples," *Built In,* updated April 5, 2024.

602. Jason Fell, "The Company Pioneering the Golden Age of Robotics: Automation is growing and this startup is ready," *Entrepreneur,* September 7, 2022.

603. Lisa M. Koonin et al., "Trends in the Use of Telehealth During the Emergence of the COVID-19 Pandemic—United States, January–March 2020," Morbidity and Mortality Weekly Report, *Center for Disease Control,* October 30, 2020 / 69(43); pp. 1595–1599.

604. Tanya Albert Henry, "74% of physicians work in practices that offer telehealth," American Medical Association, December 20, 2023.

605. "Teleradiology," *American College of Radiology.*

606. "What is text mining?" IBM, https://www.ibm.com/topics/text-mining.

607. Crystal R. China, "Leveraging user-generated social media content with text-mining examples," International Business Machines.

608. "What is speech recognition? *IBM.*

609. Jayden Khakurel et al., "Tapping into the Wearable Device Revolution in the Work Environment: A Systematic Review," *Information Technology and People* 31, no. 3 (2018) pp. 791–818.

610. Harjeevan Singh Kang and Mark Exworthy, "Wearing the Future—Wearables to Empower Users to Take Greater Responsibility for Their Health and Care: Scoping Review," JMIR Mhealth Uhealth. 2022 Jul; 10(7): e35684. Published online 2022 Jul 13. doi: 10.2196/35684.

611. Jena McGregor, "What Walmart's Patent for Audio Surveillance Could Mean for Its Workers," *The Washington Post*, July 12, 2018, https://www.washingtonpost.com/business/2018/07/12/what-walmarts-patent-audio-surveillance-could-mean-its-workers/.

612. Ian Stewart et al., "Technology and people: The great job-creating machine," *Deloitte,* www2.deloitte.com/content/dam/Deloitte/uk/Documents/finance/deloitte-uk-technology-and-people.pdf.

613. "The Future of Jobs Report: 2020," *World Economic Forum,* Centre for the New Economy and Society, 2020, p. 29, https://www.weforum.org/publications/the-future-of-jobs-report-2020/.

614. Attilio Di Battista, "The Future of Jobs Report: 2023," *World Economic Forum,* Centre for the New Economy and Society, May 2023, pp. 6, 9, & 28, https://www.weforum.org/publications/the-future-of-jobs-report-2023/.

615. George Bernard Shaw quoted in David Scott Kastan, Editor in Chief, *The Oxford Encyclopedia of British Literature,* (Oxford: Oxford University Press, 2006), p. 515.

616. Pencavel, "The Productivity of Working Hours," p. 21.

617. Heike Bruch and Sumantra Ghoshal, "Beware the Busy Manager," *Harvard Business Review,* February 2002, 80(2):62–69, 128, https://hbr.org/2002/02/beware-the-busy-manager.

618. Karen Burns, "30 Smart Time Management Tips and Tricks: Learn to Organize and Control Your Time Better," *U.S. News,* September 28, 2010.

619. Mark, Gudith, and Klocke, "The Cost of Interrupted Work."

620. Jeff Comer, "The Fallacy of Multitasking: Is Multitasking Controlling You? Here's What to Do." *Psychology Today* (blog), March 17, 2022, https://www.psychologytoday.com/us/blog/beyond-stress-and-burnout/202203/the-fallacy-multitasking.

621. Daniel B. Smith, *English Proverbs and Sayings Dictionary,* 2020, p. 106.

622. König, Kleinmann, and Höhmann, "A Field Test of the Quiet Hour as a Time Management Technique."

623. Benjamin Franklin, *Poor Richards Almanac,* 1747.

624. Henry Mintzberg, "The Manager's Job: Folklore and Fact," *Harvard Business Review,* 1990, https://hbr.org/1990/03/the-managers-job-folklore-and-fact.

625. "Want to improve productivity? Make friends at workplace."

626. Emma Seppälä and Marissa King, "Having Work Friends Can Be Tricky, but It's Worth It," *Harvard Business Review,* August 8, 2017.

627. Ian Cook, Would They Call You Their Best Boss Ever? (United States: *Leader's Beacon,* 2012), pp. 58–59.

628. "Your slow recruiting process costs your organization more than lost revenue."

629. Blenko et al., *Decide & Deliver,* p. 88.

630. Helliwell et al., "Happiness at Different Ages."

631. Sattar Bawany, "Managing Your Boss: The Two-Way Conversation of Management," *Leadership Excellence Essentials;* Aurora, Vol. 31, Iss. 10 (Oct 2014): p. 47.

632. Mintzberg, "The Manager's Job: Folklore and Fact."

633. Bawany, *Managing Your Boss,* p. 34.

634. Amy Gallo, "How to Disagree with Someone More Powerful than You," *Harvard Business Review,* March 17, 2016, https://hbr.org/2016/03/how-to-disagree-with-someone-more-powerful-than-you.

635. Harry S. Truman quoted in Franziska Frank, *The Power of Humility in Leadership: Influencing as a Role Model,* New York: Productivity Press Book, 2023, p. 45.

636. "Survey: 84 Percent of U.S. Workers Blame Bad Managers for Creating Unnecessary Stress."

637. Jo-Ann Lorber, "Executive Officer Leadership: Cultivating Effective Union-Management Relationships," January 2018.

638. "National Labor Relations Act," National Labor Relations Board, https://www.nlrb.gov/guidance/key-reference-materials/national-labor-relations-act.

639. "Introduction to the NLRB," National Labor Relations Board, https://www.nlrb.gov/a

640. 1947 Taft-Hartley Substantive Provisions," National Labor Relations Board, June 23, 1947.

641. "Labor-Management Reporting and Disclosure Act of 1959, As Amended," U.S. Department of Labor, 29 USC § 402 (i).

642. "Labor-Management Reporting and Disclosure Act of 1959, As Amended."

643. "Collective Bargaining Rights," National Labor Relations Board, https://www.nlrb.gov/about-nlrb/rights-we-protect/the-law/employees/collective-bargaining-rights.

644. "National Labor Relations Act."

645. "Employee/Union Rights and Obligations," National Labor Relations Board, https://www.nlrb.gov/about-nlrb/rights-we-protect/your-rights/employer-union-rights-and-obligations.

646. "Right-to-Work States: What Employers Should Know," Indeed for Employers, accessed April 21, 2025, https://www.indeed.com/hire/c/info/right-to-work-states-things-your-business-should-know#:~:text=Right%2Dto%2Dwork%20laws%20view,to%20enjoy%20the%20same%20benefits.

647. Teresa J. Tschida, "Unions and Management: A Blissful Marriage?" *Gallup Business Journal,* March 9, 2006, https://news.gallup.com/businessjournal/21727/unions-management-blissful-marriage.aspx.

648. Bill Fotsch and John Case, "How to Cut Through Labor-Management Hostility," *Forbes,* October 18, 2015, https://www.forbes.com/sites/fotschcase/2015/10/18/how-to-cut-through-labor-management-hostility/?sh=4bbc4cec599f.

649. Bill Fotsch and John Case, "The Business Case for Open-Book Management," *Forbes,* July 25, 2017, https://www.forbes.com/sites/fotschcase/2017/07/25/the-business-case-for-open-book-management/?sh=3fad94dd5883.

650. Kamala D. Harris and Martin J. Walsh, "White House Task Force on Worker Organizing and Empowerment: Report to the President," Executive Order 14025 establishing the Task Force on Worker Organizing and Empowerment, February 2022, p. 3.

651. Justin McCarthy, "U.S. Approval of Labor Unions at Highest Point Since 1965," *Gallup,* August 30, 2022, https://news.gallup.com/poll/398303/approval -labor-unions-highest-point-1965.aspx.

652. Harris and Walsh, "White House Task Force on Worker Organizing and Empowerment: Report to the President," pp. 3, 4.

653. "Union Membership Summary," U.S. Bureau of Labor Statistics Economic News Release, January 23, 2024, https://www.bls.gov/news.release/archives /union2_01212011.pdf.

654. Harold Meyerson, "Generation Union: Millennials and Gen Zers are the most pro-union generation since the 1939s and '40s – and probably more so," *The American Prospect,* October 2022, https://prospect.org/labor/generation-union/.

655. Drew Desilver, "2023 saw some of the biggest, hardest-fought labor disputes in recent decades," Pew Research Center, January 4, 2024, https://www .pewresearch.org/short-reads/2024/01/04/2023-saw-some-of-the-biggest -hardest-fought-labor-disputes-in-recent-decades/#:~:text=Through%20the%20 end%20of%20November,than%20any%20year%20since%202000.

656. Tim Kurkjian, "'Oh my God, how can we do this?': An oral history of the 1994 MLB strike," ESPN, August 12, 2019.

657. Edmund P. Edmonds, "MLB Minimum and Average Salaries 1967–2012," Notre Dame Law School, February 2, 2012.

658. Peter Chawaga, "Changes In MLB Pace Of Play Fueling Increasing Attendance," *Forbes,* June 19, 2024.

659. Alia Wong, "The Ripple Effect of the West Virginia Teachers' Victory," *The Atlantic,* March 7, 2018, https://www.theatlantic.com/education/archive/2018/03 /west-virginia-teachers-victory/555056/.

660. Ashley Wong, "Tensions Rise at Columbia as Strikers Fear Retaliation from University," *The New York Times,* December 8, 2021, https://www.nytimes .com/2021/12/08/nyregion/columbia-grad-student-strike.html.

661. Ashley Wong, "Student Workers at Columbia End 10-Week Strike After Reaching a Deal," *The New York Times,* January 7, 2022, https://www.nytimes .com/2022/01/07/nyregion/columbia-student-workers-strike-ends.html.

662. Joanna Slater, "As Buffalo baristas stage vote on unionization, Starbucks delivers executive visits, more staff," *The Washington Post,* November 28, 2021, p. A3.

663. Heather Haddon and Allison Prang, "Union Efforts at Starbucks Gain Steam Across the U.S.," The Wall Street Journal, January 22–23, 2022, p. B3.

664. Josh Eidelson, "Starbucks employees are petitioning to unionize at 50 U.S. stores," *Bloomberg,* January 31, 2022.

665. Lauren Kaori Gurley, "Judge orders Starbucks to reinstate seven fired baristas," *The Washington Post,* August 18, 2022.

666. "Union Membership Summary."

667. Teresa J. Tschida, "Unions and Management: A Blissful Marriage?" Gallup, March 9, 2006.

668. Warren Buffett interview by Savanah Guthrie, "Buffett Reminds Entrepreneurs to 'Delight' Customers," *Bloomberg* (YouTube), June 13, 2016, 2 minutes and 5 seconds, https://www.bloomberg.com/news/videos/2016-06-08/buffett -reminds-entrepreneurs-to-delight-customers

669. Christian Nordqvist, "Customer—definition and meaning," *Market Business News,* October 3, 2016, https://marketbusinessnews.com/financial-glossary /customer-definition-meaning/.

670. Richard L. Oliver et al., "Customer Foundations, Findings, and Managerial Insights," *Journal of Retailing,* Vol. 73, No. 3 (Autumn 1997): pp. 311–336.

671. Alison DeNisco Rayome, "91% of top companies use AI to boost customer service, improve branding," *Tech Republic,* October 11, 2017, https://www.techrepublic .com/article/91-of-top-companies-use-ai-to-boost-customer-service-improve -branding/.

672. "Study: 'Iconic' Companies Use Artificial Intelligence to Increase Customer Satisfaction," *Networks Asia,* October 19, 2017.

673. "What is corporate social responsibility?" *bdc,* accessed April 21, 2025, https:// www.bdc.ca/en/articles-tools/entrepreneur-toolkit/templates-business-guides /glossary/corporate-social-responsibility#:~:text=It's%20an%20ongoing%20 process%20built,their%20local%20communities%20and%20environments.

674. Lucas Thompson, "The Air Force has released its first plan to reduce its carbon footprint and adapt to climate change," *NBC News,* October 5, 2022.

675. "New Study Finds Brand Loyalty Hinges on Customer Support Experiences," *Globenewswire,* December 6, 2017, https://www.globenewswire.com/news -release/2017/12/06/1234043/0/en/New-Study-Finds-Brand-Loyalty-Hinges -on-Customer-Support-Experiences.html.

676. Tom Peters, "Under Promise, Over Deliver," *Tom Peters! Writing,* 1987, https:// tompeters.com/columns/under-promise-over-deliver/.

677. Gates and Hemingway, *Business @ the Speed of Thought,* p.186.

678. Marcus Buckingham and Curt Coffman, *First, Break All the Rules: What the World's Greatest Managers Do Differently* (Simon and Schuster, 2014), pp. 7–8.

679. Mark Horstman, *The Effective Manager* (Hoboken: John Wiley and Sons, Inc., 2016), p. 2.

680. Wigert et al., "Re-Engineering Performance Management," p. 15.

681. Robert Rosenthal and Lenore Jacobson, "Teachers' Expectancies: Determinants of Pupils' IQ Gains," *Psychological Reports* 19 (1966), pp. 115–118, https://doi .org/10.2466/pr0.1966.19.1.115 and in Pygmalion in the Classroom: Teacher Expectations and Pupils' Intellectual Development (New York: Crown, 2003) and in Adam Grant, *Give and Take: Why Helping Others Drives Our Success* (London: Penguin Books, 2013), pp. 98, 99.

682. Mark Twain quoted in Michael Hansbury, *The Quality of Leadership,* (New Delhi: Epitome Books, 2009), p. 37.

683. Colleen Stanley, *Emotional Intelligence for Sales Success: Connect with Customers and Get Success* (New York: American Management Association, 2013), p. 178.

684. Rath, *StrengthsFinder* 2.0, p. iii.

685. Dennis and Valacich, "Computer Brainstorming," pp. 531–537.

686. Bruch and Ghoshal, "Beware the Busy Manager."

687. "How to discuss poor performance: Strategies for managers," *Business Management Daily,* updated on February 4, 2020, https://www.businessmanagementdaily.com/2663/confronting-poor-performers-6-tips-for-managers/.

688. Pencavel, "The Productivity of Working Hours," p. 21.

689. Ibid., "The Power of Praise and Recognition: Research shows they are crucial for increasing employee productivity and engagement."

690. Abraham Lincoln quoted in Michael Burlingame, *The Inner World of Abraham Lincoln* (Urbana, Il: University of Illinois Press, 1994), p. 194.

691. Phillippa Lally et al., "How are habits formed: Modelling habit formation in the real world," *European Journal of Social Psychology,* Volume 40, Issue 6, October 2010, pp. 998–1009, https://doi.org/10.1002/ejsp.674.

692. Archie Brown, *The Myth of the Strong Leader: Political Leadership in the Modern Age* (New York: Basic Books, 2014), p. vi.

693. Kathleen Doheny, "What Drives 'Kiss Up, Kick Down' Managers?" Society for Human Resource Management, October 12, 2022.

694. Patrick Darcey, "Special—Officers Eat First," *U.S. Naval Institute,* May 2012.

695. Grant, *Give and Take,* pp. 1–16.

696. "Emotional Intelligence," *Psychology Today,* https://www.psychologytoday.com/us/basics/emotional-intelligence.

697. Travis Bradberry and Jean Greaves, *Emotional Intelligence 2.0* (San Diego: TalentSmart, 2009), pp. 1–22.

698. Samiran Nundy et al., *How to Practice Academic Medicine and Publish from Developing Countries? A Practical Guide,* (Singapore: Springer Nature, 2022), p. 153.

699. James C. Collins, *Good to Great: Why Some Companies Make the Leap...and Others Do Not* (New York: Harper Business, 2001), p. 12.

700. Voltaire quoted in Wallace Alcorn, "Common sense is not so common nowadays," Austin Daily Herald, January 30, 2012.

701. "6 Tips on How to be Humble at Work," *Robert Half Solutions,* March 23, 2015, https://www.roberthalf.com/us/en/insights/career-development/6-tips-on-how-to-be-humble-at-work.

702. Collins, *Good to Great,* p. 12.

703. Mark Twain quoted in John Borek et al., *The Good Book on Leadership: Case Studies from the Bible* (Nashville, TN: Broadman & Holman Publishers, 2005), p. 61.

704. Alexander Hamilton quoted in George K. Knox, *Thoughts That Inspire: Volume I* (Des Moines IA: Personal Help Publishing, Co., 1905), p. 122.

705. Joy Ohm et al., "COVID-19: Women, Equality, and Inclusion in the Future of Work (Report)," *Catalyst: Workplaces that Work for Women,* May 28, 2020, https://www.catalyst.org/wp-content/uploads/2020/05/Covid_19_Women_Equity_Inclusion_Future_of_Work.pdf.

706. Gang Xu, "Defining Junzi and Ren: Confucius as the Father of Professionalism," *Archives of Boston Society of Confucius* 1, no. 1 (April 10, 2019): pp. 2–28.

707. Aaron P. Mikulsky, *Monday Motivation: 6 Years of Sharing Stories and Insights,* (Murrells Inlet, S.C. , 2022).

708. David Herbert Donald, *Lincoln* (New York: Simon & Schuster, 1995), p. 412.

709. Dwight Eisenhower quoted in Cornelius Ryan, *The Longest Day: The Classic Epic of D-Day, June 6, 1944* (New York: Simon & Schuster Paperbacks, 1959), p. 254.

710. Fernando Marmolejo-Ramos et al., "Your Face and Moves Seem Happier When I Smile," *Exp Psychol.* 2020; 67(1): pp. 14–22, doi: 10.1027/1618–3169/a000470.

711. Mark Stibich, "Top 10 Reasons to Smile Every Day," *Very Well Mind,* September 10, 2022.

712. Mark Twain quoted in Kay Davidson, *The Simple 6TM for Secondary Writers,* (Marion, IL: Pieces of Learning, 2008), p. 106.

713. Theodore Roosevelt quoted in David A. Holdstock, *Strategic GIS Planning and Management in Local Government* (New York: CRC Press, 2017), p. 23.

714. William Shakespeare, "As You Like It," Royal Shakespeare Company.

715. Aristotle quoted in Cathy Barker, *A Heron's Balance* (West Conshohocken, PA: Infinity Publishing, 2007), p. 76.

716. Nagesh Belludi, "Ten Rules of Management Success from Sam Walton," *Right Attitudes,* February 2, 2016, https://www.rightattitudes.com/2016/02/02/management-ideas-from-sam-walton/.

717. George Washington quoted in John C. Fitzpatrick, ed., *The Writings of George Washington from the Original Manuscript Sources, 15–1799,* Volume 29, September 1, 1786-June 19, 1788 (Washington DC: United States Government Printing Office, 1939) p. 162.

718. Clement Bellet et al., "Does Employee Happiness Have an Impact on Productivity?" *Saïd Business School WP 2019–13,* October 14, 2019, http://dx.doi.org/10.2139/ssrn.3470734

719. Shawn Achor, *The Happiness Advantage: The Seven Principles of Positive Psychology That Fuel Success and Performance at Work* (New York: Crown Publishing Group, 2010), pp. 3–4.

720. Sonja Lyubomirsky, *The How of Happiness: A New Approach to Getting the Life You Want* (New York: Penguin, 2007), p. 15.

721. Anchor, *The Happiness Advantage,* pp. 51–55.

722. Robert Zarr and Winnie Chan, "Nature: A Key Ingredient for Mental Health," *Pew Trend Magazine,* December 8, 2023.

723. Vicki Jayne, "Don't Worry Be Happy—Should Work Be Fun?" *New Zealand Management,* September 2005, p. 28, https://management.co.nz/archive/cover-story-dont-worry-be-happy-should-work-be-fun.

724. Ibid., p. 28.

725. The Buddha quoted in Naveen Kumar Chandra, *Ancient Buddhist Wisdom for A Peaceful & Happy Life,* (New Delhi: Prabhat Prakashan Pvt Ltd, 2023), pg 8.

726. Robert Waldinger and Marc Schulz, *The Good Life: Lessons From the World's Longest Scientific Study of Happiness,* (New York: Simon and Schuster, 2023), p. 10.

727. Andrew J. Oswald et al., "Happiness and Productivity," *Journal of Labor Economics,* Volume 33, Number 4 (October 2015): pp. 789–822, https://www.journals.uchicago.edu/doi/abs/10.1086/681096.

728. Sergio Rebelo, "Christine Lagarde on Income Inequality, Brexit, and the Power of M&Ms: A Q&A with the IMF managing director and Kellogg's Sergio Rebelo," Kellogg School of Management at Northwestern University, October 10, 2016, https://insight.kellogg.northwestern.edu/article/christine-lagarde-on-income-inequality-brexit-and-the-power-of-mms.

729. Booker T. Washington, *Up From Slavery: An Autobiography* (New York: Doubleday & Company Inc., 1900), p. 66.

730. Eleanor Roosevelt, *You Learn By Living,* (Lexington, KY: Westminster John Knox Press, 1960), p. 95.

731. Kevin Dugan, "Lloyd Blankfein on Gary Cohn: 'No one's perfect,'" *New York Post*, September 6, 2017, https://nypost.com/2017/09/06/lloyd-blankfein-on-gary-cohn-no-ones-perfect/.

732. "State of the Global Workplace 2024 Report," p. 2.

733. Branham, *The 7 Hidden Reasons Employees Leave*, p. 212.

734. Christine Porath, "The Hidden Toll of Workplace Incivility," *McKinsey Quarterly*, December 14, 2016, https://www.mckinsey.com/capabilities/people-and-organizational-performance/our-insights/the-hidden-toll-of-workplace-incivility.

735. Ryan Pendell, "Respect at Work Returns to a Record Low," *Gallup Workplace,* January 13, 2025.

736. Survey: 84 Percent of U.S. Workers Blame Bad Managers for creating unnecessary stress.

737. Abraham Lincoln quoted in Monty Nereim, *Survival Beneath Yucca Mountain,* (Bloomington, IN: Archway Press, 2020)

738. Winston Churchill quoted in "Quotes: Winston Churchill is one of the Most Quotable Men in History," International *Churchill Society,* 2020.

739. Harassment," *U.S. Equal Employment Opportunity Commission,* accessed April 21, 2025, https://www.eeoc.gov/harassment.

740. Ibid.

741. "Enforcement Guidance: Vicarious Liability for Unlawful Harassment by Supervisors," *U.S. Equal Employment Opportunity Commission,* https://www.eeoc.gov/laws/guidance/enforcement-guidance-vicarious-liability-unlawful-harassment-supervisors.

742. Ibid.

743. Steve Crabtree, "Global Study: 23% of Workers Experience Violence, Harassment," *Gallup,* December 14, 2022, https://news.gallup.com/opinion/gallup/406793/global-study-workers-experience-violence-harassment.aspx.

744. Kathryn Mayer, "HR's Culture Shift: Tackling Workplace Sexual Harassment While Navigating Legal Definitions," *Employee Benefit News*, March 12, 2018, https://www.benefitnews.com/news/hrs-culture-shift-tackling-workplace-sexual-harassment-while-navigating-legal-definitions.

745. Chelsea Emery et al., "10 Key Findings: Sexual Harassment in the Professional Workplace," *Financial Planning,* March 12, 2018, https://www.financial-planning.com/news/10-key-findings-sexual-harassment-in-the-professional-workplace.

746. Carrie Dann, "NBC/WSJ Poll: Nearly Half of Working Women Say They've Experienced Harassment," NBC, October 30, 2017, https://www.nbcnews.com/politics/first-read/nbc-wsj-poll-nearly-half-working-women-say-they-ve-n815376.

747. Employee Law Alliance Staff, "Employment Law Alliance Survey Takes American Pulse on #MeToo and Workplace Harassment," March 7, 2018, https://www.ela.law/articles/employment-law-alliance-survey-takes-american-pulse-on-metoo-and-workplace-harassment-.

748. Elaine Herskowitz, "Ten Misconceptions About Sexual Harassment," *Wealth Management*, January 30, 2018, https://www.wealthmanagement.com/estate-planning/ten-misconceptions-about-sexual-harassment.

749. Jena McGregor, "Intel's CEO Resigned After Violating a No-Dating Rule, More Companies are Adding Them in the #MeToo Era," *The Washington Post*, June 22, 2018, https://www.washingtonpost.com/news/on-leadership/wp/2018/06/22/intels-ceo-resigned-after-violating-a-no-dating-rule-more-companies-are-adding-them-in-the-metoo-era/.

750. "Sex-Based Discrimination," *U.S. Equal Employment Opportunity Commission*, https://www.eeoc.gov/sex-based-discrimination.

751. "Charge Statistics (Charges Filed with the EEOC) FY 1997 Through FY 2023," *U.S. Equal Employment Opportunity Commission*, https://www.eeoc.gov/data/enforcement-and-litigation-statistics-0.

752. "Supreme Court of the United States, Bostock v. Clayton County," No. 17–1618, Argued October 8, 2019—Decided June 15, 2020.

753. "Race/Color Discrimination," U.S. Equal Employment Opportunity Commission, https://www.eeoc.gov/racecolor-discrimination.

754. "Charge Statistics (Charges Filed with the EEOC) FY 1997 Through FY 2023."

755. "Charge Statistics (Charges Filed with the EEOC) FY 1997 Through FY 2023."

756. "Significant EEOC Race/Color Cases (Covering Private and Federal Sectors)," *U.S. Equal Employment Opportunity Commission*, https://www.eeoc.gov/initiatives/e-race/significant-eeoc-racecolor-casescovering-private-and-federal-sectors.

757. "Facts About Race/Color Discrimination," *U.S. Equal Employment Opportunity Commission*, https://www.eeoc.gov/fact-sheet/facts-about-racecolor-discrimination.

758. "Hooters of America, LLC to Pay $250,000 to Settle EEOC Race and Color Lawsuit," EEOC Press Release, October 22, 2024.

759. "Charge Statistics (Charges Filed with the EEOC) FY 1997 Through FY 2023."

760. "Religious Discrimination," U.S. Equal Employment Opportunity Commission, https://www.eeoc.gov/religious-discrimination.

761. "Questions and Answers: Religious Discrimination in the Workplace," *U.S. Equal Employment Opportunity Commission*, https://www.eeoc.gov/laws/guidance/questions-and-answers-religious-discrimination-workplace.

762. Sonia Ghumman et al., "Religious Discrimination in the Workplace: A Review and Examination of Current and Future Trends," *Journal of Business and Psychology* 28, no. 4 (December 2013): p. 439, https://ideas.wharton.upenn.edu/wp-content/uploads/2018/07/Ghumanneal2013.pdf.

763. "Charge Statistics (Charges Filed with the EEOC) FY 1997 Through FY 2023."

764. Christopher P. Scheitle and Elaine Howard Ecklund, "Examining the Effects of Exposure to Religion in the Workplace on Perceptions of Religious Discrimination," *Review of Religious Research* 59, no. 1 (2017), doi: 10.1007/s13644-016-0278-x.

765. "National Origin Discrimination," *U.S. Equal Employment Opportunity Commission,* https://www.eeoc.gov/national-origin-discrimination.

766. "Charge Statistics (Charges Filed with the EEOC) FY 1997 Through FY 2023."

767. "Winner Ford to Pay $150,000 To Settle EEOC National Origin Discrimination Suit," U.S. Equal Employment Opportunity Commission, November 22, 2017.

768. "Age Discrimination," U.S. Equal Employment Opportunity Commission, https://www.eeoc.gov/age-discrimination.

769. "EEOC Acting Chair Lipnic Releases Report on the State of Older Workers and Age Discrimination 50 Years After the ADEA," U.S. Equal Employment Opportunity Commission, June 26, 2018, https://www.eeoc.gov/newsroom/eeoc-acting-chair-lipnic-releases-report-state-older-workers-and-age-discrimination-50.

770. Richard Johnson and Peter Gosselin, "How Secure is Employment at Older Ages?" *Urban Institute,* December 28, 2018, p. 20, https://www.urban.org/research/publication/how-secure-employment-older-ages.

771. C. A. Viviani et al., "Productivity in Older versus Younger Workers: A Systematic Literature Review," *Work 68, no. 3 (2021): 577–618,* https://doi.org/10.3233/WOR-203396.

772. "The Advantages of Older Workers," *Mailman School of Public Health,* Columbia University, https://www.publichealth.columbia.edu/research/others/age-smart-employer/resources/guides/advantages-older-workers.

773. "Charge Statistics (Charges Filed with the EEOC) FY 1997 Through FY 2023."

774. "Texas Roadhouse to Pay $12 Million to Settle EEOC Age Discrimination Lawsuit," U.S. Equal Employment Opportunity Commission, March 31, 2017, https://www.eeoc.gov/newsroom/texas-roadhouse-pay-12-million-settle-eeoc-age-discrimination-lawsuit#:~:text=BOSTON%20%2D%20Texas%20Roadhouse%2C%20a%20national,the%20federal%20agency%20announced%20today.

775. "Americans with Disabilities Act," U.S. Department of Labor, https://www.dol.gov/agencies/odep/ada.

776. "Disability Discrimination and Employment Decisions," U.S. Equal Employment Opportunity Commission, https://www.eeoc.gov/disability-discrimination-and-employment-decisions.

777. Ibid.

778. "The ADA: Your Employment Rights as an Individual With a Disability, U.S. Equal Employment Opportunity Commission, https://www.eeoc.gov/publications /ada-your-employment-rights-individual-disability#:~:text=The%20ADA%20 only%20prohibits%20discrimination,to%20perform%20essential%20job%20 functions.

779. "Charge Statistics (Charges Filed with the EEOC) FY 1997 Through FY 2023."

780. "Persons with a Disability: Labor Force Characteristics Summary," News Release, Bureau of Labor Statistics, U.S. Department of Labor, February 22, 2024.

781. "FY 2007 Annual Report on the Operations and Accomplishments of the Office of the General Counsel," U.S. Equal Employment Opportunity Commission, https://www.eeoc.gov/reports/fy-2007-annual-report-operations-and-accomplishments-office-general-counsel.

782. "Equal Pay/Compensation Discrimination," U.S. Equal Employment Opportunity Commission, https://www.eeoc.gov/equal-paycompensation-discrimination.

783. "Global Gender Pay Gap Survey," *Glassdoor, 2015,* https://media.glassdoor.com /pr/press/pdf/GD_Survey_GlobalGenderPayGap.pdf.

784. "Charge Statistics (Charges Filed with the EEOC) FY 1997 Through FY 2023."

785. "Dell to Pay $75,000 to Settle EEOC Equal Pay Lawsuit," U.S. Equal Employment Opportunity Commission, September 7, 2021.

786. Richard Fry, "Young women are out-earning young men in several U.S. cities," *Pew Research Center,* March 28, 2022, https://www.pewresearch.org/short-reads /2022/03/28/young-women-are-out-earning-young-men-in-several-u-s-cities/

787. Smith, "Work-life Balance Perspectives of Future marketing Professionals," p. 434.

788. "Entering Year Three of the pandemic, American workers face new challenges and changes," *Prudential,* March 8, 2022, https://news.prudential.com /latest-news/prudential-news/prudential-news-details/2022/Entering-Year -Three-of-the-pandemic-American-workers-face-new-challenges-and-changes -03-08-2022/default.aspx.

789. Carey Oven, "Peace of mind: Inclusive culture + paid family leave: Caring for caregivers as they grow careers," Deloitte, accessed April 21, 2025, https:// www2.deloitte.com/us/en/pages/about-deloitte/articles/inclusion-family -leave-well-being-parental-caregiver.html.

790. Ellie Harrison, "Resurfaced tale details how Toy Story 2 was saved after being deleted—twice," *Independent,* February 17, 2022, https://www.the-independent. com/arts-entertainment/films/news/lightyear-toy-story-2-deleted-b2017238 .html#:~:text="Eight%20people%20met%20us%20with,and%20the%20 film%20was%20saved.

791. James Carlson, "What Is Financial Wellness? Determining the Characteristics of a Real Financial Wellness Benefit," *Employee Benefits and Wellness Excellence Essentials,* February 2016.

792. "Bank of America Study Finds 84% of Employers Now Say Offering Financial Wellness Tools Helps Increase Employee Retention," *Bank of America*, September 27, 2022, https://newsroom.bankofamerica.com/content/newsroom/press-releases/2022/09/bank-of-america-study-finds-84-of-employers-now-say-offering-fi.html.

793. Rebecca Henderson and Andrew Dunn (editor), "Paycheck to Paycheck Statistics: 66.2% of Americans Report Struggling Between Paydays," *MarketWatch Guides*, August 9, 2024, https://www.marketwatch.com/guides/banking/paycheck-to-paycheck-statistics/.

794. Stephen Miller, "SHRM Benefits Survey Finds Renewed Focus on Employee Well-Being," *Society for Human Resource Management*, September 12, 2021, https://www.shrm.org/topics-tools/news/benefits-compensation/shrm-benefits-survey-finds-renewed-focus-employee-well.

795. Peter Boersma, Lindsey I. Black, and Brian W. Ward, "Prevalence of Multiple Chronic Conditions Among US Adults, 2018," *Preventing Chronic Disease* 17 (2020), https://doi.org/10.5888/pcd17.200130.

796. Dan Witters and Sangeeta Agrawal, "The Economic Cost of Poor Employee Mental Health," *Gallup*, updated December 13, 2022, https://www.gallup.com/workplace/404174/economic-cost-poor-employee-mental-health.aspx.

797. E.P. Terlizzi and J.S. Schiller, "Estimates of Mental Health Symptomatology, by Month of Interview: United States, 2019," *National Center for Health Statistics*, March 2021, https://www.cdc.gov/nchs/data/nhis/mental-health-monthly-508.pdf.

798. "Anxiety and Depression: National Pulse Survey," National Center for Health Statistics, Centers for Disease Control and Prevention.

799. "Nearly One in Five American Adults Who Have Had COVID-19 Still Have 'Long COVID,'" Centers for Disease Control and Prevention, last reviewed June 22, 2022, https://www.cdc.gov/nchs/pressroom/nchs_press_releases/2022/20220622.htm#:~:text=Health%20Statistics%20Home-,Nearly%20One%20in%20Five%20American%20Adults%20Who%20Have%20Had,19%20Still%20Have%20"Long%20COVID"&text=New%20data%20from%20the%20Household,symptoms%20of%20"long%20COVID."

800. "Long COVID or Post-COVID Conditions, Centers for Disease Control and Prevention," accessed September–November 2022, https://archive.cdc.gov/www_cdc_gov/coronavirus/2019-ncov/long-term-effects/index.html.

801. "Nearly One in Five American Adults Who Have Had COVID-19 Still Have 'Long COVID.'"

802. Rod Baxter, *Enterprise Excellence Handbook: A Step-By-Step Guide to Success* (Naples, FL: Value Generation Partners, LLC, 2016), p. 136.

INDEX

ABOUT THE AUTHOR

Garry Stanberry was a successful manager for more than 45 years. During his 29 years as an Air Force officer, he served as a hospital commander, a joint task force deputy commander (forward), a regional hospital senior administrator, and the director of the Medical Service Corps. Garry later worked as a senior healthcare information technology (IT) consultant and an associate director of a federal government agency. He has extensive experience in corporate-level management, medical administration, IT, and human resources.